Lean Six Sigma
for Service

*How to Use Lean Speed and Six Sigma
Quality to Improve Services and
Transactions*

Michael L. George

McGRAW-HILL

New York   Chicago   San Francisco   Lisbon   London
Madrid   Mexico City   Milan   New Delhi   San Juan
Seoul   Singapore   Sydney   Toronto

5 6 7 8 9 0 DOC/DOC 0 9 8 7 6 5 4

ISBN 0-07-141821-0

Library of Congress Cataloguing-in-Publication Data applied for.

This publication is designed to provide accurate and authoritative information in regard to the subject matter covered. It is sold with the understanding that neither the author nor the publisher is engaged in rendering legal, accounting, or other professional services. If legal advice or other expert assistance is required, the services of a competent professional person should be sought.

—From a Declaration of Principles jointly adopted by a Committee of the American Bar Association and a Committee of Publishers

McGraw-Hill books are available at special quantity discounts to use as premiums and sales promotions, or for use in corporate training programs. For more information, please write to the Director of Special Sales, McGraw-Hill, 2 Penn Plaza, New York, NY 10121. Or contact your local bookstore.

 This book is printed on recycled, acid-free paper containing a minimum of 50% recycled de-inked fiber.

Contents

PART I
Using Lean Six Sigma for
Strategic Advantage in Service

Part II
Deploying Lean Six Sigma
in Service Organizations

Part III
Improving Services

Acknowledgments

Many people have helped this book become a reality. They contributed detailed case studies or reviewed the manuscript, making great personal sacrifices along the way. I greatly appreciate their help and their organizations' support. Special thanks go out to:

Lockheed Martin: Mike Joyce, Manny Zulueta, James Isaac, George Sanders, Kevin Fast, and a special thanks to Myles Burke, who made substantial contributions to the text

Bank One's National Enterprise Operations (NEO) group: Mike Fischbach, Darryl Greene, Jim Kaminski, Tim Williams

Stanford Hospital and Clinics: Karen Rago (now of UC–San Francisco), Nick Gaich

The City of Fort Wayne: Mayor Graham Richard, Roger Hirt, Michele Hill

Caterpillar, Inc: Rod Skewes

A special note of thanks to the Lean Six Sigma pathfinders: Lou Giuliano of ITT Industries; Dave Burritt and Geoff Turk of Caterpillar; Jerry Henry, Steve Hochhauser, and Dick Cunningham of Johns Manville; Lew Fischer of Bank One; Vance Coffman of Lockheed Martin; Mayor Graham Richard of the City of Fort Wayne... "You have given others the courage to accomplish their own greatness."

I'd like to give special thanks to all of my outstanding George Group colleagues, who are continually pioneering the work of Lean Six Sigma to drive real shareholder value creation with our clients. In particular, I'd like to single out a few people whose contributions are reflected in this book and its predecessor, *Lean Six Sigma*:

James Works—for creating a strategic deployment architecture to leverage the power of Value Based Management, Lean Six Sigma, Leadership Effectiveness and Conquering Complexity to drive incredible, sustainable value for our clients around the world

Bill Kastle, Mark Price, Kevin Simonin—for proving that Lean Six Sigma works by leading some of the largest, most ambitious and most successful Lean and Six Sigma deployments ever undertaken

Rick Hardcopf, Walt Mores, Jeff Howard and John Maxey—for their outstanding contribution to the advancement of our knowledge of Lean Six Sigma and capture of Voice of the Customer

Paul Jaminet—for his ground-breaking contribution to the development of the ideas and implementation strategies for "Conquering Complexity"

Kimberly Watson Hemphill, Ken Jacobson and Chuck Cox—for their continuing development and application of truly innovative Design for Lean Six Sigma

I'd also like to thank **Bob DeLeeuw**, **Bryan Carey**, and **Joe Walsh** of DeLeeuw Associates who are using our Lean Six Sigma principles to reshape the banking industry.

A last word of thanks to **Kim Bruce** for helping to keep this book moving forward, and to **Sue Reynard**, a gifted writer who has expertly translated my consultant-speak into English.

About the Author

Michael George, Chairman and CEO of George Group Consulting, is an effective change agent for *Fortune* 500 companies. He has worked personally with CEOs and executive teams at companies such as ITT Industries, Caterpillar, Colgate-Palmolive, Xerox, Johns Manville (a Berkshire Hathaway company) and Ingersoll-Rand. His primary emphasis is on the creation of shareholder value through application of process improvement initiatives including Lean Six Sigma, Lean Manufacturing, and Complexity Reduction. His recent book, *Lean Six Sigma* (McGraw-Hill, 2002), describes the philosophy and implementation for maximizing business growth and economic profit. Mr. George holds a BS in Physics from the Univ. of California and a MS in Physics from the Univ. of Illinois. He began his career at Texas Instruments in 1964 as an engineer. In 1969, he founded the venture startup International Power Machines (IPM), which he subsequently took public and sold to a division of Rolls Royce in 1984. This enabled him to study the Toyota Production System and TQM first hand in Japan, resulting in the book *America Can Compete*, which led to the founding of George Group in 1986.

Introduction

An interesting thing happened after the publication of my previous book, Lean Six Sigma: Combining Six Sigma Quality with Lean Speed. People could easily grasp the need for Lean Six Sigma, and its fundamental truth: quality improves speed and speed improves quality. But I heard one question over and over again: How do I apply Lean Six Sigma to a service organization?

When I looked over the content of that book, I had to admit that I and my co-writers had fallen into a trap that has hobbled many Lean and Six Sigma consultants: though we had included examples of applying Lean Six Sigma in services, by and large they were discussed using a jargon that has arisen from manufacturing roots. This jargon, especially for Lean, has made translating the methods to service environments more difficult than it has to be.

This book breaks that paradigm: almost all the applications of Lean and Six Sigma are for services and transactions. The case studies demonstrate how Lean Six Sigma can be used in service organizations just as effectively as in manufacturing—and with even faster results. Here for the first time, you'll read about how classic Lean tools, such as "Pull systems" and "setup reduction," are being used in procurement, call centers, surgical suites, government offices, R&D, etc. (Those who want shopfloor manufacturing applications of these topics can find examples in Lean Six Sigma.)

During the journey that has produced this book, I've been impressed by the range of people I've met doing extraordinarily fine work in improving service functions and entire organizations using Lean Six Sigma methods.

Take Karen Rago, for example. She's been in the medical field for more than 25 years, starting out as a nurse and rising to vice president at Stanford Hospital and Clinics before moving to the University of California at San Francisco. She has only recently become aware that her work in reducing the complexity related to surgical supplies and improving patient "flow" through the hospital was groundbreaking.

And then there's Myles Burke. He's a Master Black Belt at Lockheed Martin and one of my principal collaborators on this book. Though he comes from a manufacturing engineering background, his application of Lean Six Sigma in procurement operations has helped elevate the very nature of the buyers' jobs at Lockheed Martin.

I think Mike Fischbach, Darryl Greene, and a host of others from Bank One—including their inspirational leader, Lew Fischer—are creating an industry standard in how to use Lean Six Sigma as a strategic business tool. They are routinely cutting 30–80% of the wasted time and costs from their operations and providing a model for the whole organization.

All of these people and their organizations were impressive, but it's the city of Fort Wayne, Indiana, that really amazed me—perhaps because I, like most people, had low expectations when it came to government services of any sort. Once you know that Mayor Graham Richard has spent more than a decade living and breathing "quality" in its many manifestations, it probably isn't surprising to know that he walks the talk. What's really intriguing are the dozens of city employees who are reducing lead times, streamlining processes, providing better quality service to citizens, and holding down costs.

You'll hear more about each of these organizations and their employees in this book, along with numerous case studies describing how they've been able to achieve their impressive results.

Why a Book for Service?

"Service" in this context encompasses both service organizations (healthcare, banking, government, retail) and the service infrastructure in both service and manufacturing organizations (marketing, sales, accounting, hiring, production control, engineering, R&D, and so on). In short, everything except "the making of goods and articles by hand or especially by machinery" (that is, the direct manufacturing processes). Why is a book needed for these applications in particular?

One reason is **because of the huge opportunity.** Empirical data have shown that the cost of services are inflated by 30–80% waste—that is, the processes are riddled with activities that add no value from the perspective of the customer.

Here's another reason why a book on service is needed: **because service functions really need Lean Six Sigma tools, data skills, and process thinking.** The manager of a marketing call center claimed his 40 telephone marketing people were not productive because half the incoming calls were misdirected calls unrelated to marketing. Data showed that in fact only a third of the incoming calls were misdirected, but, more importantly, they consumed less than 5% of the call center's time. This manager would have to find other improvement opportunities to find something with a significant payback in terms of increasing customer contact time.

Service departments have little or no history of using data—in fact, needed data may not exist, and most service people are not as "numerically literate" as some of their manufacturing counterparts. But this is no obstacle to success. *Lean Six Sigma for Service* shows how easy it is to get started with relatively simple statistical and Lean tools that can effectively remove cost and delays from processes. Learning how to capture the important data within a service process gets you more than halfway to substantial Lean Six Sigma results.

And here's a final reason for this book: because of the factors just listed, **service functions have a harder time applying Lean and Six Sigma principles and tools.** The manufacturing roots of Lean and Six Sigma have made it unclear how to apply these tools to services, and this book makes that translation. For example, you'll find descriptions in Chapters 2 and 10 of one of the most important Lean tools for accelerating the speed of a process: the *Four Step Rapid Setup Method.* In manufacturing, this tool is used to reduce the changeover time from producing product A to product B. Many people in a service environment aren't aware that they have "setup" time and have no idea how the concept applies to their

Lean Principles, not Lean Manufacturing

Some people always couple the word Lean with manufacturing (Lean Manufacturing). That's a mistake. Lean is a set of principles that accelerates the speed of all processes across the enterprise.

process. But Lockheed Martin's System Integration Business Area (SIBA) MAC-MAR procurement center credits this tool with being a key enabler for cutting procurement costs by 50%—and this is a place where people sit at computers and talk on the phone the majority of the time.

What *Lean Six Sigma for Service* Can Do for You

This book provides real-world examples from situations where the critical determinants of quality and speed are the flow of information and the interaction between people. Here are some other important features of the book that will make reading it worth your while:

1) **Discover how to apply Lean tools to achieve greater speed in service processes.** Many books claim that Six Sigma can reduce cycle times and make the company more responsive and faster. This is merely wishful thinking unless Lean tools are integrated within Six Sigma—a statement based on a combination of theory, empirical observation, and data, all of which you'll see in Chapter 2. Lean principles, such as the need to improve process speed, apply to all processes in an organization. This book discusses Lean principles, not Lean manufacturing. It provides the necessary analytical framework needed to apply Lean to any process.

2) **Discover how to integrate Lean and Six Sigma.** Few books address Lean Six Sigma as an integrated methodology applied to service applications, and none to our knowledge show that Six Sigma and Lean must be applied side by side, not as independent improvement or "first one then the other" approaches. The fact is that Six Sigma is limited to process *quality* tools and does not have the process *speed* tools. Nowhere was this made more evident than by Jack Welch's famous assessment of the shortcomings of the Six Sigma implementation at GE, which initially contained no Lean. After three years he lamented:

"We have tended to use all our energy and Six Sigma science to move mean [delivery time] to…12 days. The problem is, 'the mean never happens,' and the customer is still seeing variances in when the deliveries

actually occur—a heroic 4-day delivery time on one order, with an awful 20-day delay on another, and no real consistency...Variation is evil."

Similarly, Lean does not possess the tools to bring a process under statistical control, nor does it define a sustaining infrastructure or emphasize customer focus as does Six Sigma. Thus, achieving the goals of your enterprise—ultimately to improve Return on Invested Capital (ROIC) by gains in customer satisfaction and waste reduction—requires both Lean and Six Sigma.

3) **See how you can use shareholder value to drive project selection—without needing an MBA.** Most experts will tell you that Lean Six Sigma reaches its full potential only when projects are linked to the CEO's strategic objectives and used to drive the most basic of business goals, such as shareholder return. Yet most books on Lean or Six Sigma do not even have metrics like ROIC and Net Present Value (NPV) in the index. They are written by very competent quality or manufacturing specialists whose experience is remote from the challenges faced by a CEO. This book brings these metrics and the underlying methods within the capability of managers, Champions, and Black Belts who often lack an MBA or other financial training. The result: The CEO's strategy drives tactical execution through Lean Six Sigma.

4) **Discover how Lean Six Sigma can cut costs by reducing complexity.** The internal and external diversity and complexity of your services/products is a major cost cutting opportunity for all organizations. Reducing the cost of complexity adds a third dimension to Lean and Six Sigma in opening new vistas for higher growth of ROIC. The quantitative value of complexity reduction versus traditional process improvement is presented in this book for the first time (see Chapter 5, which discusses methods for reducing complexity).

Structure of *Lean Six Sigma for Service*

This book is intended both for those who have never heard of Six Sigma or Lean as well as those who might already be using one or both of these methods:

Part I: Using Lean Six Sigma for Strategic Advantage in Service makes the case that Lean Six Sigma is an essential tool for driving shareholder value, and all that entails (such as increasing customer satisfaction, and simultaneously improving quality, speed, and costs, not to mention reducing complexity).

Part II: Deploying Lean Six Sigma in Service Organizations describes the basic elements of successful deployments. It include insights from corporate leaders who have already "walked the talk," which will accelerate your own journey.

Part III: Improving Services shows how Lean Six Sigma methods and tools work in service applications in the real world. It includes several chapters on using DMAIC effectively on existing processes (including numerous frontline case studies) and one on using Design for Lean Six Sigma to invent new services/processes.

PART I

Using Lean Six Sigma
for Strategic Advantage
in Service

"So what is the strategic significance of Lean Six Sigma? I want us to invest in the knowledge in people's heads. I'm not asking for capital or computers. I'm asking for an investment in people so we can have long-term sustainability of the kinds of results we've seen already."

—Mike Joyce, VP of LM21, Lockheed Martin

CHAPTER 1

The ROI of Lean Six Sigma for Services

"The lack of initial Six Sigma emphasis in the non-manufacturing areas was a mistake that cost Motorola at least $5 billion over a four year period."

—Bob Galvin, former CEO of Motorola

S ervice operations now comprise more than 80% of the GDP in the United States and are rapidly growing around the world. Even within manufacturing companies, it's common to have only 20% of product prices driven by direct manufacturing labor—the other 80% comes from costs that are designed into the product or costs associated with support and design functions (finance, human resources, product development, purchasing, engineering, etc.).

Moreover, in service applications, the costs related to work that adds no value in your customers' eyes ("non-value-add") is higher than in manufacturing, in both percentage and absolute dollars. The revenue growth potential of improving the speed and quality of service often overshadows the cost reduction opportunities. For example, as you'll see in the case studies later in this book, **work that adds no value in your customers' eyes typically comprises 50% of total service costs.** This represents enormous "white collar" potential for achieving significant speed, quality, and cost improvements, all of which can give organizations a major strategic advantage over their competition.

Here are some typical organizations that needed Lean Six Sigma in their services and business processes:

Like many of its counterparts in the banking industry, Bank One had been reincarnated several times throughout the 1990s. Mergers and acquisitions meant that heroic efforts were needed every day just to get the basic business work accomplished. In an industry as competitive as finance, this condition couldn't last long—and they had a long way to go to get the process under control, let alone achieve any kind of competitive advantage.

# # #

In 1999, Lockheed Martin (LM) set a goal of eliminating $3.7 billion in costs. At the time, LM was a relatively young organization, having been formed by a series of mergers and consolidations in the aerospace industry in 1995. Its workforce was a conglomeration of almost 20 separate companies, cultures, and processes, with a core manufacturing operation surrounded by a much larger "service" component (procurement, administration, design/engineering, etc.). How could they bring everyone together to achieve such a challenging goal?

# # #

At Stanford Hospital and Clinics (SHC), the future was clear: Patient volume was dropping because SHC kept losing contracts due to high costs. Physicians and management alike recognized that if they didn't do something soon, they would continue to lose current patients and be unable to attract new ones. It's one thing to want to provide high-quality patient care, but the pragmatists operated under this slogan: "No margin, no mission."

# # #

When Graham Richard, an entrepreneur and businessman, was elected as Mayor of Fort Wayne, Indiana, he had a simple vision: "I want Fort Wayne to be a safe city. I want it to have quality jobs. I want it to have excellent service and attract new businesses." He knew the city couldn't keep doing "bureaucracy as usual" if it was to implement this vision. But was there an alternative that would work in government?

Though these organizations come from a range of sectors, they represent significant service opportunities for applying Lean Six Sigma. Their goals and objectives may be different, their needs range from providing medical care to patients to providing logistical support for manufacturing, but they are all in the vanguard of a new movement. They realized the most effective way to achieve their objectives was by integrating Lean and Six Sigma principles and methods to improve service operations.

- **Bank One's** use of these principles and methods started with an initiative in their National Enterprise Operations called **Focus 2.0.** Launched in February 2002, it began with a series of carefully selected, strategically important projects. As a result of their efforts, the NEO group has the opportunity to generate millions of dollars in revenue per year due to improvements in one operation and saved thousands of dollars in cost avoidance and waste reduction in others.

- **Lockheed Martin** developed a clear goal: "We want Lean processes with 6s capability." They can cite a long list of service processes from procurement to design that now take a fraction of the time and cost they took before. In fact, over 1000 projects have been completed in the past few years in service areas alone. Their debt is down, revenues are healthy, they are going to exceed their cost-reduction target, and there are a record number of orders backlogged. They were able to offer their newest missile (with all the customer-required capabilities) at half the cost and one-third the cycle time of its predecessors due to significant and widespread use of Lean Six Sigma, not by using cheaper materials or cutting corners! They won the Joint Strike Fighter contract, which has an estimated value of over $100 billion. "There are a lot of reasons that contribute to these kinds of results," says Mike Joyce, a vice president at Lockheed Martin, "but a fundamental contributor is LM21 (Lockheed Martin 21st Century), our organizational effectiveness initiative that's based on Lean Six Sigma."

  At the 4000-person Lockheed Martin Naval Electronics and Surveillance Systems plant, 75% of the Black Belt projects have been in non-traditional manufacturing or white collar areas, generating $5 million in savings in its second year alone.

- In just four years, **Stanford Hospital and Clinics'** application of Six Sigma concepts (data, customers, quality) and Lean thinking (process flow, the preventable costs of unnecessary complexity) put them in a position to deliver higher quality patient care with lower costs—and regain market share from local competitors. Here's an example of their results: mortality from coronary artery bypass graft surgery dropped by 48% at the same time costs in the cardiac unit dropped by 40%. Overall, material costs throughout the hospital are now running $25 million below previous levels per year.

- **Fort Wayne** Mayor Graham Richard has authorized the launch of numerous projects citywide that draw on Lean and Six Sigma principles and methods. Many city departments have seen improvements in some aspect of its citizen services (clearer communication, faster response times to queries or complaints), a significant drop in costs, or better use of city resources. A change in construction permits, for example, has dropped the response time from almost two months to less than two weeks, and removed the kind of hassles that dissuaded many companies from wanting to do business with the city. (See Case Study # 3 in Chp 12 for details.) Improvements in garbage collection have reduced costs nearly $200,000 a year for the subcontractor while providing better services.

Each of these organizations recognized several fundamental truths: (1) getting fast can actually improve quality, (2) improving quality can actually make you faster, and (3) reducing complexity improves speed *and* quality. However, this cycle doesn't happen unless you apply *both* Lean and Six Sigma.

What Does Lean Six Sigma Mean for Services?

Lean Six Sigma for services is a business improvement methodology that maximizes shareholder value by achieving the fastest rate of improvement in customer satisfaction, cost, quality, process speed, and invested capital. The fusion of Lean and Six Sigma improvement methods is required because:

- Lean cannot bring a process under statistical control
- Six Sigma alone cannot dramatically improve process speed or reduce invested capital
- Both enable the reduction of the cost of complexity

Ironically, Six Sigma and Lean have often been regarded as rival initiatives—Lean enthusiasts noting that Six Sigma pays little attention to anything related to speed and flow, Six Sigma supporters pointing out that Lean fails to address key concepts like customer needs and variation. Both sides are right. Yet these arguments are more often used to advocate choosing one over the other, rather than to support the more logical conclusion that we need to blend Lean and Six Sigma.

How is it that Lean and Six Sigma are complimentary? Chapter 2 goes into more detail about what each of these methodologies brings to the party, but here's a quick overview:

Six Sigma...

- emphasizes the need to recognize opportunities and eliminate defects as defined by customers

- recognizes that variation hinders our ability to reliably deliver high-quality services

- requires data-driven decisions and incorporates a comprehensive set of quality tools under a powerful framework for effective problem solving

- provides a highly prescriptive cultural infrastructure effective in obtaining sustainable results

- when implemented correctly, promises and delivers $500,000+ of improved operating profit per Black Belt per year (a hard dollar figure many companies consistently achieve)

Lean ...

- focuses on maximizing process velocity

- provides tools for analyzing process flow and delay times at each activity in a process

- centers on the separation of "value-added" from "non-value-added" work with tools to eliminate the root causes of non-value-add activities and their cost

- provides a means for quantifying and eliminating the cost of complexity

The two methodologies interact and reinforce one another, such that percentage gains in Return on Invested Capital (ROIC%) is much faster if Lean and Six Sigma are implemented together. (Some people might question whether ROIC is a valuable metric for service businesses, and the answer is yes: Many service businesses—hotels, airlines, restaurants, health care—are very capital intensive. In most other service business—software development, financial services, government, etc.—the biggest costs are salaries/benefits, so invested capital is really the "cost of people.")

In short, what sets Lean Six Sigma apart from its individual components is the recognition that you can't do "just quality" or "just speed." Empirical proof of the need to use Lean and Six Sigma in combination is found throughout this book; additional support is gained by analyzing performance data using specialized software (see sidebar and Figure 1.1).

Applying Lean Six Sigma to Services— It's Not Just for Manufacturing!

The roots of both Lean and Six Sigma reach back to the 1980s (and beyond), a time when the greatest pressures for quality and speed were on manufacturing. Lean arose as a method for optimizing automotive manufacturing; Six Sigma evolved as a quality initiative to eliminate defects by reducing variation in processes in the semiconductor industry. It's not surprising, therefore, that the earliest service applications of Lean and Six Sigma arose in the service support functions of manufacturing organizations—GE Capital, Caterpillar Finance, ITT, Lockheed Martin, etc. These companies were already adept at key Six Sigma and Lean skills: value stream mapping, data collection, analysis of variance, setup reduction, design of experiments. It's impossible for outsiders to know how much of the stated gains in these companies are due to improvements in service operations vs. improvements in manufacturing, but Jack Welch stated that Six Sigma added $2 billion to GE's 1999 profits of $10.7 billion—and service applications dominate profit at GE. In the May 2000 issue of *Industry Week*, Lou Giuliano (CEO of ITT Industries) announced increased profits of over $130 million in the second year of Lean Six Sigma implementation (based on a $12 million investment).

How Speed and Quality Are Linked

Approximately 30 to 50% of the cost in a service organization is caused by costs related to slow speed or performing rework to satisfy customer needs. The development of value calculations discussed in Chapter 4 provides the means for mathematically proving that only a fast and responsive process is capable of achieving the highest levels of quality, and that only a high-quality process can sustain high velocity.

Figure 1.1: Only Lean + Six Sigma = Lowest Cost

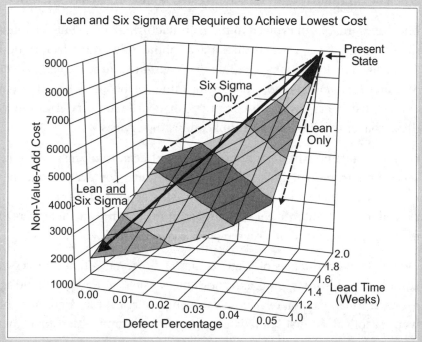

This figure shows the output from these calculations. The horizontal axis depicts the defect rate (the target of Six Sigma); the axis that goes into the page shows cycle time (the target of Lean).

The value of greatest interest on this chart is the vertical axis, representing costs that add no value to your product or service. The ideal state is in the lower left front corner—where costs are lowest. As you can see, reducing defects alone or reducing lead time alone bring some gains, but you can achieve the lowest cost only if you simultaneously improve both quality and speed.

Many people in service environments have heard about Six Sigma, the improvement methodology focused on achieving extraordinarily high levels of quality that has contributed well-publicized millions to the bottom line of companies like GE, Allied Signal, ITT, and Lockheed Martin. In contrast, few people outside manufacturing know much about Lean applications. Which is the problem. People hear "Lean" and automatically think "manufacturing" because that's the way it's always been used. In fact, Lean creates process **speed** (by reducing cycle time) and **efficiency** (minimal time, capital invested, and cost) in *any* process.

Like Six Sigma, Lean evolved in the manufacturing arena, but even more than Six Sigma, Lean sounds like it is at home only on the factory floor. Terms like *batch processing, WIP, setup, workstation turnover, Pull systems, 5S's,* and *Kanban* have no inherent meaning for people whose job is to talk to customers, type at a computer, or coordinate services. And yet these concepts have powerful applications in services.

Here's one example from Stanford Hospital of Lean thinking at work in a service environment: It is standard in medicine for every surgeon to specify his or her own surgical tray of instruments and supplies for any procedure. In Stanford's cardiac surgical unit, that meant there were six different surgical trays for each type of case, one for each surgeon.

One of the central tenets of Lean Six Sigma, however, is that unnecessary complexity adds costs, time, and enormous waste. Stanford got all the surgeons to collaborate on developing a *common* surgical tray. Naturally, they were skeptical at first. But when pushed to examine the issue more

---

Learning to Recognize Waste

When applying Lean to a service environment, one challenge is calling something that's accepted as "just the way work happens" by a new name: waste. All organizations need to develop Stanford's willingness to challenge themselves: "Which of these costs contribute to improving patient outcomes?" The traditional mindset would have been, "How can we prepare each of these surgical trays most efficiently," not "Are all these different trays really necessary?" The former mindset leads companies to do things like training staff to handle all the complexity—and completely ignore the hidden costs inherent in supporting that complexity! (See Chp 5.)

closely, the surgeons realized that having six different trays **had little impact on the quality of care provided to patients**. Within the space of a few meetings, they were able to agree on a standard surgical tray.

Stanford went on to apply this simplicity principle and other Lean Six Sigma concepts throughout the hospital. The result? As noted earlier, annual material costs have dropped by $25 million.

Here is another example from the City of Fort Wayne. The transportation department has an annual budget of $2 million. Once a bid for any large expenditure was accepted, that money would get "locked up," in their terms, inaccessible to other uses. Sounds like proper procedure, right? But what if the job came in underbudget? That would mean there was money sitting around that wasn't needed but that the department couldn't use for other jobs. Or say the job had cost overruns... then the city would have to scramble to find money it likely didn't have.

The team assigned to work on this problem realized, for the first time, that there was a lot of variation between the bid price and the actual price of most jobs—ranging from about 23% below bid to 22% over. Their first step was to set a goal of having bids come in ±10% of actual cost. (Was that a good target? No one knew at first! The point was that the city had never had a target before.) By Lean-ing the process (defining the flow of work and eliminating complexity) and using data to pinpoint problems, the team was able to greatly reduce the amount of variation in the bid-to-actual amounts, freeing up nearly $200,000 a year that would previously have been "locked up."

Making the manufacturing-to-service translation

From a Lean viewpoint, the unavailability of money in a service environment is just like unavailable production capacity in a factory, with the same types of consequences. This book's predecessor (*Lean Six Sigma*, pp. 57–58) showed that machine downtime coupled with variation in demand caused large amounts of work-in-process (WIP) and subsequently long delays in completing that work. In Fort Wayne, the unavailability of money had the same effect: projects whose costs varied on the high side had to remain as work-in-process (delaying completion) until the funds became available.

These examples are typical of the gains that can be achieved when Lean and Six Sigma tools are applied together in service applications.

Why Services Are Full of Waste— and Ripe for Lean Six Sigma

There are three key reasons why service functions need to apply Lean Six Sigma (the following chapters go into more detail):

- **Service processes are usually slow processes, which are expensive processes.** Slow processes are prone to poor quality… which drives costs up… and drives down customer satisfaction and hence revenue. The result of slow processes: more than half the cost in service applications is non-value-add waste.

- Service processes are slow because there is **far too much "work-in-process" (WIP)**, often the result of unnecessary **complexity** in the service/product offering. It doesn't matter whether the WIP is reports waiting on a desk, emails in an electronic in-box, or sales orders in a database. When there is too much WIP, work can spend more than 90% of its time *waiting*, which doesn't help your customers at all and, in fact, creates or inflicts substantial waste (non-value-add costs) in the process.

Does Lean Apply to You?

Lean methods and tools apply to anyone who…

- Chases information in order to complete a task (an "information shortage" in service is equivalent to material shortage in manufacturing)
- Must jump through multiple decision loops
- Is constantly interrupted when trying to complete a task
- Is engaged in expediting (of reports, purchases, materials, etc.)
- Does work in batches (collect a certain number of items requiring the same kind of work before embarking on the pertinent tasks)
- Finds work lost in the "white space" between organizational silos
- Doesn't know what they don't know

- In any slow process, **80% of the delay is caused by less than 20% of the activities**. We only need find and improve the speed of 20% of the process steps to effect an 80% reduction in cycle time and achieve greater than 99% on-time delivery.

In short, people working in service functions typically find that most of the steps in their processes *add no value* to the service in their customers' eyes. (You'll find quantifiable proof of this in the case studies in Chapters 12 and 13.) Identify and quantify the non-value-added waste, eliminate it using Lean Six Sigma, and the results follow as the day follows the night.

This isn't cost reduction, it's process change

"What really irks me is that investment analysts always talk about ITT's Value-Based Six Sigma effort, or other efforts like it, as cost reduction," says Lou Giuliano, the CEO of ITT. "It's not cost reduction. If you're doing cost reduction you're taking out people, you're skimping here, you're cutting back on an investment there; that's cost reduction. This is process change. Yes, you might take out resources, whether they be capacity, dollars, people, material, whatever it is, but it's not because you're cutting them, it's because you don't need them; you've found a better way to get the work done."

The Strategic Imperative of Investing in Lean Six Sigma

In manufacturing businesses, a significant investment in equipment may be required to improve labor productivity. In contrast, service operations are primarily driven by intellectual capital. According to Warren Buffett, "the best kind of investment to make is one in which a huge return results from a very small increment of invested capital" (*Berkshire Hathaway*, 1984).

By application of Lean Six Sigma, the numerator of the ROIC equation can be increased without increasing financial investment. At Lockheed Martin's procurement center, for example, the key investment that enabled a reduction of 50% of procurement cost had a 5 month payback.

At Stanford Hospital and Clinics, big savings came from bringing together a group of surgeons without any capital investment at all (details were provided earlier in this chapter). If Buffett likes this kind of investment, so will your shareholders.

The concept of linking Lean Six Sigma efforts to shareholder value is critically important but seldom discussed. If the link isn't made, your organization may realize some gains, but it will be a crapshoot as to whether your investment in Lean Six Sigma will help drive your strategic goals.

To illustrate the principle of driving shareholder value, Tom Copeland, a renowned authority on business valuation whose credentials were established while a consultant to McKinsey, compiled the actual stock market value of several hundred firms (see Figure 1.2, next page), including data on their...

- **Market to Book Value** (vertical axis), which measures the premium that the stock market will pay for the net assets (book value) of the company. Some companies trade at 1 times, others at 6 times, their book value.

- **Economic Profit** (the y-axis that goes into the page), which captures the "spread" (difference) between the percent Return on Invested Capital (ROIC%) and the percent Cost of Capital (COC%), i.e., how much the percentage earned on assets exceeded the percent that could be earned if those assets were invested in a T-Bill plus some equity risk.

- **Revenue Growth** (horizontal axis), another key driver of shareholder value if Economic Profit is positive.

The graph in Figure 1.2, which was generated from stock market data from real companies not theoretical models, shows that ROIC—the ratio of profit to invested capital—is the strongest driver of high stock market multiples of book value (indicated by the steep rise as ROIC increases). Revenue growth is a strong second.

If Economic Profit (EP) = 0%, then the company's ROIC% = Cost of Capital, and empirical stock market data shows that the company trades at about book value. If the ROIC% is 5% higher than its cost of capital,

Figure 1.2: The "Value Mountain": ROIC Drives Shareholder Value

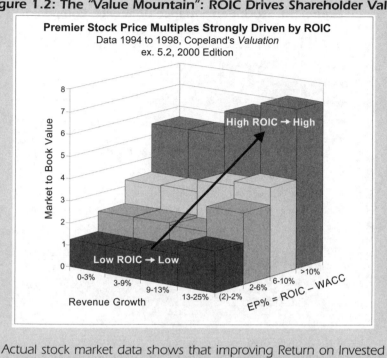

Actual stock market data shows that improving Return on Invested Capital (ROIC) is the best way to drive shareholder value. Here:

$$ROIC = \frac{Profit\ After\ Tax\ (PAT)}{Invested\ Capital}$$

...where invested capital is the total assets of the organization minus the current liabilities.

the company trades at 4–5 times book value. Companies that can grow at 10% or more per year with 10%EP stand a good chance of trading at 10 times their book value!

Thus there is huge value leverage in increasing ROIC. For this reason, all Lean Six Sigma projects should be prioritized based on their ability to contribute to ROIC% of the corporation—consistent with P&L managers' judgment. (Chapter 4 goes into more detail on how this is accomplished.)

But does it really work? Figure 1.3 compares the performance of companies who have reached full deployment of Six Sigma or Lean Six Sigma (= 1% of the workforce is Black Belts) versus the S&P 500.

Figure 1.3: Stock Performance of Service Companies with 1% Black Belt Population

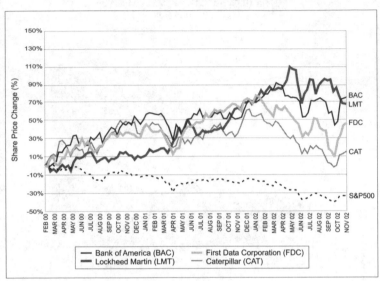

Here we see the stock performance of four Lean Six Sigma practitioners—Bank of America, First Data, Lockheed Martin, and Caterpillar—compared to S&P 500 performance.

Revenue Growth Drives Shareholder Value

Besides increasing ROIC by lowering costs and capital investment, Lean Six Sigma has an important role to play in **revenue growth**. This is only true for organizations or operations that earn more than their cost of capital. Here's the basic financial argument first: As Warren Buffett says,

> "The value of any business is determined by the cash inflows and outflows—discounted at an appropriate interest rate" (*Berkshire Hathaway Annual Report*, 1992).

This quote may sound exotic, but it really isn't. What Buffett means is that a dollar earned next year is worth less than a dollar earned this year because of inflation. For example, if inflation is at 5%, the "discounted value" of $1.00 next year is only $0.95:

Discounted Value = $1 / (1+ .05) = $.95

A dollar earned two years from now would be $\$1/(1+.05)^2 = \$0.90$, and so on. The notion of discount value is important because it affects the value of revenue growth, which must be captured as the "discounted value of growing cash flows" (yes, you may project that revenue may grow by $100,000 next year, but its real value to your organization should be represented as only $95,000 at 5% inflation). This principle is the same as the discounted value of Economic Profits.

If you are in the business of comparing potential Lean Six Sigma projects, you need to make three- to five-year projections for returns on those projects and represent them as their discounted (present) value, using best-estimate growth rates. That's the only fair way to compare the expected return on different projects, and the only way to make sure your Lean Six Sigma projects will have the biggest impact on shareholder value. Is all revenue growth good? Remember the huge valuations of the dot.coms? Some grew at fantastic rates but generated no profit-after-tax, and hence their Economic Profits were strongly negative. If you look back at Figure 1.2, you can see that **growth without Economic Profit creates no value**—as you move right on the horizontal axis (= growth without profit), the curve barely rises at all, meaning little value is added.

Conclusion

Lean Six Sigma for services is about getting results *rapidly*. The kind of results that can be tracked to the bottom line in support of strategic objectives. The kind that leaves delighted customers wanting to do *more* business, that creates value for your shareholders, and that energizes employees.

What accounts for the rapid results? Lean Six Sigma incorporates Lean's principles of speed and immediate action into the Six Sigma improvement process itself, increasing the velocity of improvement projects and hence results. Lean Six Sigma also incorporates the Six Sigma view of the evils of variation and reduces its impact on queue times. Finally, Lean Six Sigma uniquely attacks the hidden costs of complexity of your offering.

Combine Lean Six Sigma's ability to achieve service improvements with its focus on shareholder value and you have a powerful tool for executing the CEO's strategy, and a tactical tool for P&L managers to achieve their annual and quarterly goals. How you do that is the subject of the rest of this book.

CHAPTER 2

Getting Faster to Get Better:
Why You Need Both Lean and Six Sigma

"So far, we were able to reduce the cost of procurement by 50% while reducing the lead time for puchase order processing by over 40%—greatly improving our internal customers' productivity and satisfaction."

—Myles Burke, Master Black Belt, Lockheed Martin

#   #   #

One of the most expensive aspects of medical care is hospital stays… which puts providers in a quandary: how to reduce costs but still provide high-quality care. In the cardiac unit of Stanford Hospital and Clinics, an analysis of process flow found a capacity constraint in the "step-down unit," used for post-operative patients who no longer required intensive care. Limited capacity in that unit resulted in patients staying longer in more expensive intensive care than was necessary. Rather than simply hiring more nurses or assigning more beds to increase capacity, a team examined the protocols used in the step-down unit, studied guidelines for determining discharge readiness, and evaluated factors that contributed to longer stays to determine if there was anything the hospital could do to mitigate or avoid those issues (such as changing guidelines for using certain drugs). A number of changes were instituted, all of which resulted in increased capacity in the step-down unit without major investment.[1]

Speed. Quality. Low cost. These universal goals have been around as long as there has been competition in business. Bryan Carey, an executive VP at the consulting firm of DeLeeuw Associates, has worked in the finance industry for about 20 years, 17 of those with Bank of America. He and his colleagues have worked with countless banks and other financial institutions, and recently he's noticed a big change:

> "Historically, any change initiative at a bank always involved a negative conversation about tradeoffs. People looked at the pyramid of quality, time, and cost and thought, 'I'm not going to be able to optimize all three.' Line-of-business managers were all used to making autonomous decisions within their silo, never having to make decisions as a team. There'd be the CFO who cared about cost, a change manager who cared about getting quality results, and the executive sponsor of the project for whom speed was most important. They all had different priorities.

> "What I've seen from Lean Six Sigma is that we now have a mechanism for getting everyone to talk the same language. And people are starting to realize that you CAN have all three. It's no longer a conversation about trade-offs, it's conversations about how to leverage them together. This is the first time you can have all the players at the table engaged in a positive conversation about quality, speed, and cost."

Many separate disciplines have evolved to achieve these goals. As Carey discovered, only Lean Six Sigma lets you work on all three simultaneously because it blends Lean, with its primary focus on *process speed*, and Six Sigma, with its primary focus on *process quality*.

Some firms have adopted Lean or Six Sigma to the near exclusion of the other, or even allowed competing camps to emerge. Myles Burke, a Master Black Belt at Lockheed Martin, recalls a time a few years ago when he was challenged to choose: "People were either die-hard Six Sigma or die-hard Lean. There was no middle ground," says Burke. "Once we had conflicting schedules of Six Sigma and Lean training. When I went to Lean training, my Black Belt friends said, 'What are you doing? Are you abandoning ship?'" (Such conflicts no longer arise at Lockheed Martin due to the integration of Lean and Six Sigma into what they call their LM21 program, described later in this book.)

But it is also true that Lean advocates do not always understand the importance of Six Sigma tools in their ability to achieve Lean goals. A simple mathematical derivation (available at www.profisight.com) shows how a 10% scrap rate (= defects) increases process cycle time by 38% and the number of things-in-process by 54%. And that ain't Lean!

Viewing Lean and Six Sigma as competing practices entirely misses the central theme introduced in Chapter 1: you can't achieve maximum speed without also improving quality, nor can you achieve maximum quality without also improving velocity. And you can't maximize ROIC unless you do both. This chapter reviews the key elements of Six Sigma and Lean, then explains how they are complimentary and why you need them both.

Defect-free Service: What Six Sigma has to offer

Zero defects, re-engineering, Baldrige, ISO 9000, TQM... any number of approaches have evolved over the years to improve quality. Yet with all of these to choose from, why would executives from companies such as GE Capital, Quest Diagnostics, Starwood Hotels, Bank One, ITT Industries, Bank of America, and Mt. Carmel Hospital embrace Six Sigma as their preferred execution tool? No other quality initiative can claim such an illustrious roster of advocates.

The answer lies in one of the simplest but most powerful Six Sigma concepts: that the *outcomes* of any process are the result of what goes *into* that process. In Six Sigma texts, you'll find this notion captured in the simple "Y is a function of X" equation that relates an output (Y) to inputs or process variables (Xs):

$$Y = f(X_1, X_2, X_3, \ldots)$$

This equation holds true at the organizational level as well: any output (Y), such as profit, growth, or ROIC, is dependent on the process variables (Xs) such as quality, lead time, offering attractiveness, non-value-add cost, etc., that go into it. In order to improve the results we see ("drive the Y" in Six Sigma parlance), we have to find and focus on the critical Xs that affect that result.

There's a deeper meaning to this equation that you'll learn to appreciate the more you get involved in Lean Six Sigma. It's not just that "Y is a function of some Xs"—but that it's our job to *discover* the Xs that will really drive the Y. Want to increase profits? What *inputs* do you have to affect to do that? Want to improve quality of one of your services? What are the key inputs to the service that affect quality the most?

The more that leaders appreciate this equation, the more they start to change their behavior. They will no longer simply call for a 10% improvement in results. Rather, they'll support Lean Six Sigma efforts so people can study and improve the processes that *produce* that result. When Lou Giuliano conducts a review with a P&L center, he begins by asking for a presentation on the Black Belt projects. The CEO's focus on the Xs (which determine the Ys) supports the cycle of improvement and signals that continuous improvement is the "way we do business."

Core Elements of the Six Sigma Prescription

Six Sigma started out as a metric and an organized group of quality tools (most of which had been around for decades). The typical business manager could not understand why it was different from TQM, and therefore why he or she should pay any attention to it. But over the past decade, Six Sigma has proven itself superior to its predecessors in several unique and decisive ways:

1) **CEO & Managerial Engagement.** A company has one set of shareholders for whom ROIC is the common goal, one set of resources to apply to the highest value-creating opportunities. The speed, quality, and cost advantages provided by Lean Six Sigma are the drivers of ROIC. That's why the CEO has to be out front in the support of the initiative and why failure of a P&L manager to "get on board" is not an option. The CEO should regularly communicate and demonstrate his or her engagement in the change process, and everyone on the management team should be trained on how to lead in the new culture.

2) **You have to allocate appropriate resources (= staff and time commitments) to high-priority projects.** One promise of Six Sigma is that full-time Black Belts can generate $500,000 per year of increased operating profit that can be tracked to the bottom line. There are two components to this equation: the number and nature of the resources, and the processes used to select projects. Companies achieving those

The Importance of Executive Engagement

Chapters 6 to 9 discuss a number of cultural practices that can help boost Lean Six Sigma commitment and results. Of those, the most important by far is senior management involvement.

For example, Vance Coffman, CEO of Lockheed Martin, has set a mandate that investment in LM21 is a bottomline competitive advantage that customers and shareholders will "see and feel" in the company's results. This message is emphasized in each of his quarterly reviews. Early in the launch of LM21, Coffman demonstrated his personal commitment to learning and practicing Lean Six Sigma by clearning time from his schedule to participate in basic Lean Six Sigma training (see Figure 2.1).

Figure 2.1: CEO Vance Coffman Leads By Example

Lockheed Martin CEO Vance Coffman is a CEO who leads by action, not just words. Here, he joins Dick Watham, Cindy Waun, and Dennis Stuart in a Lean Six Sigma training project with a "statupult" device used for training simulation exercises.

kinds of results have typically committed about 1% of their best people—future leaders of the business—as full-time resources (Black Belts, Master Black Belts, and Champions), and another 3% of employees have received Green Belt training. (See Chapter 8 for a discussion of these various roles, including a discussion of whether Black Belts need to be full-time.) They have also developed a rigorous process—usually led by the corporate Champion—for identifying, scoping, and selecting projects based on rational criteria, such as maximizing ROIC and/or the potential effect on customers' Critical-to-Quality issues. And, finally, they are good at tracking projects and knowing when to pull the plug if one is not performing to plan.

3) **Everyone affected by or involved in Six Sigma should receive some level of training.** All executives and managers need to be educated about Six Sigma. The extent of the training depends on how directly the group or individual will be involved in selecting, guiding, managing, or implementing improvement. (See Chp 8 for details).

4) **Variation has to be eliminated.** Reducing variation is a concept woven into the warp and woof of a six sigma organization. Variation in meeting a customer Critical-to-Quality (CTQ) requirement is regarded as a key initiator to guide the improvement process. Attacking and eliminating variation is accomplished by the Define-Measure-Analyze-Improve-Control (DMAIC) problem-solving methodology and supporting tools that require management to make *data-driven* decisions.

Speed & Low Cost: What Lean can contribute

Whereas Six Sigma is most closely associated with defects in quality and elimination of variation, Lean is linked to speed, efficiency, and elimination of waste. The goal of Lean is **to accelerate the velocity of any process by reducing waste in all its forms.**

The overarching benefit of Lean is the ability to see cost and lead time reduction opportunities where you never saw them before. Through application of the Lean concepts and tools, you will find that the process steps you once thought were essential are unnecessary, and their costs and delays removable *after* Lean tools have been applied. You'll start to see the difference between standards and practices that are meaningful and those that are adding cost for no benefit to your customers.

Here's an example: Any business that was considering building in Fort Wayne was soon warned: doing business with the city was difficult at

Origin of the Six Sigma terminology

Six Sigma terminology arises from the relationship between the variation in a process or operation and the customer requirements associated with that process. In this normal distribution in Figure 2.2, the largest concentration of values is around the mean (average), and tails off symmetrically. The distance between the center line and the inflection point (where the curve starts to flatten out) is known as sigma (σ), the standard deviation. Sixty-eight percent of the data falls within one standard deviation above or below the mean, 95% within 2σ, and 99% within 3σ. (So the range from -3σ to +3σ represents 99% of the data.)

Six Sigma numbers represent how the distri-

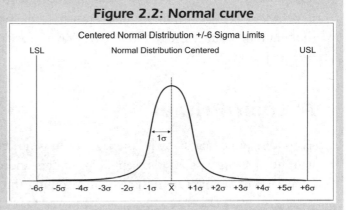

Figure 2.2: Normal curve

bution of actual output compares to the range of acceptable values (customer specifications). A defect is any value that falls outside customer specifications. The more of the distribution that fits within the specifications, the higher the sigma level. To make sure different processes can be compared, it's customary to standardize by reporting a defect "rate" (defects per million opportunities) rather than raw counts.

Sigma Level	Defects per Million Opportunities	Yield
6	3.4	99.9997%
5	233	99.977%
4	6,210	99.379%
3	66,807	93.32%
2	308,537	69.2%
1	690,000	31%

Being "six sigma capable" means having a process that produces only 3.4 defects per million opportunities despite expected fluctuations.

best. Among other things, it often took close to two months (avg = 51 days) just to get the proper permits. Benchmarking by a city team revealed they were at a definite competitive disadvantage against other cities that got the equivalent work done in under a month.

A team assigned to improve the permitting process soon identified the most critical steps, eliminated unneeded activities, and developed standardized procedures with clear directions. With the new process in place, 95% of permit requests are now processed within 10 days. The progress is being noticed by a number of customers, the contractors who once thought they would never build in Fort Wayne. (See p. 323 for details on this project.)

A Lean Primer

Every discipline has its own language; Lean is no different. There are a handful of terms you'll find essential for understanding and appreciating what Lean has to offer (and that you'll encounter throughout this book).

Lead time and process speed

Lead time is how long it takes you to deliver your service or product once the order is triggered. Understanding the drivers of lead time is much simpler than you might think thanks to a simple equation known as **Little's Law** (named after the mathematician who proved it):

$$\text{Lead Time} = \frac{\text{Amount of Work-In-Process}}{\text{Average Completion Rate}}$$

This equation tells us how long it will take any item of work to be completed (**lead time**) simply by counting how much work is sitting around waiting to be completed (**work-in-process**) and how many "things" we can complete each day, week, etc. (**average completion rate**).

Little's Law is a lot more important than it may look. Most of us don't have a clue what our average delivery or lead time is, let alone what the variation is. And the thought of having to track an order through every step in the process is daunting, especially if you have a process that takes days or weeks to complete. (Think about the permit applications staff in Fort Wayne—can you imagine having to trace one permit for 51 days?) Now we can get a reasonable estimate of any of the factors in this equation if we have data or reliable estimates of the other two. E.g., if you know your WIP and completion rate, you can estimate lead time. If you know your lead time and completion rate, you can estimate the amount of WIP in your process.

WIP (work-in-process)

Some people in service environments are uncomfortable with the term "work-in-process" (WIP) because it sounds like a manufacturing line. But the concept applies

> "Lean is simply creating an environment where you have the right amount of resources—where work is paced and content targeted according to customer demand. More importantly, Lean is having the ability to rapidly respond to a signal from the customer through a standardized process—which means it is predictable, controllable, and sustainable."
>
> —Jim Kaminski, Ass't VP, Bank One

to any and all processes. If it helps you translate Lean to your own application, think of WIP as TIP (number of "things-in-process"). Those "things" can be customer requests, checks waiting to be processed, phone calls you have to return, reports you need to complete, etc.—any work that is officially in the process and isn't yet complete. You'll see the term WIP referenced on most pages in this book: whenever you see it, think about your own job and how many tasks there are sitting on your desk or in a computer program or voicemail log waiting for you to work on them. That's WIP.

Delays/queue time

Whenever you have WIP, you have work that is *waiting to be worked on*. In Lean speak, this work is said to be "in queue" (in line); the time it sits around waiting is "queue time." Any time that work sits in queue is counted as a delay, no matter what the underlying cause.

Value-add and non-value-add

As you begin to track the flow of work, it soon becomes obvious that some of the activities *add value in the eyes of your customers* (and hence is called **value-added** work). Another way to look at value-added work is to ask yourself whether your customers would be willing to pay for it if they were given the option of whether to pay for it if they knew it was part of their purchase price. If they would likely refuse to pay if given the choice, or would take their business elsewhere to find another supplier who didn't have those costs, then that work is **non-value-added.**

Process efficiency

The critical metric of waste for any service process is what percentage of the total cycle time is spent in value-added activities and how much of it is waste. The metric used to answer this question is **process cycle efficiency (PCE)**, which relates the amount of value-add time to the total lead time of the process:

$$\text{Process Cycle Efficiency} = \frac{\text{Value-add Time}}{\text{Total Lead Time}}$$

A PCE of less than 10% indicates that the process has a lot of non-value-add waste opportunity.

Waste

As you've just seen, waste is anything—time, costs, work—that adds no value in the eyes of your customer. All organizations have some waste that, because of how their processes operate today, is *required* to compensate for internal weaknesses. The amount of waste at each activity is proportional to how long it delays the work. Lean shows us how to recognize and eliminate waste and not simply accept it as "the way work is done around here." There are seven specific forms of waste identified in Lean practice, which are discussed in Chapter 10.

Basic Lean Lessons

The principles discussed above come together in a handful of deceptively simple but incredibly powerful lessons that allow us to achieve rapid gains through Lean. Here are the principles discussed below:

1. Most processes are "un-Lean"—that is, have a Process Cycle Efficiency of <10%

2. A primary goal is reducing controlling WIP (if you can't control WIP, you can't control lead time)

3. Every process should operate on Pull, not push, to eliminate variation in lead time

4. Only 20% of the activities cause 80% of the delay

5. Invisible work can't be improved: we need visual management, based on data

Lean Lesson #1: Most processes are "un-Lean"

You probably won't be surprised to learn that in "un-lean" service processes, most of the work—at least 50% and often more—is non-value-added. This point is easily illustrated by using colors or other techniques to visually separate value-added from non-value-added work on a process map. Figure 2.3 (next page), for example, shows the start of a basic flowchart done by a team at Lockheed Martin that discovered 83% of the activities performed between placing a purchase order and receiving the goods was non-value-added (waste)—work done to correct for mistakes, contact the vendor for a quote (when it could have been a pre-negotiated item), get a corrected drawing, or procedures to correct delays made earlier in the process. (There are more examples of this type of flowchart in Chps 12 and 13.)

Won't speed hurt quality?

All of us have been in situations where exhortations to "work faster" only led to quality problems, and likely slower processes as well. So the natural concern is that Lean's focus on process speed will hurt quality. But that doesn't happen. Why? Because Lean practices reduce time by reducing non-value-add activities, eliminating queues, reducing the time spent between value-add activities, and so on. The key steps that your customers value are generally left untouched by Lean tools. Application of Six Sigma tools to value-add activities can help reduce defects, which in turn can speed up value-add steps, but since they are typically less than 10% of the processing time, speeding up value-add work has relatively little impact until after the non-value-add activities are eliminated.

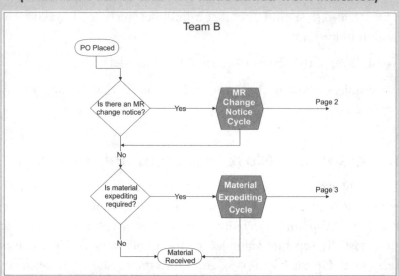

**Figure 2.3: Simple Flowchart
(with value-added and non-value-added work indicated)**

A team from Lockheed Martin's procurement center discovered that most of the work from placing a purchase order to receiving materials was waste (non-value-added)—rework done to compensate for errors, omissions, delays in earlier parts of the process, or for the large variety of different tasks (complexity). By drilling down the value stream (showing 248 steps in sufficient detail), then reducing complexity through standardization, they were able to eliminate most of this waste. Gains from such improvements allowed them to cut procurement costs in half.

Lean Lesson #2: A primary goal should be reducing WIP

Take another look at Little's Law:

$$\text{Lead Time} = \frac{\text{Amount of Work-In-Process}}{\text{Average Completion Rate}}$$

This equation isn't simply some theoretical construct; it has a lot of practical implications. First of all, it shows that the two ways to control lead time are either limiting work-in-process (WIP) or increasing the average completion rate. In any operation that doesn't deal directly with customers—that is, where WIP is orders or calls or emails or reports, not people—controlling WIP is much easier than improving completion rate. In fact, you can speed up any process—reduce lead time—by reducing the amount of WIP, *even if you do nothing to improve completion rate.*

This conclusion explains how people can achieve such quick gains by applying Lean principles. Wherever and whenever possible, they simply have to limit how much work they allow into the process at any given time. (Examples later in this book discuss what to do when WIP is "people" and the best way to maintain lead time becomes adding capacity to keep the completion rate up there.)

Why should we focus on WIP first? It only costs intellectual capital to reduce WIP. It takes the investment of financial capital or payroll to increase the average completion rate, both of which hurt ROIC and hence shareholder value. Lean tools can reduce the work-in-process and eliminate waste, hence boosting ROIC. Little's Law provides the mathematical foundation that allows us to apply Lean to *all* processes.

Lean Lesson #3: "How the heck can I reduce WIP?" (Creating a Pull system)

Look around your workspace. Is your In-Box stuffed to overflowing? Do you have a long list of new emails that will take you days to get through? Is your voicemail box rejecting new messages? Are people waiting for your work output?

All of those items represent WIP, work that someone else—a coworker, a customer—is requesting of you. As a newly converted Lean thinker, you know that you need to reduce that WIP if you want to stand a chance of improving cycle time and reducing waste. You know that WIP is like cars on a freeway: adding more cars doesn't speed up a congested freeway! But how to do it?

Naturally, putting a limit on WIP isn't possible in customer-facing processes when that WIP is really people waiting to be served or trying to purchase a product (in those situations, there are other ways to maintain or improve lead time, see p. 34).

For any work that isn't an actual customer standing in front of you, the secret to reducing WIP is found in Little's Law. In a Lean service process, there is a step that *precedes* the actual process, a step where input (work requests, orders, calls, etc.) are collected together. Someone then controls the release of these "materials" into the process.

Let's look at one example. The independent distributors for one company needed to get proposal information from the marketing department in order to quote construction jobs. The distributors were unhappy with the 2 to 3 weeks it took marketing to develop the needed information. The required turnaround to delight these customers was 3 days.

A team collected data over a few weeks that showed the marketing staff could process an average of 20 quotes per day. The distributors wanted a *reliable* 3-day turnaround; the data showed that because of variation in the process, the marketing staff would have to aim for a target closer to 2.4 days in order to meet that customer request.

How much WIP could they allow in the process? They turned to Little's Law and plugged 20 into the completion rate and 2.4 days into lead time, to come up with a maximum WIP of 48 quotes in process at any time:

$$\text{Lead Time} = 2.4 \text{ Days} = \frac{\text{Amount of Work-In-Process} = 48 \text{ quotes}}{\text{Average Completion Rate} = 20 \text{ quotes/day}}$$

To manage this system, they created a visual board that showed how many quotes were in process. The cap on WIP was 48 requests, so unless the number dipped to 47, no additional quotes could be delivered by the clerk, as shown in Figure 2.4 (next page).

The secret to making this system work is captured in the lower left-hand corner of Figure 2.4, in the bin labeled "input." (The bin can be a physical compartment or an electronic database, depending on the nature of your work.) These requests are not officially *in* the process until they are released from the raw material bin. **The only trigger for releasing the work *into* the process is having an item *exit* the process—and that's what a Pull system is.** The guaranteed service level of about two-and-a-half days' turnaround doesn't start until the request enters the process.

Figure 2.4: Pull System for Sales Quotes

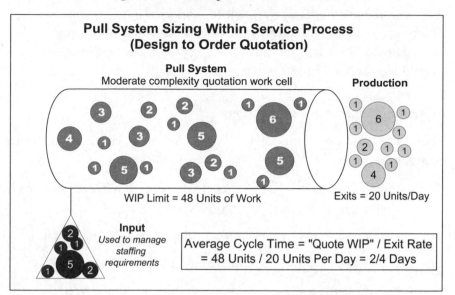

In other words, a Pull system in service environments means making deliberate decisions about the timing of work released into process. Just how you make those decisions is critical; it gives you another opportunity to live out a focus on "value." For example, in this case the question was *which request will be released into the process when another request is completed.* "First in, first out" didn't cut it here because some requests represented highly likely, high-dollar-potential orders; others were much less likely to be accepted, represented difficult bids, or were for smaller orders.

The answer lie in **triaging** the bid opportunities. Each request was rated on a scale of 1 to 3 on each of three criteria:

- Difficulty to bid
- Competitive advantage
- Gross profit dollars

The scores for each criteria were multiplied for each bid opportunity. Those with the highest rating would be the next to be released into the process—even if there were other bid opportunities that had been waiting in line longer. (So a *new* request that scored a 9 would be released before an older request that scored a 6.) Using this system, the same number of marketing staff were able to book 70% more revenue and 80% more gross profit. (An alternative, of course, would have been for this company to hire a lot more marketing staff—at great expense—so they could increase capacity.)

Creating Your Own Pull System

How can you make this system work for you? Here's a suggested sequence:

1. Identify/confirm the service level you want to achieve. (Ask your customers what service level they want.)

2. Determine your work group's completion rate (based on data).

3. Use Little's Law to determine maximum WIP.

4. Cap the active work in the process at the maximum WIP.

5. Put all incoming work into an input buffer.

6. Develop a triage system for determining which incoming work should be released into the process next.

7. Continue with other process improvements so you can improve completion rate and further reduce lead time.

The contribution of Lean Six Sigma in situations like this is two-fold: For the first time, data (on demand variation, WIP, and completion rate) are captured in a service environment and used as the basis for decision making. Secondly, speed and quality tools can then be brought to bear by people who have the time and energy to drive home the results.

Careful! Don't treat customers like inventory or raw materials!

The Pull system described above works when the input is paperwork, email, phone call messages, etc. But in customer-facing process, you have to keep the response time and the capacity of the service offering at acceptable levels, come what may. When the "things" in process are customers, you can't put them in inventory, nor can you make them wait longer to receive service, hence the lead time cannot increase. Looking at Little's Law, we can tell that the only option left is increasing the average completion rate.

One challenge of customer-facing operations is they show high variation in demand, with customer numbers bunching up at some hours and slacking off at others. If the pattern is predictable, you can increase completion rate by changing staffing patterns, having additional staff at peak times much like call centers do. If variation in demand is unpredictable, the solution is to apply Queuing Theory, equations that allow you to calculate how different factors—such as variation in supply or demand—affect WIP (and hence lead time). For example, Figure 3-11 from Lean Six Sigma (reproduced below as Figure 2.5) shows that that if you have 20% back up capacity, variation in demand has virtually no impact on the time a customer waits (queue time).

Taking a Counterintuitive Leap

Pull systems sound counterintuitive to many people. Most of us think that the best way to get faster is to push work into the process as soon as possible. What Lean teaches us is the exact opposite: we can only speed up process time by controlling (and usually slowing) release of work into the process.

Figure 2.5: Impact of Variation Is Worst When Capacity is High

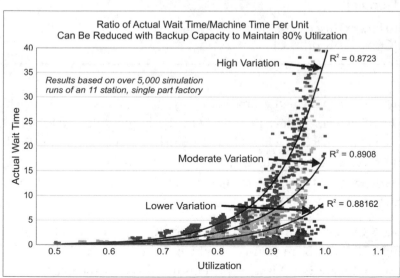

Ratio of Actual Wait Time/Machine Time Per Unit
Can Be Reduced with Backup Capacity to Maintain 80% Utilization

High Variation — $R^2 = 0.8723$

Results based on over 5,000 simulation runs of an 11 station, single part factory

Moderate Variation — $R^2 = 0.8908$

Lower Variation — $R^2 = 0.88162$

Actual Wait Time

Utilization

You can get backup capacity using personnel from other departments who are cross trained; or using triaging (just like the Pull system described above), where, for example, harder or more difficult services are funneled to more-experienced staff.

Lean Lesson #4: Process Cycle Efficiency allows you to quantify the opportunity

Typical process cycle efficiencies in services run at about 5% (see Table 2.1), meaning that work spends 95% of its "in process" time just waiting. Sound bad? It is. And it's not just the delays that are a problem. The old adage is true: the longer the work stays in process, the more it costs. **A Lean process is one in which the value-add time is more than 20% of the total cycle time of that process.**

Table 2.1: Cycle Efficiencies		
Application	Typical Cycle Efficiency	World-Class Cycle Efficiency
Continuous Manufacturing	5%	30%
Business Processes (Service)	10%	50%
Business Processes (Creative/Cognitive)	5%	25%

Don't be surprised if the processes in your organization initially have cycle efficiencies of less than 5%. On the bright side, experience has shown that you'll find a lot of low-hanging fruit and will be able to eliminate at least 20% of your cost by application of basic Lean Six Sigma tools. (Several of the case studies in Part III of this book led to even greater gains—near 50%.)

Process Cycle Efficiency can be dramatically displayed by differentiating value-add times from non-value-add times on a Time Value Map, as shown in Figure 2.6. (Visual depictions like this cause people to really sit up and take notice!)

Figure 2.6: Time Value Map

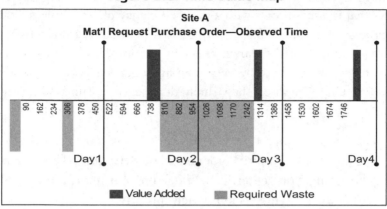

A time value map is generated by tracking a work item through the
process and tracking where it spends its time. Only work that is seen
as value-added by the customer is plotted above the midline; everything else is waste in their eyes.

The concept of a Time Value Map is simple enough. Just track any work
item as it flows through the process and classify the time into one of
three categories: (1) Value-added work, (2) waste that is required for
business reasons (work the customer doesn't necessarily want to pay for,
but is needed for accounting, legal, or regulatory reasons), and
(3) delays/waste. Then draw a timeline and mark off the time segments
for each of these categories. In this Lockheed Martin purchasing example, you can see there is a four-day cycle from the time the material
request reached the procurement center to the time the purchase order is
placed. The value-added work (shaded portions above the centerline)
shows the buyer is only working the order for 14 minutes of those
4 days. The majority of the time, delineated by the blank space, is idle
queuing time. This process initially had a Process Cycle Efficiency of less
than 1% (14 min out of 4 days, or 1920 minutes).

Lean Lesson #5: 20% of the activities cause 80% of the delay

The only way to achieve the primary Lean goal—speed—is to remove
anything that is slowing a process down. Mapping a process and collecting data on cycle time, variation, and complexity allows you to calculate

the delay time that each activity contributes to the process. Experience shows that in *any* process with a cycle efficiency of 10% or less, 80% of the process lead time is chewed up by less than 20% of the activities—another example of the Pareto effect in action! These 20% are called **Time Traps**, which become very obvious when creating value stream maps (see Chp 4) and can be visually depicted in a Time Value Map as in Figure 2.6.

As you'll see in Chapter 4, finding the Time Traps is the critical piece in attacking problems in priority order based on delay time. This is tremendously liberating: you get terrific leverage on your improvement dollars if you select the right targets in the right priority.

Lean Lesson #6: Invisible work can't be improved

If there really is such large cost and lead time opportunities in services, why hasn't Lean Six Sigma been applied more often?

One clear advantage that people in manufacturing have is the ability to physically see and trace the *flow* of work. You can walk down a production line and follow the work-in-process (WIP) as raw materials or products are turned into finished product as they move from workstation to workstation. This flow is always documented in a "router" which shows the path of value-add work. Similarly, there are constant physical reminders of any waste (rework, scrap, delays) in the form of piles of in-progress or soon-to-be-discarded material.

In services, work is largely invisible. Someone hits a computer key and a report zips through circuits to another office down the hall or across the world. Someone else hits a button on a phone and a customer is transferred from one workstation (perhaps customer service) down to another (technical support).

It's not just the work *flow* (process) that is harder to see in services; it's just as hard to judge the amount of work-in-process. Yes, some of us can judge WIP by looking at the stack of paper on our desks or counting the number of people standing in line waiting for service. But it's much more common to have the "work" be something less visible: an electronic file of reports or orders waiting to be processed, 20 emails awaiting responses, 10 customers "on hold."

Even though it can be difficult to visualize flow in service environments, understanding the flow of work and being able to evaluate WIP are pre-requisites for applying Lean concepts to improve speed and reduce waste. Different types of process maps are typically employed to "make the invisible visible," including a variety called **value stream maps** that you'll encounter frequently in this book (see the example in Figure 2.7).

Figure 2.7: Value Stream Map (A process flow map)

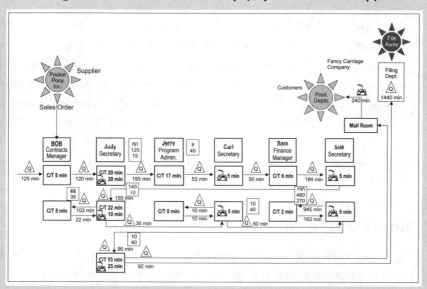

This value stream map, based on an actual process, captures the main sequence of activities in the boxes across the top line. The triangles and other notations show wait times (delays) and rework loops (another form of waste). Notice that the order begins by waiting 125 minutes "in queue" at Bob's activity before he spends 8 minutes adding value, then waits 120 minutes at Judy's station before she adds 20 minutes of value, etc. The order makes several loops back and forth between Judy, Bob, and Sue. Creating a map like this highlights wasted time and effort that usually isn't apparent to people mired in the process. Why the long queue times? Because there is a lot of work-in-process that has to be handled before any new item of work can be handled.

Figure 2.7 also demonstrates how unnecessarily complex many administrative processes are. One company had an Engineering Change Notice (ECN) approval process that required signatures from seven managers, and it usually took weeks for the approval form to make it through all seven in-baskets. This service process inflicted major problems on the manufacturing process because it prevented the correction of defective engineering drawings (and the products based on those drawings). The long cycle time on this decision process meant that rework had to continue long after a quality problem had been detected, even after *new* artwork had been prepared that would have allowed them to produce defect-free products.

When they looked more closely at the purposes of having all seven signatures, this company realized that five of the managers had no particular expertise they could contribute to the process. These five could therefore be changed to an "FYI notification status" without harming the process (they were still copied on the form because knowing that changes were happening was helpful to them, but they were not truly part of the decision-making process). Now it takes less than a week for the two remaining managers to review the form, resolve any issues, and set the rest of the process in motion.

Visual Management

The benefits of having WIP, waste, and employee ownership visible are why Lean encompasses so many visual management tools used to:

1) Establish and display work priorities

2) Visually display daily process performance ("was today a good day or a bad day?")

3) Support communication within a work area or between management and staff

4) Provide feedback to team members, supervisors, and managers and make it possible for all employees to contribute to continuous improvement

At its simplest level, visual management can include things like posting process maps that document how the process should operate, or posting data charts on a bulletin board so that everyone and anyone in the work area can see how well or poorly the process is performing. Figure 2.8 shows a special type of visual management tool called a **takt board** ("takt" is German for "metronome") for the marketing Pull process described above. Takt boards are used to help maintain a certain rhythm or pace in a process. The board captures figures on the desired "rhythm

Figure 2.8: Order Entry Takt Board

Takt Board: Order Entry Department				
Yesterday:		443 Orders		1.61 Orders/Hr
Today:		**440 Orders**		**1.66 Units/Hr**
Hour	Scheduled	Actual	+/- Diff	Comments
7-8 AM	60	53	-7	System Down f/5 min
8-9 AM	60	59	-8	
9-10 AM	45	48	-5	
10-11 AM	60	61	-4	Took late lunch
11-12 PM	30	31	0	
12-1 PM	60	59	-1	
1-2 PM	50	50	-1	
2-3 PM	40	41	0	
3-4 PM	35	35	0	Over 7 min: Software issue
Totals	440	440		

Step 1: Write in the number of orders processed and the orders/hour from yesterday.

Step 2: Write in the number of orders to process and the orders/hour goal for today. Confirm the takt rate for each hour (account for breaks and lunch).

Step 3: Each hour, write in the number of orders processed in the previous hour.

Step 4: Write in the cumulative difference between the scheduled orders processed and the actual orders processed.

Step 5: Write in any comments (network/system down, ran out of forms, etc.) As a reason for meeting or not meeting the takt rate.

A takt board is a simple visual tool that helps people maintain a certain pace or rhythm in the process required to meet customer demand and not exceed a maximum level of work-in-process (which allows them to maintain the lead time). Produce too fast, and you end up with excess WIP and a slowed process. Produce too slow, and you end up with unhappy customers. The takt board shows the desired schedule for work, differences in actual work produced, and reasons for those differences (which helps process operators discover patterns in delays).

of production" (which is based on customer demand and caps on WIP) and the actual rate achieved by the process operators. Based on the original work done by this group to establish a WIP limit, this board is used to maintain a level of 48 requests-in-process. (Other visual management tools will be covered later in this book.)

A Recap of Lean Thinking

A Lean process...

- Operates at a process cycle efficiency >20%

- Has a maximum cap on WIP to control velocity

- Uses a Pull system where new work is released into the process only when work has exited to the next process

- Uses visual controls to manage and monitor the process (e.g., by showing the status of various items or service in-process, and a list of additional lead-time reduction ideas)

Service Example of "Hard" Lean Tools

A few years ago, Lockheed Martin's Systems Integration Business Area (SIBA) centralized the majority of its procurement operations in its Material Acquisition Center–Mid-Atlantic Region (MAC-MAR), which serves 14 or more different locations (MAC-MAR's "customers"). Many of these sites were acquired during the 1990 defense industry consolidations and operate with different legacy computer systems.

Each buyer was responsible for the procurement of a certain number of commodities. They would log onto one site's computers, process its purchase requests, then move onto the next site. This logging on and off was a problem. Because of legacy computer issues, it often took a buyer an average of 20 minutes to log off one site and log on to another site. The Lean description of this situation is **long setup time**, although no one in purchasing at that time—prior to the LM21 initiative—had been trained in Lean and hence did not call it or even recognize it as setup time or understand its impact.

And it wasn't just the physical setup time, switching from one computer system to another, that was killing the MAC-MAR buyers. The **mental setup** ("learning curve") was tough as well; the legacy of many systems meant buyers had to constantly switch from one set of rules to another, try to remember 14 different part numbers, and so on.

What would you do in such a situation? Just what these buyers did: process all the purchase requirements for one site before moving on to the next. On average they would stay locked on one customer's site for about a day before switching. While buyer productivity in terms of orders placed per hour might be high, much of their time was spent placing the wrong orders if looked at in terms of priority. Any time a lot of WIP is in a system, you can be sure that the lead times will be very long in accordance with Little's Law.

Figure 2.9 represents how buyers processed orders prior to the improvements. Because they could only log onto one site at a time, they would tend to complete all the purchases at that time, regardless of whether an individual request was hot or cold.

Figure 2.9: Partial screen capture from initial buyer program

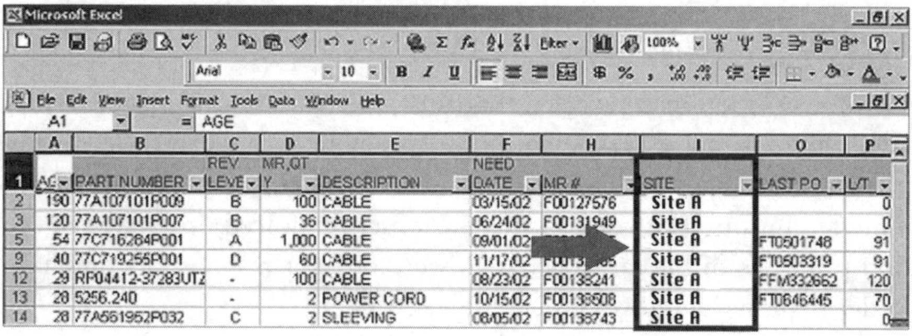

Because of Lockheed Martin's many legacy computer systems, buyers at the centralized procurement center could only log onto one site at a time. It could take as much as 20 minutes for them to move to another site... so naturally they would tend to handle all the orders at one site before switching.

The problem, of course, was that this approach totally ignored the due dates of the other customers' purchase requirements—a hot order from Site D would have to wait until the buyer had completed **all** the orders for Sites A to C. As a result, it could take as many as 14 days or more (=**customer turnover time**) for a buyer to cycle through all the customer requirements, leading to long lead times, delay in major project billings, and downstream factory overtime. (See Figure 2.10, next page.) Moreover the same commodity, say an Intel Pentium chip, might be purchased 14 separate times under 14 different internal names (in 1/14 the

volume possible), increasing unit costs and perhaps creating 14 times as much administrative and expedite time.

Figure 2.10: The Inflexibility of the Procurement Process

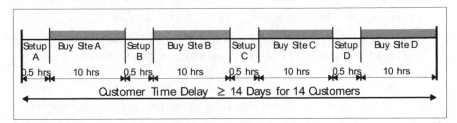

Because it was so difficult and time consuming for Lockheed Martin buyers to switch from one site to another, their standard procedure was to complete all the orders for one site, both those that were "hot" and those that were not, before moving on to the next, as depicted in the figure. The math adds up quickly—with 14 different sites to process, it could often take 14 days or more before a buyer could return to process further orders from any site.

A value creation map revealed that this particular "setup" problem created the most delays in the entire procurement process and was clearly the leading Time Trap. Unless it was solved, other improvements would only be illusory. The Voice of the Customer reinforced this analysis; the top priorities of the customer sites were quicker response to purchase order requests and lower procurement costs.

A MAC-MAR team mapped out the process, measured WIP at each step, looked at where delays were worst, identified complexity, and realized the solution to this problem was twofold:

1) Develop an application that could communicate with all legacy systems and consolidate orders for a group of commodities onto a single screen (this would eliminate the constant setup time delays when buyers switched between systems)

2) Structure the program so that buyers could sort orders by need-date and commodity

The result is shown in Figure 2.11. The new screen shows a mix of sites with the "hot" items only displayed across all sites rather than just one site. By simply clicking on an item, the purchase requisition and history

come up. Further improvements are being made by getting more products under purchase agreements, allowing the buyers to do one-click purchasing (eliminating additional setup time for all future orders), and a host of other improvements.

Figure 2.11: Buyer's "after" screen shot...

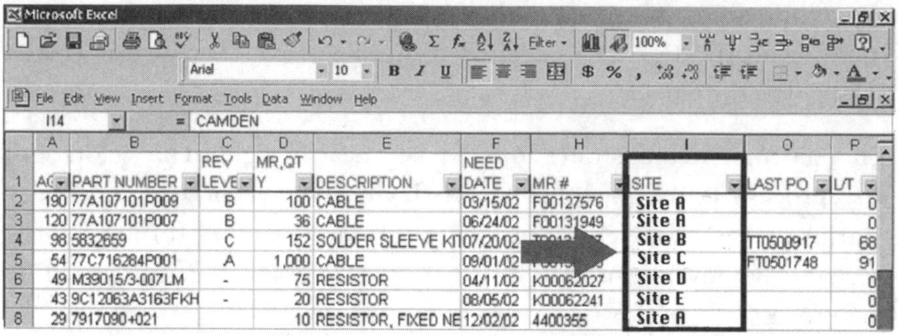

At first glance, this screen shot may not look that much different from the original screen (see Fig 2.9). But developing the ability to sort orders across all sites in order of priority meant they had to be able to compile information from many different legacy programs.

Overcoming the software legacy issues increased the flexibility of the activity (buying):

- *Setup time* dropped from 20 minutes to near zero.

- *Batch sizes* are now 1 because the buyer isn't hindered from jumping from site to site to place orders.

- The *cycle time interval* has dropped from 14 days to less than 1 day (e.g., if a buyer starts with Site A, he or she can complete all other *required* orders and get back to Site A within a day).

- Work-in-process: customers used to be "in process" for as much as 14 days, or an average of 7 days or 56 hours. Now they are "in process" for no more than 2 hours, or an average of 1 hour.

Do You Work at Your Convenience or Your Customer's?

If you examine your own process with "Lean eyes" you will be surprised by all the work you do "in batches" because it's convenient to you, even if not to your customer.

- The completion rate increased from one customer per 8-hour day to 14 customers every 2 hours (an equivalent of 56 per day).

The MAC-MAR team also made other process changes (such as increasing the number of prenegotiated terms). The cumulative changes allowed procurement costs to fall by 50%, lead times to be reduced 67% on commodities (from 6 months to 2 months), factory productivity to improve nearly 20% due to decreased shortages, and average unit cost of material to drop 6.4%.

This example demonstrates another key Lean insight: **The velocity of any process is proportional to its flexibility.** The original Lockheed Martin process was very inflexible (a 21-day customer turnover rate); because the buyers can switch so much more easily, they can speed up the process.

Setup Time and Batch Processing in Service Functions

Many people don't think that service applications have setup time. But if it takes you a finite period of time to transition from serving one customer to serving another, or if it takes some time to attain normal productivity, you have setup time. Similarly, any time you delay service to one customer (internal or external) because it's more convenient to continue working on your current task, you are batch processing. See Chapter 11 for instructions on how to eliminate these sources of process delays.

Why Does Lean *Need* Six Sigma?

As robust as Lean is for dealing with lead time and non-value-add costs, there are several critical problems you won't find addressed in the seminal books on Lean. Six Sigma provides robust solutions to these problems, which explains why Lean needs Six Sigma:

1. Lean does not explicitly prescribe the culture and infrastructure needed to achieve and sustain results

Most Lean resources are mute on the infrastructure needed to successfully implement Lean initiatives and achieve and *sustain* Lean speed. It is

true that many companies that have implemented Lean have been driven to develop
an infrastructure similar to that of Six
Sigma, but they did it ad hoc, rather than
use the prescriptive structure contained in
Six Sigma. Companies that only apply Lean
are sometimes *unable* to deploy it across the
whole organization and sustain results
because they lack the well-defined Six
Sigma cultural infrastructure to generate
senior management engagement, formalize
training, secure dedicated resources, and so
on. Thus the progress of Lean has been
dependent on individual initiative. I have
seen many successful Lean implementations regress when a new manager takes

> "My experience is that most people in financial industries can understand and grab Six Sigma and might say that Lean is OK for a manufacturing environment. But once they have experience with Lean, they like it better because it's faster and it's simpler. They struggle more with Six Sigma tools."
>
> —Darryl Greene, Senior VP, Bank One

over. Six Sigma is less susceptible (though not immune to) this problem:
it asserts that there is only one set of shareholders whose interests alone
must be served. Every book on Six Sigma discusses, in detail, how to sustain infrastructure; virtually no book on Lean even addresses the issue.

2. Customer Critical-to-Quality needs are not front and center

In requiring us to identify what is "value-added" in a process, Lean does
incorporate some element of customer focus, but it is introspective in its
approach. The person creating the value stream map makes the decision
as to whether an activity is value-add or not. In contrast, Six Sigma *prescribes* numerous places in improvement methods where the voices of
customers and suppliers must be included. It uses Customer Critical-to-
Quality as a key metric and requires a means of capturing the VOC in the
Define phase of DMAIC. Simply put, the customer is not front and center in Lean, yet is ever-present in Six Sigma work. (See Chapter 3.)

3. Lean does not recognize the impact of variation

Lean does not possess the tools to reduce variation and bring a process
under statistical control. Six Sigma views elimination of variation as key

"Who needs Lean? I don't have any setup time!"

Most people in service applications think that their activity has no setup time. They associate setup time with the dead zone during changeover from one product to another in manufacturing. In most service environments, there is no true dead zone. However, when switching from one task to another, there will generally be a learning curve before full output rate is achieved as we saw in the case of Lockheed Martin's MAC-MAR procurement center. This learning curve is shown in Figure 2.12.

Figure 2.12: Learning Curve Costs to Productivity

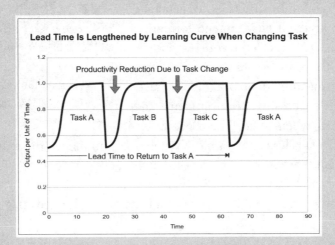

The employee is staying "locked on" a given task for 20 minutes even though current customer demand for that task only requires 5 minutes. This is similar to the one-day "lock on" period at Lockheed Martin, but the number of different "tasks" was 14, corresponding to the 14 different sites, tasks A thru N. This increases the overall lead time by a factor of four. Lean methods can be used to dramatically reduce learning curve times (see Chapter 11).

Conclusion: Anything that reduces productivity rates will result in long lead times, as people tend to remain "locked on" one type of task longer than is required to meet immediate customer demand. Lead times can be dramatically reduced by using Lean tools to allow task transitions with minimal impact on productivity. One of the primary sources of the learning curve is the complexity of the tasks performed. The larger the number of different tasks, the less often they will be repeated, and the steeper the learning curve. Thus complexity reduction prevents, while Lean Six Sigma cures, the learning curve problem.

and provides a whole arsenal for attacking variation (from statistical process control to design of experiments). As mentioned above, a 10% defect rate can increase lead times by 38% and WIP by 53%. In other words, the speed and cost gains of Lean can be erased instantly by an increase in variation!

An increase in defects is not the only source of variation that increases WIP and lead times. Variation in the demand for an offering and variation in the time it takes to perform an activity that creates that offering both have a major impact on process lead time, which Lean does not directly address. This relationship is illustrated in Figure 2.13, which graphs the outputs from one of the steps in the Lockheed Martin procurement process described earlier.

Figure 2.13: The Effect of Variation on Queue Time

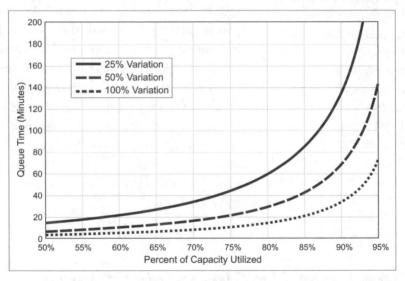

Variability in demand has a bigger effect on how long your work has to wait "in queue" the closer your process operates to capacity (as shown by the steep rise in the curve on the right). The greater the variability, the greater the effect.

Let's say that it takes Bob an average of 16 minutes to perform a particular task. However, because of the variety of tasks, 68% (one standard deviation) of process times might wander in a band about 8 minutes on either side, in which case the variation is 8/16 = 50%. Let's also assume

that the workload presented to Bob has similar variation. As you can see in the figure, if Bob is loaded up to 90% of capacity, the work backed up in queue behind Bob will wait an average of 60 minutes, which explains about half of his queue time. Encountering a particularly nasty problem could easily shoot that queue time up over 100 minutes.

Variation has little effect on processes operating at low capacity (the left side of the diagram). But most service organizations function at or near full-capacity—and that's when variation has a major impact on how long the work (or a customer) has to wait "in queue." Customer-facing service processes often experience a lot of variation in demand because we have no control over when customers will contact us. The lesson? The larger the variation in input, the more excess capacity is needed. If there is either low variation or we can control demand in some way (which is more likely with internal processes), we can operate at a higher capacity without risking excessive delays. When I first showed this analysis at Lockheed Martin, Manny Zulueta (the VP of Lockheed Martin's MAC-MAR procurement center) said: *"This validates what we've been seeing!"*

Lean also needs DMAIC

Most descriptions of Lean methodologies dive into the Improve phase (in DMAIC terminology), going right to solutions and jumping over Define and Measure. Without a prescribed Define step to understand how big the problem is, and a Measure phase to quantify the size versus the resources, people have often bitten off more Lean than they could chew, or lost themselves in a frenzy of Lean improvement events.

Why Does Six Sigma *Need* Lean?

Just as there are gaps in Lean methodologies that can benefit from Six Sigma, let's turn the tables and see where Six Sigma falls short compared to what Lean has to offer.

The overarching message is this: As many companies have demonstrated, you can make a lot of gains with Six Sigma. But there's a hitch. No matter what tool you pick, if you don't have a Lean component to it,

if you're not focusing on improving speed and reducing WIP, any gains will eventually die. The process will still be slow and cumbersome, and its costs will be too high. More specifically, here are five reasons why Six Sigma benefits from Lean:

1. **Identifying waste**. Though process mapping is a Six Sigma tool, it does not prescribe the collection of data (such as setup time, processing time per unit, transportation, etc.) necessary to quantify which steps of which process contribute the most non-value-add work/costs to the service or product. Lean provides the powerful value stream map tool, which crosses functional silos and highlights waste and delays. Six Sigma rarely gets into a discussion of classifying activities as value-added or non-value-added, nor is elimination of non-value-add activities a central tenet of Six Sigma. Rather, Six Sigma protocol prescribes eliminating variation first, and, only if that's not possible, then redesigning the process using Design for Six Sigma (DFSS). Lean claims that process redesign is *always* required to some extent (to eliminate non-value-add activities) when cycle efficiency is less than 10%.

The waste of a lost customer

By far the biggest waste, and one that Lean admittedly fails to take into consideration, is the waste of losing a customer. You lose the associated revenue, *and* the cost of gaining a new customer is generally much higher than selling an equivalent amount of services or products to an existing customer. Virtually all the wastes that Lean explicitly defines are internal to the process, not external. It can be argued that eliminating these internal wastes will significantly decrease the odds of losing an external customer because you'll be delivering services at high speed with no waste and minimal costs. However, you can waste a lot of time and effort getting really good at delivering a service that customers don't want, and that's why Six Sigma takes a more explicit approach to capturing the Voice of the Customer and defines the loss of a customer as a defect.

2. **Improving process speed or cycle time**. Improvement in cycle time and responsiveness is often claimed as a result of Six Sigma. Six Sigma experts (and their books), however, do not make either a practical or theoretical link between quality and speed, nor do they address

instituting Pull system caps on the amount of WIP (an action that is required to make lead time a controllable parameter with limited variation). The first-order driver of cycle time is work-in-process (via Little's Law). Unless WIP is capped at some maximum value first, reduction of cycle time is just wishful thinking.

3. **Specific speed tools.** Seldom will you find any Lean tool—Total Productive Maintenance, time value analysis, 5S, etc.—included in a Six Sigma toolkit. These speed-acceleration tools are incredibly powerful, having been developed and refined over decades of experience. It's true that some translation is needed to adapt these tools to service environments (see the case study chapters later in this book), but to ignore them is to risk limiting the performance of your processes.

4. **Methods for rapid action (the Kaizen DMAIC process).** Lean methodologies include a rapid improvement method called Kaizens, which are short, intensive projects where a group of people with relevant knowledge are sequestered for four or five days and apply structured improvement methods on a targeted process or activity. The energy generated by such events is legendary, engendering a high degree of creativity by the pressure to rapidly produce tangible results. As you'll see later in the book, Kaizens have a real role to play in service environments, though some modification is often needed (see Chp 10). Still, having a time-compressed, action-oriented improvement method in your arsenal provides a good accelerator of DMAIC projects. Lean's bias for action accelerates results.

5. **Six Sigma quality is approached much faster if Lean eliminates non-value-add steps.** The Six Sigma Research Institute once pulled together a chart (see Figure 2.14) that examined rolled-throughput yield, which looks at the cumulative effect of defects on yield. For example, consider an invoicing process that has 20 activities, each operating at 4σ (99.379% yield). The overall rolled-throughput yield would be $(.99379)^{20} = 88\%$, which is not atypical for service processes. This low yield creates accounts receivable problems and sparks the need for manual collection procedures and rework.

With Lean tools, it is quite realistic to quickly (within a few weeks at most) remove the non-value-add activities—likely at least half (= 10)

of the steps. So instead of having a 20-step process, the invoices now only have to travel through 10 steps. Even without making any other quality improvements, it seems obvious that a 10-step process has far fewer opportunities for error than a 20-step process.

The rolled-throughput yield will then rise to $(.99379)^{10} = 94\%$. The higher yield will provide a significant return on your improvement investment, and, even more significantly, the velocity of the process will double—which not only allows you to provide your output to customers more quickly, but doubles the feedback rate on using the quality tools, making them twice as effective.

Figure 2.14: Rolled-throughput yields

Overall Yield vs. Sigma (Distribution Shifted ± 1.5σ)				
# of Steps	±3σ	±4σ	±5σ	±6σ
1	93.32%	99.379%	99.9767%	99.99966%
7	61.63%	95.733%	99.839%	99.9976%
10	50.08%	93.96%	99.768%	99.9966%
20	25.08%	88.29%	99.536%	99.9932%
40	6.29%	77.94%	99.074%	99.9864%

Lean reduces non-value-add steps

Six Sigma improves quality of value-add steps

Source: Six Sigma Research Institute, Motorola University, Motorola, Inc.

Lean Six Sigma drives quality, speed, and cost simultaneously

The message of this chart is that it's much harder to achieve high levels of quality with processes that have a lot of steps, and vice versa, low quality has a much greater cumulative impact on complex process. The most efficient way to achieve 6 Sigma levels of performance is therefore to simultaneously improve quality and apply Lean principles to eliminate non-value-added process steps.

By combining Lean and Six Sigma, it's quite possible you could not just eliminate steps but improve quality levels in each remaining activity to, say, 5σ, which would raise the rolled-throughput yield to $(.99976)^{10}$=to 99.8%.

Internal benefits of faster speed

"An ITT service unit that basically sold high-tech labor had a goal of increasing revenue. One of their early projects was how to hire more effectively and more rapidly. They found it was taking them 105 days on average to hire new employees. The goal was 20 days. They went through the [Value-Based Six Sigma] process because their sales dollars were directly impacted by how many people they had working these contracts. Not only were they able to reduce the cycle time, but they found out they got better quality people by being faster—it didn't take the better people 105 days to find a job."

—Lou Giuliano, CEO, ITT

A challenge for Six Sigma advocates

The question sometimes arises whether it's better to first optimize a process (without removing non-value-added process steps) using Six Sigma or to eliminate non-value-added steps first through Lean and then optimize the process through Six Sigma. Some Six Sigma advocates suggest that Lean methods (like Pull systems) should be applied only *after* a process has been brought under control and optimized. This viewpoint is easily challenged: "How could it hurt anything to use Lean and implement a Pull system so you can control the velocity and reduce cycle times during Six Sigma implementation?" The answer is you do both simultaneously with the Lean Six Sigma tool kit and a business culture to be the best. Projects should be selected based on their impact on increasing ROIC, not on whether solving the problem is more likely to require Lean vs. Six Sigma tools.

Blending Lean and Six Sigma to Optimize Service

The fact is that Lean Six Sigma is a powerful tool for executing the CEO's strategy, and a tactical tool for P&L managers to achieve their annual and quarterly goals. If executives aren't engaged in Lean Six Sigma, the company will likely be out-competed by companies whose executives embrace Lean Six Sigma.

Blending the key themes of Lean and Six Sigma provides us with five "laws" that provide direction to our improvement efforts. Here are the first four (which we number from "0" because the first list is fundamental to all the others):

0: **The Law of the Market:** Customer Critical-to-Quality defines quality and is the highest priority for improvement, followed by ROIC and Net Present Value. We call it the Zero Law because it is the foundation upon which all else is built.

1: **The Law of Flexibility:** The velocity of any process is proportional to the flexibility of the process (see Fig 2.10).

2: **The Law of Focus:** 20% of the activities in a process cause 80% of the delay.

3: **The Law of Velocity:** The velocity of any process is inversely proportional to the amount of work-in-process (or number of things-in-process). Little's Law states that:

The number of things in process in turn is increased by long setup times, rework, the impact of variation in supply and demand, time, and the complexity of the product offering.

There's one final Lean Six Sigma law we'll examine in Chapter 4:

4: **The Law of Complexity and Cost:** The complexity of the service or product offering generally adds more non-value-add costs and WIP than either poor quality (low Sigma) or slow speed (un-Lean) process problems.

> "I faced a typical challenging task–to consolidate the purchasing from 22 locations in 9 months with little budget and a mandate to not affect the cost and to be seamless to the customer. The only way I knew it could be accomplished was to apply my Lean Six Sigma thinking and challenge my team to remove waste, mistake proof the process, and get every employee involved."
>
> —George Sanders, Director of Sourcing
> (Northern Material Acquisition Center), Lockheed Martin

Endnotes

1. Remember that Stanford's cost achievements were made at the same time that mortality decreased substantially.

SUCCESS STORY

#1

Lockheed Martin
Creating a New Legacy

Lockheed Martin was formed by the merger of Lockheed and Martin-Marietta (part of a long series of consolidations) in 1995, so on paper it is about seven years old. But ask the people who work there and they'll tell you it feels even younger because, until about two years ago, most people were more strongly aligned with their parent organization; Lockheed Martin was more an amalgam of 18 different corporations than one cohesive unit.

What changed two years ago was the advent of "LM21 Operational Excellence," Lockheed Martin's initiative built around Lean Six Sigma. According to Mike Joyce, the Vice President of LM21, Lean Six Sigma is the enabler that's given them a common thread to unite employees in working together to achieve shared business goals. Here's how they've made it happen.

The Burning Platform

Lockheed Martin's success is strictly dependent on invention, breakthroughs, and execution. This helps explain why such a large portion of its improvement work has been done in the service support areas: design, purchasing, engineering, lifetime support, hiring people, billing customers, legal, etc. Procurement is an example of a service application that has come to the fore, as approximately 50–60% of the cost of each product is purchased or subcontracted.

As Joyce says, "It would be absolutely ludicrous for us to think that we're going to use a 1975 radar in a new fighter, yet we found it perfectly acceptable to use 1975 processes for operating our supply chain. We need to not only engineer the new radar, we need to engineer exactly how the business process is going to function as that radar comes together."

Lockheed Martin describes its government contract work as the "programmatic invention business"—developing customized solutions for highly specific customer needs. As they describe it, "breakthrough technology is part of our daily routine." To that end, about 50,000 of LM's 125,000 employees are scientists and engineers.

The issue of legacies is a major factor at Lockheed Martin. The progenitors of Lockheed Martin include divisions from a wide range of premier companies—among them General Dynamics, GE, IBM, Goodyear, Westinghouse, Loral, and Ford—each with their own strong heritages. Bringing together 18 different companies meant there were at least 18 different computer systems, 18 different part numbering systems, 18 different ways of purchasing, 18 different ways of developing specifications, of hiring, of paying the bills.

Furthermore, all of these progenitors had a history with one or more of the incarnations of quality improvement: Quality circles, SPC, continuous-flow manufacturing, Six Sigma, TQM, Lean manufacturing. A major factor behind Lockheed Martin's improvement strategies has

Insights into Lockheed Martin's use of Lean Six Sigma have come from Mike Joyce, Vice President of LM21 (Lockheed Martin's operational excellence program), Manny Zulueta, Vice President of the SIBA Material Acquisition Center–Mid-Atlantic Region (MAC-MAR), James Isaac, the Director of Procurement Excellence, George Sanders, the Director of Sourcing (Northern Material Acquisition Center), and Myles Burke, a Certified Black Belt and Manager of Supply Chain Excellence.

Lockheed Martin has about 125,000 employees divided into four major business areas worldwide: aeronautical systems, space systems, systems integration, and technology services.

therefore been the need to allow people to carry forward the pride in their corporate heritage, but still come together as one team.

Progress towards this goal began in 1998, when Lockheed Martin's management realized that there were pockets of excellence throughout this new enterprise. They created an initiative called "LM21 Best Practices" as a way to capitalize on that knowledge by spreading it throughout the company.

> "LM21 encompasses all the enterprise functions. It permeates throughout the business, providing productivity targets and performance improvements."
>
> —Manny Zulueta, VP, Material Acquisition Center

Though sharing best practices was a good start, it had some limitations:

- **What does "best" mean?** In today's business environment, the pace of change is accelerating. So a focus on only best practices ignored waste and opportunities in much of the business.

- **People could get complacent.** Lockheed Martin wants every employee to feel the pressure of continuous improvement and never feel that they already have "the best." Best is only a moment in time.

- **There was too much flexibility in the Best Practices system.** Originally, it was up to the various plants and divisions to decide which Best Practices they wanted to adopt. "But when the Lockheed Martin star goes on a product, it's got to mean something in terms of a standard of excellence," says Joyce. "We can't let any of our sites opt out of improving quality by saying, for example, that they want to go after best practices in business development. Quality and speed cannot be optional."

Therefore, two years into LM21, its focus was changed from Best Practices to Operating Excellence, with an overarching goal of *Lean processes operating at Six Sigma capability*.

"This encompasses Lockheed Martin's entire operating system," says Joyce, "everything that we do, from how we bill a customer or buy

inventory, to how we design a product and hire people." The new LM21 approach is based explicitly on the principles of Lean Six Sigma: taking a hard look at all work that is done, categorizing it as value-enhancing or as waste, eliminating the waste, and improving what remains. Most importantly, LM21 is not positioned as something extra or above the work of the organization. "It is a strategy for helping managers achieve ambitious annual goals and targets and putting in place processes that assure we can sustain business results over the long term," says Joyce. "Getting the job done and improving how the job gets done is everybody's task."

Preparation and Rollout

The rollout of LM21 at Lockheed Martin embodies the essential elements of a Six Sigma infrastructure. For example:

1) There is highly visible top management involvement and support

Lockheed Martin's CEO, Vance Coffman, has explicitly stated his commitment to LM21.

2) Top management has been trained in Lean Six Sigma concepts and application

Coffman and his executive committee all received four-and-a-half days of training (two-and-a-half in the classroom and two days of practice fixing a process), which covered...

- Lockheed Martin's 5 **Principles of Excellence** (see sidebar)

- A half-day on defining value from the customer's perspective, including a panel discussion with customers who talked about what it's like doing business with Lockheed Martin

- Exploration about value streams and process flow, including a simulation training on work system designs

- Activities around structured problem solving

Lockheed Martin's 5 Principles of Excellence*

Mike Joyce says it was important for Lockheed Martin to define principles of excellence up front because they are essential criteria for deciding how work gets done. Elements of both Lean and Six Sigma are incorporated in these principles:

1. Understanding value from the customer's perspective. Customer's value you not only on what you give them but what it was like doing business with you. Everyone needs to understand how their customers define value. Getting this right is the first step because they can use that understanding to categorize all work as either value-enhancing or waste. If you get this wrong, then by definition all that follows is waste!

2. Understanding the value streams. Managers need to have deep knowledge of where product and service value are created in the organization. No guessing allowed: you have to have it written down, documented, and be able to answer questions like, "When was the last time we observed it? Where is the data on the observation?"

3. Understanding work flow. Engineers always refer to what's at the "top of the requirement pyramid," the overriding need that must be met for a product or service, the thing that has to come before anything else. To achieve Operating Excellence, the top of the requirement pyramid is designing systems of work that optimize the flow of data, and the flow of molecules. If you don't optimize for flow, you won't get to optimal performance.

4. Focusing on cycle time and pull. The goal is to shrink the time it takes to do everything to its absolute minimum so that you can approach an instantaneous response to a changing customer need.

5. Striving for Perfection. For Lockheed Martin, that means achieving Six Sigma levels of quality at Lean speed.

*Based on work done by James Womack, author of such books as *The Machine that Changed the World* and *Lean Thinking*.

There are two other important aspects of this leadership training:

- At first, many members of Vance Coffman's executive team were less than enthusiastic about trying to find four-and-a-half days on their calendar for this training. At one meeting, Mike Joyce challenged them: "How many of you have been formally trained in this way of thinking?" Out of the 20 people in the room, only 2 raised their hands (one had had exposure to Six Sigma, the other to Lean). Joyce then pointed out that if this team was going to lead the corporation implementing Lean Six Sigma, they should know what it means. After the training, every one of the executive team said it was probably the best training they had ever had in their careers. As Joyce puts it, "The goal wasn't to turn them into Black Belts, nor even improve a process dramatically in two days. But we hoped it would embolden them to lead in this direction and support LM21 efforts."

- Second, the executive team at Lockheed Martin received their LM21 and Lean Six Sigma training within their divisions, not as a separate team. Why? As Joyce told them, "Eventually LM21 needs to reach out to everyone in the company. So rather than training all you guys together, I want each of you to go through training with your staff at the operating company, so that they can see leadership commitment to making this happen."

3) The basic training has reached all levels of management

Once the executive team was trained, Lockheed Martin made the requirement that *anybody who has incentive compensation* has to go through the basic class, which in their organization meant anyone with the title of director or above. They ran these five-day Lean Leadership training sessions at the sites, in groups of 50, until they got through all 5000 managers. (Now the program has expanded to include customers and supplier executives for quick-hit projects.)

4) Implementation began with value stream mapping

The starting point strategically for Lockheed Martin is doing a value stream map at the program level because the optimization of flow *across functions* has to occur at that level (a program is a set of processes used to provide one or more products or services to a specific customer). A value stream map captures the current reality, what is going on right now in the workplace. Value stream maps provide a way to start evaluating operations against the principles of excellence: Are you providing value as the customer defines it? What are your gaps? What can you do to close those gaps?

5) They continue to develop a strong infrastructure

All employees are reached by involving them in improvement projects and providing just-in-time training. Projects run under the LM21 banner depend on an internal cadre of Black Belts, Green Belts, sponsors, and what Lockheed Martin calls "subject matter experts" (SMEs).

- The primary responsibility for identifying and selecting projects resides with line management (such as departmental managers), who in turn often serve as project sponsors. They are usually the process owners as well, the people responsible for seeing that processes are maintained and improved.

- Subject matter experts (SMEs) are a core group of 20 seasoned professionals who report directly to Mike Joyce at the corporate level. In that sense they are similar to Six Sigma Champions in other organizations, but at Lockheed Martin they play a much broader role. These 20 SMEs represent different functional disciplines: business operations, cash management, supply chain management, operations, engineering, human resources, customer relations, logistic management, software, and so on. Their purpose in life is to get an accelerated learning of what LM21 is about and help deploy it at every site, within every function. Their purpose is to serve as catalysts at Lockheed Martin's 36 sites to make sure that what the sites are doing is consistent with corporate methodology and standards.

- Lockheed Martin has a goal of training 1% of its population as certified Black Belts ("certified" means that they've gone through the multiweek training program, completed a series of different types of projects, and mentored Green Belts to the satisfaction of their sponsor and the LM21 office).

- Anybody who wants to can take the 40-hour Green Belt training. The only requirements are that they have to run a project team afterwards that has its financial savings certified. For example, to date, 43 of the 160 people in the Systems Integration group at the Material Acquisition Center have taken the training, and 32 are certified.

6) Their methods meld Lean and Six Sigma

LM's training curriculum and improvement methods combine all the basic tools and principles of both Lean and Six Sigma, such as the DMAIC process, identifying the seven forms of waste (a Lean concept), mapping processes, working towards shorter cycle times, and so on.

7) As soon as was feasible, they began reaching out to suppliers

"Like most manufacturers, we used to do a lot of inspection to make sure incoming materials met our specifications and engineering drawings," says Manny Zulueta, the VP of Lockheed Martin's Material Acquisition Center. "Then we started five or six different initiatives where we work with our critical suppliers in incorporating Lean and Six Sigma at their plants, which makes them better suppliers... and we get near-perfect material coming in. Now, when we receive material, we just do a count to make sure the quantity is right and a quick check of condition, then put it into our stockroom."

The supplier partnerships have ranged from having Lockheed Martin staff train and coach suppliers' employees on Lean Six Sigma, to hosting symposia where suppliers can learn from each other.

There is a practical limitation, however. With thousands of suppliers, Lockheed Martin simply can't work with all of them. "So we basically did a process where we set out factors that would indicate whether a

supplier was important or not, weighted them, scored them," explains Zulueta. "The factors included things like how well they're doing compared to our requirements, whether they have critical technology, their potential to impact production, and so on. Now we've got a list of about 200 key suppliers that we all agree are the ones we want to work with."

The secret to supplier partnerships, says Zulueta, is connecting with the suppliers' leadership. "This only works if we engage their senior management, because we want them to work on substantive process improvement," says Zulueta. "And we work with them for months at a time. We need senior leadership buy-in for that. If their president or CEO or general manager isn't interested, we have a high probability of failure."

Results

To date, LM21 has encompassed more than 5000 projects, with more than 1000 of those in transactional areas (management, financial management, closings, purchasing, etc.). Their initial target was to take out $3.7 billion in cost over a four-year period—they're actually on track to achieve around $4 billion of documented savings. As Mike Joyce points out, in an organization the size of Lockheed Martin, it's impossible to say that all of that is the result of LM21, but the focus on excellence certainly has been a major contributor. Other business metrics are also

---

LSS Experience Leads to Advancement

James Isaac is an example of how LM21 is being used as for executive development. He is currently the Director of Procurement Excellence at MAC-MAR, a job he's only had since the spring of 2002. Before that, he spent two years as a Subject Matter Expert. "We received a lot of coaching and mentoring," says Isaac, "as well as personal training on management skills around successfully managing projects and improving productivity."

Isaac had only indirect experience in supply management before he took his current position. "I spent 18 years with Lockheed as a systems engineer before becoming an SME," he says. "It's interesting being on the other side of the equation, looking at design from the supply side. I have a newfound respect for what happens with the designs I used to create."

improving: orders are at a record level; debt is down considerably from the post-acquisition levels; they are generating a billion dollars in cash every year. As noted in Chapter 1, these changes (many in the service aspects of its business) have allowed Lockheed Martin to deliver its next-generation cruise missile with the same mission capability of other products but at *half the cost* and *a third of the cycle time*. At the department and project level, Lean indicators are up across the board. Many processes operate with far fewer handoffs then before (which improves cycle time and customer satisfaction).

Similar results are visible in many non-core-manufacturing areas throughout Lockheed Martin. The Naval Electronics and Surveillance Systems group, for example, is providing products, services, and the integration of advanced naval shipboard electronic weapons and communications suites in battle fleets around the world, with comparable gains in speed and cuts in cost. Results are also evident in Lockheed Martin's ability to capture new business. Recently, for example, they were selected as one of the key contractors on Deepwater, the largest and most ambitious U.S. Coast Guard program ever undertaken.

Growing your business

According to Mike Joyce, it's important that management not equate "eliminating waste" with "eliminating people."

"We use LM21 not for the purpose of firing people once the waste is eliminated, but to help us improve the work we do, and to make sure that our people are deployed to value-enhancing tasks, not consumed by waste," he says. "If we can eliminate the waste, we can provide customers with a better deal and grow our business."

As with any business, Lockheed Martin acknowledges they cannot guarantee lifetime employment. But their LM21 efforts are contributing to their ability to win major new contracts. And those employees who participate in LM21 training and projects are becoming equipped with the skills to better serve customers and increase their lifetime employability. "With customers, come jobs," says Joyce. "Therefore sustained employment is everybody's end goal."

Lockheed Martin will be the prime integrator on this multi-billion dollar program to rebuild the fleet infrastructure. The LM21 Lean Six Sigma tool set has already been used extensively to define customer value, develop critical-to-customer requirements, apply Design for Six Sigma, and establish new supplier partnerships in the initial efforts of this 20-year program.

Challenges

Think about how *you* get 125,000 people thinking and working in a new way and you'll begin to appreciate Lockheed Martin's challenges. Its goal is to get 60% of the employee population—about 70,000 people—through either a one-week Green Belt training or a one-week project by 2004. In the meantime, they are well on their way to value-stream mapping all 2000 of its programs. Other challenges include:

- **Increased expectations of program managers.** Up until this point in their careers, most program managers were just told to make sure they delivered to the customer what they contracted for: "Here's the cost and schedule curve. Deliver on that." Now, they're being told that's not enough: they have to not only deliver on the cost and schedule curve, but also be driving improvements in how the work happens inside their programs. It's like changing the rules of the game mid-course," says Mike Joyce. "We have to make sure they have the knowledge and tools to meet the increased expectations."

- **Keeping every part of the business in sync.** Suppose Lockheed Martin had focused solely on streamlining its manufacturing operations until they were

> "I know that by using Lean Six Sigma tools.my team has done its homework, has the facts, and I can then approach our internal Lockheed Martin customers to initiate joint Kaizen evens to realize break-through performance."
>
> —George Sanders, Director of Sourcing (Northern Material Acquisition Center), Lockheed Martin

the epitome of Lean manufacturing: fast, efficient, working just-in-time with no wasted investment in inventory. All that work could be wasted if their scheduling people were still releasing orders in batches, or if procurement had not eliminated shortages, or suppliers had not improved quality or designs. These kinds of problems can affect any organization that doesn't keep a systems view of its operations, making sure that the pieces of the puzzle continue to fit together. Keeping track of all the puzzle pieces helps companies avoid a classic failure mode that limits the return companies see from their Lean Six Sigma investment.

- **Convincing people they need Lean Six Sigma.** There are two predictable responses you'll find if you try to take Six Sigma and especially Lean into a service area, and Lockheed Martin heard them both. The first: "It doesn't apply here... It doesn't have anything to do with software... with legal services... with ___ [fill in the blank]." Or you'll hear, "Oh, yes, we've done that already, we did it 10 years ago. It doesn't work." Mike Joyce deflects these resistances by simply responding, "Okay, let's go observe your process and find the current reality." He invites people to "attach" themselves to a document going through their process, observe what happens, and get data on the current reality. Invariably, people are surprised by what they discover... and aware of their many opportunities for improving quality, cost, and speed!

CHAPTER 3

Seeing Services Through Your Customers' Eyes:
Becoming a customer-centered organization

"It was not the fair market value of inventories, receivables, or fixed assets that produced [See's Candies'] premium rates of return, rather it was a combination of intangible assets, particularly a pervasive favorable reputation with consumers based on countless pleasant experiences they have had with both product and personnel. Such a reputation creates a franchise that allows the value of the product to the purchaser, rather than the production cost, to be the major determinant of selling price."

Berkshire Hathaway Annual Report of 1983

\#　\#　\#

"Charlie and I, not fully aware of the value of an economic franchise, looked at See's mere $7 million in tangible net worth (and $4.2 million in earnings) and said $25 million (not $30 million) was as high as we would go (and meant it). Fortunately, the transaction was not derailed by our dumb insistence on $25 million. Over the past 20 years, See's has distributed $410 million to Berkshire Hathaway for an increase in retained earnings of only $18 million!"

Berkshire Hathaway Annual Report of 1991

Warren Buffett is renowned for his view that value is created by "sustained rates of return higher than the cost of capital." It's a view supported by the stock market data shown in Figure 1.2

in Chapter 1, which demonstrated that companies with the highest market-to-book value showed strong revenue growth and economic profit.

No one would consider Buffett anything but a self-interested investor, but his comments on See's Candies reinforce a long-standing improvement theme at the heart of Lean Six Sigma: quality and value can be defined only by the customer. In order to provide quality, we therefore have to learn to see through our customers' eyes, learn to judge what we do and don't do the way that they would judge us.

Much has been written about techniques for gathering Voice of the Customer (VOC) data (see sidebar, next page, for a quick review). The purpose of this chapter is broader: to create a vision of what it's like when customer awareness pervades every aspect of business operations. We'll cover four topics:

1) Incorporating customer information into strategic decision making

2) Using VOC data in product/service design

3) Weaving VOC data into process improvements

4) Shaping job descriptions/skill sets around customer needs

VOC Use #1: Strategic business decisions

At the broadest level, an understanding of your customers (and the markets they create) should be an integral part of decisions about your organization's market positioning and strategic goals. Five types of customer-related information are useful for this purpose:

- How well your current services/products meet (or don't meet) customers' needs

- What customer needs exist that you are not currently meeting (market opportunities)

- What offerings customers feel are unnecessary (product/service line analysis)

- How your offerings compare to the competition

- What world-class levels of performance are (benchmarking)

The first lesson that comes with collecting any of the above data is to make sure you're speaking your customer's language. "We sit down with our internal customers—who measure everything in great detail—and discuss their metrics and our metrics," says Manny Zulueta, the VP of Lockheed Martin's MAC-MAR procurement center. "The question is

---

Review of VOC collection

There are two basic ways to gather VOC information: to go out and get it (proactive methods) or let it come to you (reactive methods).

Reactive methods mean that information comes to you through a customer's initiative. It encompasses customer calls (complaints, compliments, queries, technical support, sales), web page hits, emails or cards that customers send to you, point of sale survey cards they fill out, contract negotiations, referrals, and so on. Having well-developed methods for gathering, tracking, and using this information is absolutely vital in retaining current customers because it tells what they think about your current offerings. Because customers are more likely to contact you when they have problems or questions, reactive methods are better at detecting product/service weaknesses than strengths. They may also be biased in terms of representing some customer segments more than others.

Proactive methods mean that you take the initiative to contact customers. They include surveys/questionnaires, focus groups, interviews, site visits or tours, point-of-sale contact, and so on. Because you control the timing and content of the contact, proactive methods can be used for a wider range of purposes than reactive methods, including product/service design, process improvement, performance monitoring, market analysis, and so on. In recent years, it has also become increasingly popular to include representatives from one or two customers on problem-solving/process improvement teams.

Remember that data "costs." So if you're going to be investing time and dollars in gathering VOC data, make sure you use that investment wisely by getting timely, accurate, reliable customer information that is easy for employees to use and easy for them to access.

---

whether these metrics are still important, how they would prioritize them. That way we make sure we're measuring something that is important to them. These 'critical-to-customer' metrics form the basis of integrating our initiatives with our customers.' Done properly, the results we get contribute directly to achieving our customers' goals. Our never-ending goal is to always exceed their expectations."

An example of how such information can be used is shown in the "Bubble" diagram below (Figure 3.1). This company has five value streams (in this case corresponding to brands) and simply began an analysis of their strategic position by gathering Voice of the Customer data ("how well do our offerings compare to the competition"). Such research can focus on any combination of price, features, related support services, and so on.

Figure 3.1: "Bubble" diagram of strategic position

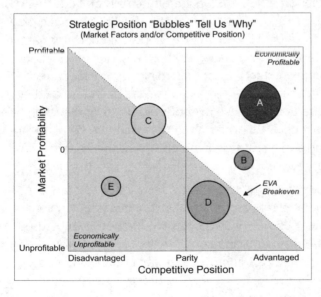

The Y axis shows whether the industry as a whole for each product or service is on average producing economic profit. The size of the circles reflects the revenues for that brand; the location on the graph is a combination of competitive position and market profitability. Brand A is in the best position: it generates a lot of revenue (it's a big circle), it's in a profitable market (indicated by being in the upper half of the graph), and it is competitive (it's on the right side of the graph). Brand E is in the opposite position: it's small, and in the lower left corner of the graph (meaning it generates few revenues and is in a bad competitive position in an unprofitable industry).

A product/service line in which the industry as a whole earns negative Economic Profit is an "unattractive industry." This is not to say that no company does well, just that the average company will not. (For example, from its inception, the airline industry has earned negative economic profit. But competitively advantaged companies, like Southwest Airlines, have had a positive Economic Profit.)

The analysis shows that Brand C is in an attractive industry but is competitively disadvantaged. The company could decide to abandon this brand line, but since the market is profitable, it's more likely they would choose to capture VOC data and implement Lean Six Sigma improvements to improve Brand C's competitive position.

(The analysis can't stop here: obviously this company needs to make decisions about what to do with each of its brand lines. But you'll have to read Chapter 4 to find the answers.)

VOC Use #2: Product/service evaluation and design

The strategic use of VOC information relies on broad market-level patterns; here, the focus is much narrower, on customers' reactions to specific product or service designs, features, functionalities, etc. The two situations where you typically need this information are:

A. Evaluating how well current services/products match Critical-to-Quality (CTQ) needs

B. Gathering VOC data to generate design requirements for new or redesigned services/products

Both of these uses revolve around understanding what is important to your customer and what isn't.

A: Do your priorities match your customers'?

Customers don't purchase a service or product based on overall market trends. They react to individual features or functions. That's why you

should always check whether the features/functions of your service or product match what your customers need.

An example of this type of analysis is shown in Figure 3.2 (below). This company asked an important customer to identify what they thought was most important in the company's offering, then rate how well this company and several competitors did. The bars on the chart indicate the customer's importance rating; each line tracks how well one of the companies did relative to those ratings. The most important takeaway from this chart is that the company did poorly on the customer's top seven attributes; they only did well on the remaining eight attributes, which weren't all that important to the customer!

Figure 3.2: Do Your Priorities Match Your Customers'?

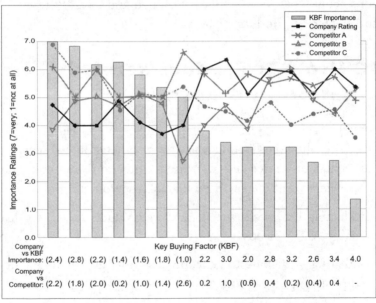

As you can see, none of the companies performed consistently well relative to the customer's top priorities; most of them performed much better on attributes that weren't nearly as important to the customer. If the company that did this analysis can improve performance across all customers' priorities, they could gain an advantage compared to their competitors.

In short, this company (and its competitors) had mistakenly focused on attributes that were lower in importance to the customer. The results

showed up in the offering's poor financial performance. Whether the company can afford to stay in this market and fix this offering would take further investigation.

B: Using VOC in design decisions

You can avoid situations like that shown above by weaving the Voice of the Customer into your service/product design decisions. The standard Six Sigma methodology used for this purpose is called Quality Function Deployment (QFD), a technique for converting customers *needs* into specific product/service design *features*. There are two basic steps in this process, depicted in Figure 3.3 (below).

1. Determine VOC (understand what is critical to customers)

2. Use QFD to transform customer needs into *functional requirements* then into *design requirements*

Figure 3.3: Turning Customer Needs into Design/Performance Requirements

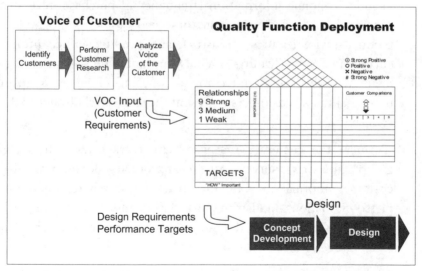

Service/product design process needs to start with the Voice of the Customer—what your customers say they want. Quality Function Deployment is a rigorous methodology for converting these requirements into a final design. The conversion happens through a series of steps, captured in a form called the "house of quality" where issues like functionality are related to product capabilities.

These steps encompass very specific and sometimes sophisticated procedures. Going into detail is beyond the scope of this book; here's a quick overview to give you a taste of what's involved.

Step 1: Determine the Voice of the Customer

The objectives here are to understand what your customers want and need from your service/product (their Critical-to-Quality requirements), organize that information, analyze the patterns it contains, then develop priorities and strategies. The output is a complete and organized list of customer requirements; the highest priority requirements are the input for design. The process is...

a) **Identify the customers** (external, regulatory, internal) **of the given product/service: whose needs must it meet.** You'll need to decide whether different subsets of customers are likely to have significantly different needs (speak with different "voices"). If so, you'll need to gather information from different **segments**, and look for differences between segments. Typical segmentation factors include **economic information** (frequency of purchase, revenues generated, etc.), **descriptive factors** (geographic, demographic, product/service features, industry), and **product/service preferences** (price, value, features). What you want to do is focus on segments that align with your company's business strategy. Keep in mind that not all customers represent the same level of value to the company.

b) **Perform the customer research.** Use market research, focus groups, interviews, surveys, etc., as appropriate. Besides proactive customer information, look into market research reports, completed evaluations, industry reports, competitor assessments, web page hits. Capture your decisions in a Customer Research Plan (see Figure 3.4).

c) **Analyze the information.** The goal is to translate VOC input into customer requirements. The tools used most often here are affinity diagrams (to identify themes) and tree diagrams (to organize the themes in increasing levels of detail).

Figure 3.4: Example of customer research plan

Customer Segment	Interview	Focus Group	Survey/Other
• Conference / Meeting guests	• Willingness to provide pre-register information • Paired comparison ranking of competitors	• Determine needs/wants of check in (their scope) • Best/worst experiences • Dissatisfiers / Delighters	• All segments - buy external research for accurate segmentation • Payment type/arrival info • Segment needs ratings
• General business travelers	• How is hotel selected - critical factors • Paired comparison ranking of competitors	• Determine needs/wants of check in (their scope) • Best/worst experiences • Dissatisfiers / Delighters	• Payment type/arrival info • Segment needs ratings • Who selects hotel • Who plans trips/meetings
• Pleasure / leisure guests	• None - not primary customer segment	• None - not primary customer segment	• Reasons for selecting a premier hotel • Buy data to better understand customer profile
• Conference / Meeting coordinators	• Understand needs to frame focus groups (gather/validate but not prioritize)	• Lead time for planning • Selection criteria • What info can/will they provide in advance • Typical changes & type • Typical complaints	• Buy info to determine leading providers • Survey based on feedback from focus groups
• Corporate travel planners and agents	• Understand needs to frame focus groups (gather/validate but not prioritize)	• Role in travel • Limitations imposed • Info that could be provided • Typical complaints	• # of days planning time • How paid • Other needs based on focus group feedback

A customer research plan helps organize a team's decisions about which market segments to pursue, how representatives from each segment will be contacted (interviews, focus groups, surveys), and for what purpose.

Table 3.1: VOC Gathering Methods for Different Purposes

Current level of knowledge	Research method	Output (what you get)
No knowledge	Interviews & focus groups	Customer wants and needs (general ideas, un-prioritized, not clarified, all qualitative)
Know preliminary wants and needs	Interviews & focus groups	Customer wants and needs (clarified, more specific, preliminary prioritization) Customer input to list of competitors, best-in-class
Qualitative, prioritized customer wants and needs	Surveys Face to face Written/mail Telephone Electronic	Qualified prioritized customer wants and needs Competitor comparative information

Making sense of qualitative data is an iterative process, involving interpretation and prioritization. You will likely go through several rounds of data gathering as you refine your understanding of customer needs (see Table 3.1, previous page).

Investigate Quality, Cost, and Speed Attributes

It used to be that customer research was largely focused on quality- and cost-related attributes. But now that your organization is becoming more Lean-focused as well, be sure to include questions about lead time, delivery time, etc., in your research.

Step 2: Use QFD to translate the VOC into design/performance requirements

Quality Function Deployment (QFD) is a very customer-focused method for product and service design. It emphasizes "outside in" quality (bringing the VOC into your company, rather than relying on internal experts to take their best guesses. QFD is a more efficient, effective planning method, reducing the cost and time of development (see Figure 3.5).

Figure 3.5: QFD gets you to market sooner than traditional methods

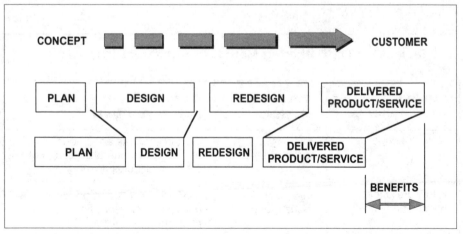

A traditional service/product development process puts too little emphasis on planning and capturing VOC information. As a result, the design phase usually takes a long time, as does the redesign phase as conflicts are worked out. By putting in more emphasis up front, in the planning phase, a QFD process avoids many problems further on, leading to a shorter overall cycle time and an earlier release-to-market.

QFD encompasses a series of analyses linked to the construction of a "House of Quality" that succinctly captures an enormous amount of information: what customers said they wanted, what importance was attached to those needs, how the needs translated into functional requirements, and how the proposed product/service compares to the competition. An example from a company studying their loan process is shown in Figure 3.6.

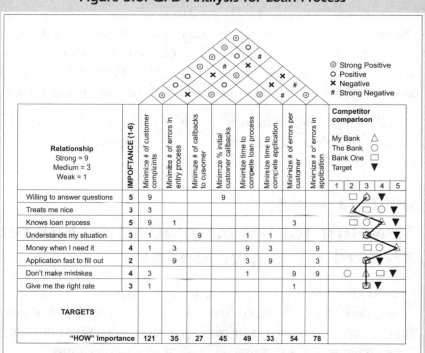

Figure 3.6: QFD Analysis for Loan Process

This format, called the House of Quality, is a central feature of a QFD process. It summarizes key discoveries and decisions made by a team throughout the design process. The left side lists functionalities the customers want and the importance to them (here, what they want as they experience the loan application process). The top shows capabilities the company could use to address those requirements and interactions between the capabilities (the "roof" with the symbols). The right side shows the company currently compares to the competition in meeting customer requirements. As a team goes through the QFD process, they methodically fill in the House of Quality piece by piece.

Rather than go into detail here, see Chapter 14 for an example of how an internal company process was designed using the QFD methodology and more explanation around the House of Quality and its role in service/product design.

VOC Use #3: Process improvement and problem-solving

The DMAIC (Define-Measure-Analyze-Improve-Control) methodology associated with Six Sigma is very good at reinforcing VOC awareness. In the Define stage, for example, instructions for creating a team charter include capturing any available VOC information relevant to the project and defining targets based on customer needs. (If the information is not available, teams are instructed to gather VOC data before proceeding.)

In addition, it's becoming increasingly popular for teams to include customer representatives on their teams. (See Chps 12 and 13 for examples of projects where customers were included.)

VOC Use #4: Shaping job descriptions & skill sets around customer needs

Organizations that are truly learning to see through their customers' eyes usually take steps to build customer awareness (internal or external, as appropriate) among *all* employees, not just those involved in Lean Six Sigma projects, not just managers making strategic decisions.

An example of how this works comes from Nick Gaich, the Vice President of Materials Management and Customer Service at Stanford Hospital and Clinics (SHC). His area encompasses a combination of several logistic departments (mail delivery, etc.) surrounded by professional areas such as purchasing and contract management.

"Materials management touches every customer in some way, every day," says Gaich. "So our first step was getting the Materials group to understand how well and how far they contribute to ultimate patient care." As part of this effort, which began a number of years ago, Gaich recalls drawing a bull's-eye: patients were at the center, surrounded by a ring of caregivers, which was surrounded by the rest of the organization. "Every activity we do daily hits one of those points in the bull's-eye, and if we're hitting those points it means we have a *value* to what we do ultimately in the delivery of care," says Gaich.

What Gaich was trying to achieve should sound familiar to any organization dedicated to providing superior customer service: "Our role in purchasing is to understand our clinicians' needs so well that we can [identify] opportunities they couldn't identify themselves in contract negotiations, in technology advancements, and so on. Our main objective is to contribute at such a high level of service that our work promotes and fosters the continued advancement of our clinical programs."

This growing focus on customer needs didn't stop at this general level. Gaich's group imbues a customer-focused awareness of *value* into every job. Here's one example: The mail room at SHC has a relatively small (but expert) staff, handling well over 100,000 pieces of mail each week. "If you look at mail services, ultimately the biggest **trigger point** [for providing value to our customers] is the sorting of the mail," explains Gaich. "Some of the secondary outcomes, obviously, are the final distribution and timing of when mail is delivered, but if you take a look at the amount of mail coming through that small mail room, if we don't have the skills and quickness in how we sort that mail, we're either delivering the wrong mail to the wrong areas, wrong individuals, or patient mail isn't getting through on a timely basis." The mail room group, therefore, worked to build the knowledge and enhance their individual skills to help support that function.

Annual evaluations like this allow the Materials Management group to keep on top of the changing needs of the organization and refine or expand their skill sets accordingly.

This work not only improves the services offered to internal staff and patients, but has helped elevate the status of many within the materials management group: "For our purchasing director and his staff, for example, it took them from a world of measuring how many POs are cut a day and how many line items there are on a PO, to allowing them to be more professional in what they do, both in understanding the market well enough to provide the technologies and opportunities for clinicians, and to be the best negotiators in-house, to provide the best economics to the decisions we're bringing in based on clinical need."

Creating this awareness and working to change the professional image among those within the Materials group and, more importantly, beyond that to other groups in SHC was not simple. "We went through a progression where materials management was once an afterthought to changes being made in the organization," says Gaich. "Now we've progressed to where we have become an integral part of the organization's preplanning process because we are now offering what I call **intelligent services** based on a strong professional knowledge base. That is a great feeling for both the individual and the materials management department as we consistently strive to raise our level of professionalism with our peers in the organization."

Eliminate the Complexity of Outdated Services

The type of approach used by Nick Gaich's Materials Management group to constantly re-examine whether what they are doing is still adding value to the organization is a model that can be adapted for any service, whether internal or external focused. Allowing outdated services to linger in your suite of offerings creates excess complexity and its associated costs (discussed in Chapter 5).

Conclusion

Meg Whitman, CEO of on-line superstar eBay, describes how developing a true customer focus can happen and the importance of listening to the Voice of the Customer in a recent interview with *American Way* magazine (April 15, 2002).

AW: In addition to online and phone input from customers, you fly some of them to headquarters to talk face-to-face. With all of the comments you already get, is that really necessary?

MW: You're referring to our "Voice of the Customer" program. Every two months, we invite about 12 eBay users to San Jose to learn firsthand about their trading experiences on eBay. The users meet with the senior managers of virtually every department, such as marketing, customer support, policy, technology, and community outreach. During these sessions, we get a great deal of feedback about the features and services that work well and how others could be improved. Following their visit to San Jose, we reassemble the group each month for six months via conference calls to discuss emerging issues. This program provides us with invaluable, ongoing feedback from an instant "focus group" of steady, reliable, and active users.

AW: When you revamped your Collectibles category, nearly 10,000 customers gave you suggestions for changes. Isn't that overkill?

MW: We rely on the feedback of our users for almost all changes to the site. Our users know the site really well – some are on the site up to eight hours a day. As our Collectibles team was looking to restructure the ever-expanding category, we tapped the expertise of our users on how they use the site. The result is a Collectibles page that is much like a portal tailored to the collector. The updated structure is more convenient and easy to use, while better reflecting the trading areas that are important to our users.

The immediate interaction we have with our users allows them to be part of the product-development team, so to speak. Their involvement multiplies the strength of our own management team. For example, one of our users suggested a way to speed up auctions for impatient bidders, so we introduced "Buy It Now," a feature that lets bidders end an auction at a set price. Now, 45 percent of listings use this feature, which attracts more buyers and helps close auctions much faster.

As you can see eBay's approach involves direct contact between customers and the company's leaders as well as project teams.

The benefits of such an approach are illustrated by the quotes about See's Candies at the beginning of this chapter. They provide the basis for establishing a relentless focus on serving customers. Making *your* organization a delight to work with is key to maximizing long-term economic profit. *Quality can be defined only by our customer.*

SUCCESS STORY

#2

Bank One
Bigger... Now Better

Like other major banks in a consolidating industry, Bank One has been getting bigger. A few years ago it realized it also needed to get better. And that's why Lew Fischer, the Division Executive of National Enterprise Operations (NEO) launched an initiative that has brought Lean Six Sigma thinking and methods to NEO. He has led the change by creating an operating architecture and the culture to support it. This operating architecture has engaged every level of the organization and brought with it simple problem-solving tools and thinking. As it continues to mature, it has started to incorporate more complex Lean Six Sigma methods.

The Burning Platform: Survival... then Excellence

If you ask Bank One's NEO staff why their division is investing so much in improvement efforts, the first thing they'll tell you is that the reasons they're doing it today aren't the same as when they got started.

Mike Fischbach, senior VP of the National Enterprise Operations (NEO) group, says that with all the changes that occurred in the company in the 1990s, the driving force initially was basic survival. "We needed to take what was unpredictable and make it predictable and sustainable," he says. "We weren't striving for best in class, just getting control over our operations."

Just two years into their efforts, the situation is quite different. The talk now is around goals such as…

- Sustaining the fundamentals

- Service excellence

- Supporting revenue growth

- Creating a high performance culture

The measures of success have changed, too, from "can we meet basic customer needs," to hard core metrics like earnings per share. Which if you're in a business like banking, means having the Lines of Business maximizing revenue and the back office operations reducing costs. "We can improve what we do every day," explains Fischbach, "but if we don't take out the infrastructure, the buildings, the equipment, the waste, our earnings per share won't increase." In other words, focusing only on quality won't get Bank One where it needs to be; they also have to focus on speed and cost. "We're not trying to use this to do anything but drive return for the bank," says Fischbach. "That's really our purpose."

The Bank One story comes to us from Mike Fischbach, Senior Vice President of Implementation Services of National Enterprise Operations (NEO), Darryl Greene, Senior VP of NEO's National Performance Consulting group (NPC) and two of his direct reports, consultants Jim Kaminski and Tim Williams.

Additional insights into the banking industry were provided by Bob DeLeeuw (President), Bryan Carey (executive VP), and Joe Walsh (executive VP) of DeLeeuw Associates.

Focus 2.0: A Pathfinder Approach to Improvement

The first improvement efforts in the NEO division were centered around measuring performance and identifying opportunities. What became "Focus 1.0" was introduced as a simple problem-solving approach to address gaps. Senior VP Darryl Greene likens Focus 1.0 to GE's "Workout": a simple, collaborative problem-solving strategy where everyone gets in the same room, looks at the issues, and quickly comes to resolution on tactical actions that they have ownership over. But Lew Fischer, NEO Division Executive, recognized that one method would not be sufficient to address the improvement needs of NEO.

That's when a new generation of improvement was born, called Focus 2.0. Launched in early 2002, it differs from Focus 1.0 in having a lot more emphasis on Lean goals (eliminating complexity, increasing process velocity). Rather, Focus 2.0 illustrates a pathfinder approach: using pilot and demonstration projects to generate success that creates pull for Lean Six Sigma methods. The rollout is designed to occur in three phases:

2002	2003	2004
Prove Concept	Create success aligned	Fully deploy
Build momentum	with operating plans	
Build capacity	Continue building capacity	

"One of the biggest obstacles to getting started is having faith in the process," says Senior VP Darryl Greene, who himself is a 6 Sigma Master Black Belt and has led organizations in implementing three major improvement approaches (Lean Manufacturing, Six Sigma, and Design for Six Sigma). "One of the ways of getting over that obstacle is selecting opportunities that are important to the people who have to implement and support the effort. Initially, people hesitated until we said, 'We'll do it on your project, and we're going to give you resources to facilitate the process. And that's when they said, 'Okay, we're willing to give it a shot.'"

Because they are in a demonstration phase, where the primary interest is creating what engineers would call "proof of concept" for Lean Six Sigma, the main priority was not in building a critical mass of knowledge and support (such efforts were begun later in their deployment plan). That's why Bank One delayed two of the most common first steps companies engage in:

1. **Massive corporate training.** There has been no widespread training beyond a core group of experts (next page). Though the knowledge base has been building slowly as more and more people participate in

Focus 2.0, Jim Kaminski says, "I do not anticipate that there will be any formal training in Lean and Six until the organization has matured in total. There is still so much opportunity in areas just doing the fundamentals of problem solving using simpler tools."

2. **Creating project teams.** Bank One's NEO division has avoided the typical dedicated project team model. A less-structured model has, ironically, allowed them to involve more people because there is no prerequisite for training nor requirements for long-term commitments. And the more people involved, the greater the ownership of Focus 2.0. "The amount of energy and enthusiasm the participants have is a momentum we cannot replicate with project teams," says Jim Kaminski. "Second, Bank One is sensitive to the changes that creating project teams forces onto the workforce, including the need for shuffling workloads, the unwelcome responsibility that teams face if hard choices have to be made, etc." (However, more traditional teams are likely in the cards in the future.)

Creating the Focus 2.0 Infrastructure

If NEO isn't relying on widespread training and project teams, what are they doing instead? Anyone who's studied Six Sigma knows that its prescribed infrastructure is one reason it has succeeded where previous improvement methods failed. Having formal relationships between different layers of management and various Belts of different colors creates a mechanism for better tracking of improvement projects and better linkage of results to business priorities.

However, creating a large, trained workforce of Black & Green Belts right away didn't really fit in Bank One. So they're taking a different approach to building an infrastructure that will work for them. It has two main elements: (1) a simple architecture, (2) a small cadre of internal experts.

Ingredient #1: A simple architecture

Mike Fischbach and his colleagues are all veterans of Six Sigma and other continuous improvement efforts. They've seen enough to know what hasn't worked. "Many service companies have tried to bring in sophisticated Six Sigma or Lean tools without the fundamental culture to understand how to sustain and leverage it," comments Fischbach. "They might get a few successful projects, but soon the whole program falls apart."

The conclusion was obvious: at banks and other institutions with little or no history with continuous improvement, starting from the bottom up should be considered as a viable option. "So we've been very focused on making sure that the fundamental pieces are in place and building from there," says Fischbach.

The Continuous Improvement (CI) Fundamentals, as he calls it, is an operating architecture for improving performance at every level. Starting with the frontline, as you go up in the NEO organization, each level has been provided with increasingly sophisticated tools and practices for setting goals and measuring and improving performance (conducting business reviews, closing gaps with problem solving tools, celebrating successes, etc.).

While you can find Lean and Six Sigma tools in practice, they aren't often overtly referred to within Bank One yet. Rather, the approach is to present the Fundamentals, then introduce new tools or methods as a way to add more rigor and more power. "We're not using terms like Lean at Bank One because that would only serve as a barrier," explains Senior VP Darryl Greene. "People tell us they have a problem to solve, we facilitate them through the use of problem-solving tools, and then guess what? They've just 'done Lean' without the anxiety that comes with having to be trained in a new practice, terminology, tools, etc."

Ingredient #2: Internal expertise

The second form of infrastructure is the people to help facilitate adoption of the concepts and implementation of the methods. Within Bank One's NEO division, that role is filled by the National Performance Consulting (NPC) group. NPC is staffed with people experienced in advanced problem-solving (both Lean and Six Sigma). They work collaboratively with senior, middle, and frontline staff to coach and support improvements and, on some occasions, follow up on identified action items.

If this model was followed in the long run, the danger would be in turning "quality improvement" into something that is solely the province of specialists. But remember that Bank One is using a pathfinder approach to implementation, using quick successes to spread knowledge and create pull in the organization. Also, NPC priorities are determined by priorities within the business units; NPC resources are leveraged to work on the business units' priorities. NPC and Focus 2.0 are being positioned as methods to help people meet their business goals.

Rollout of Focus 2.0

For the past several years at Bank One, each part of the NEO organization has been asked to make unit-cost productivity improvements. It is difficult to sustain significant levels of unit-cost improvement without a sophisticated look at the business. The need to achieve greater productivity improvements provided fertile ground for Focus 2.0 application. "We thought the timing was perfect to introduce Focus 2.0, because each of the departments was looking for ways to drive more improvement," says Darryl Greene. Focus 2.0 has become a means of engaging the frontline, middle management team, and senior management team by equipping them with tools and practices to improve performance.

That's why, at a practical level, the thrust of Focus 2.0 is getting an organization that has traditionally been very siloed to start thinking about the flow of work, from beginning to end. "Key operations leaders see the value of everyone in the organization thinking about their work from the customer's perspective and driving improvement accordingly," says Greene.

Establishing a vision and priorities

The rollout of Focus 2.0 within the NEO group began with an introduction of concepts to key leaders within the business unit. These people came with project ideas that they identified in their operational plans as key to achieving annual goals. This "vision event" included:

- On Day 1, NPC staff (the NEO internal consultants) interviewed participants. The interviews centered on the business unit goals and business objectives, performance against objectives, current initiatives to achieve the goals and objectives, barriers, and resource limitations.

- On Day 2, the NPC staff introduced the business unit leaders to Focus 2.0 concepts (time-based strategies, just-in-time, push vs. Pull systems, etc.). The goal of the session was for NPC and the business units to start building collaboration on future Focus 2.0 pilot projects to address cross-functional reengineering and process improvement needs.

A key outcome was having all these managers share their project ideas, talk about the opportunities, and prioritize which projects should be pursued using a process improvement approach. The NPC group then assigned their resources to work on those priorities (see Chps 12 and 13 for details on two of the projects).

Making improvement an "event"

Once business improvement priorities were identified, they were implemented through a similar event model. In fact, Focus 2.0 is built around a series of **improvement events,** a model based on a Lean technique called Kaizen, in which a group of people is brought together for an intensive multiday session. In Bank One, a Focus 2.0 event lasts five days, with an objective to identify and implement solutions across the value stream Here's how it works:

- **The purpose is to take a cross-functional view of the process or work area.** In the new approach, the goal was to look at the business from an end-to-end perspective, using collaborative sessions among areas affected.

- **Participants are people who are directly involved in (and usually responsible for) various parts of the process.** Typical resource commitments include 8 to 12 people who often represent different cross-functional areas. The "event" team composition is divided into thirds: one-third are very hands-on (operators, supervisors); a third are managers and internal suppliers; and the final third are outsiders, people who can look at the process with fresh eyes—typically, it is the members of the NPC group that fill this role. "NPC also stays engaged with the team after the Focus 2.0 event to assist them in overcoming implementation barriers and to provide project management support," says Assistant VP Tim Williams.

91

- **Participants are pulled off their jobs**, for several days at a time. This is perhaps the most difficult aspect of the "improvement event" approach. Nobody wants to be pulled off their jobs. But the NPC group has worked hard to ensure that every event is centered on priority issues and generates quantifiable successes. This approach minimizes the negative effect that would occur if the time away was wasted on trivial problems or limited gains.

- **The work leverages a Lean format** (with DMAIC concepts where possible). The goal of each event is to come away with concrete Improve action items that are linked to well-defined problems in the process or area being studied.

The basic improvement event structure is always the same, with the specifics tailored to fit different situations.

Day 1 is typically an afternoon spent with NPC training participants on topics that cover basic concepts focusing on three Lean concepts: why cycle time matters, how to distinguish between value-added and non-value-added work, and identifying waste. NPC also reviews activities that the team will undertake the rest of the week.

Day 2 is spent looking at the current process, leveraging the tools, and building on ideas from Day 1. Participants do a "unit walk," which is a tour of operations. Participants simulate being a work item flowing through the process. The group visits each step of the process, providing an opportunity for participants to hear from those who work in each area. The group then creates a value stream map (a picture of the "As-Is" situation) that captures the basic process steps, value- and non-value-add work, cycle times, number of steps, rework loops, queuing delays, WIP, transportation time, etc.

Day 3 is designed around clarifying problems and brainstorming solutions. The team then reorganizes the value stream (on paper) or creates a "Should" map that depicts how the process would need to function to solve the identified problems. The outcome includes developing action plans for implementing solutions or trial simulations for Day 4.

Day 4 is used to test the solutions, conducting a simulation within the operations if possible. The group quantifies the improvement through estimates of reduction in travel time, queuing time, work-in-process (WIP), number of steps, number of forms, and so on.

Day 5 entails a formal report out presentation by participants to the sponsor.

Keeping sponsors involved

The team leader of the Focus 2.0 event and the facilitators have an end-of-day report out to the sponsor on days 2 through 4. "We use this time to ensure the sponsor understands the issues and recommendations the team is working on, and to give the sponsor an opportunity to provide any insights and guidance. We don't want any surprises on the final report out on Day 5," says Ass't VP Tim Williams.

Results

The NEO group has quantified a number of different measures of success for each of the projects they've conducted. Their figures show that:

- Cycle time improvements have ranged from a minimum of 30% to nearly 75%, measured sometimes in minutes (one administrative process went from 20 minutes to 12 minutes) and other times in days (a complaint resolution process dropped from 30 days to 8 days).

- Fiscal indicators have all been positive as well. A project described later in this book (see p. 337) is allowing Bank One to improve revenue. Other projects have led to cost reductions or loss avoidance in the thousands of dollars.

As always, there are other intangible results as well: "Now that we have successes, we find the sponsors are asking for more application in untouched areas," states Tim Williams. "Also as we go into our annual operating planning cycle and identify priorities, we are building Focus 2.0 events in the plans as the way to achieve the established goals where and when appropriate."

Challenges

Implementing Lean Six Sigma in an environment not accustomed to improvement has naturally had its challenges:

#1: Time. Getting people to take time away from their regular jobs is very difficult. To counteract this barrier, the NPC staff work with line management to make sure that all improvement events are well scoped in advance (so results can accrue from a 5-day event) and targeted on true business priorities (so the return on investment will be worthwhile).

#2: Making physical changes to the workplace. Because service work is not as visible or physical as manufacturing work, people in service environments are seldom aware of how the physical layout of their work area affects quality and speed. In Focus 2.0 events, diagrams are used to demonstrate how the floor layout affects process flow.

#3: Making true Lean improvements. Some Lean tools and concepts bring insights that lead to relatively simple changes in a process. But sometimes the Lean changes needed to achieve the biggest gains feel counterintuitive to people working in service areas. That means teams and managers alike are sometimes unwilling to take what they see as a risky move. Other Lean challenges they've encountered include:

- **Making Lean a priority amidst the other initiatives.** People have to see that Lean tools can help them to achieve their goals.

- **Speaking in the organization's language.** As noted in Chapter 1, Lean and Six Sigma both evolved in manufacturing environments, and the language is sometimes challenging for service personnel. That's why NEO is using pilot projects to demonstrate successes with Lean and Six Sigma tools. Their education and communication now use these success stories so people can marry the terminology and tools application to a processing world they are familiar with.

- **People's ability to match their process issue/need with Focus 2.0** (Lean as their solution). People in service environments simply aren't used to recognizing waste in their processes, nor seeing that

Lean can help eliminate that waste. Building such an awareness will just take time.

Lessons Learned

The key lessons that Darryl Greene and his colleagues would share with others include:

1. Give the business units all the credit

Positioning internal Lean Six Sigma resources as a *support* to the business units is critical for acceptance. At Bank One, the NPC staff have worked hard to collaborate with line management and frontline staff to identify problems, select targets, and generate solutions. This move makes sense because ultimately the business units know their areas best, will own the changes, and will be responsible for sustaining them. NPC staff are there to *assist* in supplying the structure and create an environment for change.

2. Modify the model to fit your industry and organization

The NEO group in Bank One is modifying Lean Six Sigma to fit the financial industry, and tailoring deployment strategies to fit their organization.

- Support exists at the top, but they are creating pull from bottom up by generating success at the frontline level.

- They are not doing widespread training but instead using a demonstration phase to engage people in deployment and have them learn from experience how Focus 2.0 approaches can help them (which also creates pull).

- They avoid using Lean Six Sigma language: "My efforts at implementing Lean and Six Sigma in a services industry has shown that in their typical form, they are rejected," comments Assistant VP Jim Kaminski. "The terminology is different, the methodology is too cumbersome, the number of tools needed are excessive, it scares people, and the only proof it works is from manufacturing applications. In our event approach or pilot, we are able to design a methodology, present only essential tools, and use terminology in language that is reinforcing rather than intimidating."

3. Go at a pace that suits the organization's readiness

"When I was at GE Lighting," says Darryl Greene, "I think Six Sigma was so powerful because the infrastructure was already in place—people were familiar with metrics and scorecards, there was a history of continuous improvement, and so on. They had multiple years of double-digit productivity improvements, so there was already a culture around taking out costs, improving operations, and trying to do the best for the customer.

"Most other companies don't have that history with improvement," he continues. "DMAIC started in NEO in 2000 as a way of attacking and stabilizing the operation, which I think was a critical need. We actually slowed it down when I came on board because we discovered the opportunities linked to establishing widespread use of fundamentals was greater than doing more sophistical projects. Slowing down our use of DMAIC projects let us actually accelerate putting the infrastructure in place, which in turn is creating a high-performance culture that can sustain improvements."

By using well-chosen pilot projects, says Greene, Bank One isn't overreaching their bounds and they're getting buy-in from the ground up, which they can now leverage in other parts of the organization.

Catalysts for change

"I view participants in Focus 2.0 events as being the catalyst TO change while sponsors are the catalysts FOR change. Without daily interaction or communication between both parties, the project on its own will undoubtedly fail."

—Jim Kaminski, Ass't VP, Bank One

4. Focus on creating pull; don't force this on people

Many organizations have found it best to use CEO leadership to mandate adoption of Lean Six Sigma, as a way to rapidly build resources and capabilities and generate results. For Bank One, taking a different approach of creating pull for Focus 2.0 has proven an effective approach to implementation. They've seen that selecting projects that are high priority for sponsors tends to get the support necessary to drive improvements and be very successful, and gets people asking NPC to come in and lead improvement events. They had one project on overnight mail (see p. 337 for details), that was extremely important to the sponsor. Because of that support, all of the improvements that were identified were quickly implemented and have been sustained. More importantly, sponsors have been convinced by early successes to work with the NPC group on numerous other projects.

Pull and pressure

"It does help if senior managers support our efforts both actively and proactively," says Jim Kaminski of Bank One's NEO division. "But for us, it wouldn't work to force engagement on senior management. In our approach, we leveraged those senior managers who gave us the opportunity to pilot Focus 2.0 within their business unit. We proved the concepts…they became advocates…and in turn we promoted these early adopters. As a result, peer pressure has taken care of the rest, and other business units have begun to seek out our assistance."

5. Cross-functional problem solving

The NPC staff agree that the biggest bang for NEO's bucks has been cross-functional problem solving. "It is quite an eye opener for participants who have never seen the process of their suppliers and their internal customers," says Jim Kaminski. "Cross-functional problem solving has opened the doors to better understanding of each others' business operations and ultimate affect on the external customer."

6. A Lean focus is better suited to "events" than is quality

The NPC group initially identified two different kinds of improvement events:

- **Flow events** designed around the application of Lean concepts in order to streamline the process, reduce cycle time, eliminate waste

- **Quality events** targeted at eliminating specific defects from the process (i.e., primarily using Six Sigma approaches)

> "What's interesting is that we changed the name and used Focus 2.0, first to emphasize that we were moving to the next level of problem solving for our group, but even more importantly to avoid terms like 'Lean manufacturing.' We knew once we threw terms like that out there, people wouldn't accept it.'"
>
> —Darryl Greene, Senior VP, Bank One

What they learned is that it was much more difficult to achieve significant improvements when they focused more on defects than on process speed. "If you don't have the right data on hand, you can't do a good Six Sigma analysis in just one week," says Tim Williams. "It usually takes longer to decide what data you want and then gather it. So in our quality-oriented events, the statistics weren't very robust; the lack of data and the short time frame did not allow us to identify and test true cause-and-effect relationships. Lean tools are more easily applied in un-improved service processes, and bring immediate results."

Earning the Right to Continue

"As tough as the changes have been, getting all of our systems onto one platform, it's created a culture of working together," says Mike Fischbach. "It's taught us that getting people together with a very clear objective and a laser-like focus is a very valuable way to introduce speed into a process." He and his colleagues offer these final words of advice:

- Don't apply the tools in an area that isn't ready… it will not represent normal circumstances and therefore any benchmark data to be used with others in the organization will be inaccurate. If you try to apply Lean Six Sigma in an area that has no foundation for improving performance, it will take longer to execute projects, and results are likely to be disappointing—dynamics that no one wants to create during deployment.

- Start small… build successes… then sell, sell, sell.

- Be selective with your hosts for pilots. You need a great sponsor and someone who is respected within the organization for initial projects. That way, when success occurs, you'll have a strong, influential advocate, whose impact amongst peers is much greater than your own.

The outcomes, says Fischbach, are worth it. "The successes the pilot projects achieved has earned us the opportunity to go in and lead more events, and, more importantly, are returning value to Bank One," he says.

CHAPTER 4

Executing Corporate Strategy with Lean Six Sigma

"A good managerial record is more a function of which boat you get into rather than how effectively you row" [1]

Warren Buffett

Over the last decade, more and more companies are accepting the principles illustrated by the Value Mountain (Figure 1.2, reprinted on the next page), a graph based on actual stock market data. The main lesson is that the principal driver of shareholder value is Return on Invested Capital (ROIC). (In the nonprofit sphere, the names change to capital generation and maximizing stakeholder benefits, but the process of achieving the goals is identical.)

Thinking about ROIC is probably most familiar to senior executives and P&L managers, but it is an area of knowledge that forms a central premise of Lean Six Sigma: that decisions about investing Black Belt resources should be based on an understanding of maximum potential value creation in the organization. For that reason, it is crucial that Champions become expert in ROIC analysis, and helpful if everyone along the value chain is at least familiar with the underlying concepts.

Given the lessons demonstrated by the graph, the question is how can we identify and prioritize projects based on maximizing ROIC and revenue growth. The process reviewed in this chapter has been proven to work in practice, and is much more effective than implementations in which projects are selected solely by Black Belts or first-line management.

Figure 1.2: The Value Mountain (reprinted from Chp 1)

This graph is used to illustrate why ROIC is so critical to shareholder value. The spread of ROIC% minus the Cost of Capital% is so important that it has a special name, Economic Profit% (EP%), a factor you'll see referenced several times in this chapter. As shown in this figure, if EP% = 0 (that is, ROIC% is equal to the cost of

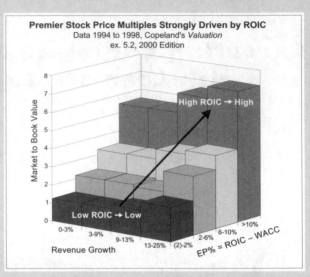

Capital%), the company trades at about book value. If EP% is 5% or greater (ROIC% exceeds the cost of capital by 5–10%), the company trades at 4 to 5 times book value. If, in addition, revenue growth exceeds 10% each year, the company will trade at 7 times book value or higher.

Applying Value-Based Management to Project Selection

The flow from high-level strategy to individual projects requires an understanding of where and how value is created in your organization. The sequence, as depicted in Figure 4.1 (next page), is to:

1) **Identify the burning platforms** of shareholder value creation at both a corporate and business unit level

2) **Identify value streams** within the business units that have the greatest potential for increasing shareholder value

3) **Identify and prioritize projects** within each value stream that will maximize value (Black Belt resources within each business units will be focused on these projects)

Maintaining the links between levels is the only effective way of measuring results at the bottom line and assuring that the business unit managers will support Lean Six Sigma and make it "the way we do business" instead of an additional task. Most companies will have performed some if not all of the initial work described below as part of their annual strategy planning. This is not a book on valuation or strategy, but we'll summarize the process in full to show how value can be carried seamlessly from corporate strategy to Black Belt project execution.

Figure 4.1: From Strategy to Projects

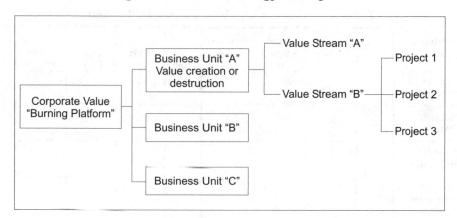

Stage 1: Identifying the Burning Platform of shareholder value creation

The backdrop for the analysis presented in this chapter is that your organization knows what its biggest competitive or strategic challenges are. Every company is in competition for customers (to drive revenue); public companies also compete for shareholders (to drive share price). How well your company is doing on both these fronts can be determined by comparing your performance to that of your competitors.

There are two elements to this analysis:

A) **Corporate shareholder value analysis**, which will reveal the potential for shareholder value creation

B) **Business unit analysis** for determining the Economic Profit and revenue growth of different components of your business

Step 1A. Corporate Shareholder Value Analysis

The general idea behind this analysis is to use data available in public records to compare how your company is performing in the marketplace at the broadest level. Table 4.1 (see below) shows the most common indicators included in such an analysis. For our purposes in using this as part of a drive towards selecting Lean Six Sigma projects, the most important figure is Economic Profit% (calculated as the % change in ROIC minus the (weighted) % cost of capital) as an overall indicator of company performance, and Growth Rate.

Table 4.1: Shareholder Value Analysis Format

Strategic Issue	You	Compe-titor A	Compe-titor B	Compe-titor C	Avg	s (Std Dev)	CEO Goal	Share Price A
Economic Profit %								
Growth Rate								
Market to Book								
Owner Earnings/ Profit								

When you plot your own figures versus that of your competitors, you'll come up with a customized version of Figure 1.2, as shown in Figure 4.2, next page. You'll probably want to plot share price movement for your nearest competitors or similar kinds of companies over the last three years, as well as project where you think your share price can move to *if* you achieve your the strategic vision (through Lean Six Sigma).

By comparing your value to similar kinds of companies, you will generally find opportunities. An analysis of similar "conglomerate" type companies drove ITT Industries' Lean Six Sigma process. The CEO said:

"We noticed in our analysis that while some companies get a conglomerate discount, there are others like GE, who got a conglomerate premium. And guess what? It all depends on performance, and if we could get our performance up, we felt we'd be able to earn those types of premiums. We had to convince our management teams that even though

Figure 4.2: Identifying Your Burning Platforms

You can use the Value Mountain to highlight your competitive challenges vs. your competitors. On the graph, Revenue Growth is included because it affects shareholder value through the benefits of future Economic Profits. Add these additional profits and investments to compute the future Economic Profit %.

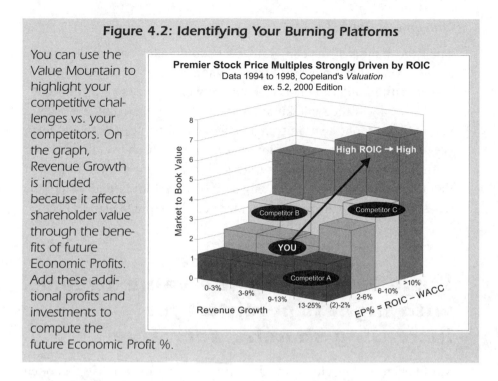

they were doing well in their individual industries, when you measured them against multi-industry, premier peers—the GEs, Danahers, ITWs of the world—we were mediocre. That's how we started Value Based Six Sigma."

Like the companies depicted in Figure 1.3 (p. 16), ITT's stock has more than doubled in a time period when the S&P has dropped.

Step 1B. Business Unit Analysis

The data that needs to be taken at the business unit level is the same as at corporate, assuming you can find "pure play" competitors to compare against your unit's business (they have a single line of business similar to your own for which data are available). So you would fill in Table 4.1 for each business unit, adding in data on relative Gross Margin and SG&A% (Selling, General, and Administrative costs). This will tell the CEO how much value is being created or destroyed by the business unit. Economic Profit % by customer and geography should also be analyzed at the business unit level.

Outcome of Stage 1

The data analysis at the corporate level should allow you to determine, at the broadest level, what the biggest factors are that you need to be concerned with in order to drive shareholder value (revenue growth, ROIC, etc.). Looking at the same kind of data at the business unit level allows you to focus in on those units that are contributing most to the problem (i.e., perhaps it's just one division that is holding back overall corporate value growth). The next step is to dive down one more level, to look at the value streams within the targeted business units and determine where your improvement investment would have the biggest impact.

Stage 2: Mapping the value streams with highest potential for increasing shareholder value

Most business units offer many different products and services that often do not share common value streams. One option, of course, would be to simply launch a lot of projects throughout the unit. But you can be much more effective in your resource investment if you figure out how each value stream in a business unit contributes to value creation or destruction. Value streams are usually defined within a business unit by product or service type, and include suppliers' processes and internal processes, and extend to customers and often their processes. (In this context, a value stream is defined as an entire process that transforms supplier inputs into outputs that satisfy a customer need.)

The metric to look at first is once again Economic Profit, this time segmented out by value stream. When you arrange the results in descending order of value creation vs. value destruction, you end up with a **waterfall** diagram like that shown in Figure 4.3 (see p. 109).

One note if you do this type of analysis yourself: the allocation of overhead cost and invested capital can be challenging if performed in detail. For the purposes here, it's just as effective to use a reasonable estimate with ranges of values as a first step. This will give you a *directionally*

Continued on p. 108

The Right Fiscal Indicator: Profit After Tax or Owner Earnings?

The discussion in the accompanying text provides empirical reasons for placing Voice of the customer (Critical-to-Quality) measures and ROIC center stage in any process for making strategic choices about where to invest Lean Six Sigma resources.

But ROIC as it traditionally calculated $= \dfrac{\text{Profit After Tax (PAT)}}{\text{Invested Capital}}$

has a significant flaw: We have recently seen companies inflating Profit After Tax (PAT) by classifying current costs as investments such as Capex or Inventory, or claiming false revenue that inflates accounts receivable.

The alternative? Buffett defines owner earnings as the cash that is generated that can be used for the benefit of shareholders for

- reinvestment in the business (if ROIC > WACC, growth opportunity)
- valid acquisitions (Purchase price < NPV of target)
- repurchase of shares (Market price < NPV of business)
- dividends to the shareholders (when none of the above pertain)

His formula for owner earnings (from Berkshire Hathaway Annual Report 1986) is:

Owner Earnings = (PAT) – (Capex) + (D&A) – (Increase in working capital)

Since Capex fluctuates, it's best to use an average of three years.

A company that attempts to hide current expense in either Capex, inventory, or receivables may be found out by Owner Earnings (unless the transactions are not on the balance sheet, e.g., Enron). Thus in computing ROIC, replace PAT with Owner earnings. A company that is able to reduce working capital, receivables, and Capex accelerates the velocity with which investments are transformed to cash inputs at a given revenue level.

It's true that the Owner Earnings equation does not yield the (deceptively) precise figures of GAAP (e.g., Capex is an average). Despite this problem, owner earnings, not the GAAP figure, is more relevant for valuation purposes—both for investors in buying stocks and for managers in buying entire businesses. We agree with John Maynard Keynes' observation:

"I would rather be vaguely right than precisely wrong."

correct answer (whether the value stream is destroying or creating value). This analysis usually detects large discrepancies in Economic Profit; there are clear winners and losers.

But Figure 4.3 represents only half the story. As you may recall from Chapter 3, another component of "value" is the potential for revenue growth. This is measured as attractiveness to customers and Economic Profit of the market. In fact, Figure 3.1 was based on the same five value streams. In that chart, the profitability of each value creator was compared to its competitive position (based on market data). The size of the circle indicated the relative revenue of each offering. Combining the two gives us a more complete picture, as shown in Figure 4.4. These charts are based on actual data. After completing this analysis, the company decided to:

- **Sell (or shut down) Value Stream** E, which loses out on both sides of the analysis: The left-hand graph in Figure 4.4 shows thatvalue stream E generates the largest *negative* Economic Profit (EP); the right-hand graph shows that it is also at a significant competitive disadvantage and has relatively small revenue in an industry that has aggregate negative EP. Barring some breakthrough there are much better opportunities to invest improvement resources. While Lean Six Sigma emphasizes the need to listen to the Voice of the Customer, this shows one situation where the customers' business will never earn a positive economic profit. Companies have to consider whether effort applied to a Value Stream like E would be better applied to a different set of customers, products, or geographies. If that is the case, then they should make a graceful exit from that business and focus improvement efforts on businesses that can earn a positive economic profit. (If E is a whole division, the company should consider offering it for divestiture, as discussed later in this chapter.)

- **Undertake a major initiative to improve the position of value stream D**, which, though it showed negative EP, was at an advantaged position. Though value stream D was competing in an unprofitable industry overall, customers preferred D to the market competition. This meant that D was a value stream well worth

Continued on p. 110

Figure 4.3: "Waterfall" of Value Stream Assessment

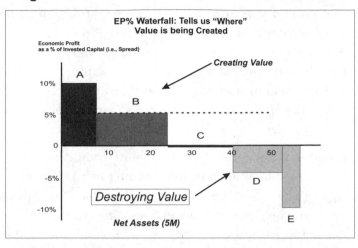

This company calculated Economic Profit for each of five value streams within one business unit, then plotted the results in order of decreasing EP%. The X axis is the amount of invested capital. The Y axis is the Economic Profit, which is defined as the difference between the ROIC% and the cost of capital. The width and direction of the bars indicate the net assets of each value stream and whether it is creating or destroying value. In this case, value stream A has relatively little invested capital (the bar is narrow) but the highest EP%. Overall, value streams A and B are creating value, C is neutral, and D and E are destroying value.

Figure 4.4: Combined Economic Profit Analysis

Value stream analysis (Fig 4.3) with
strategic position analysis (Fig 3.1)

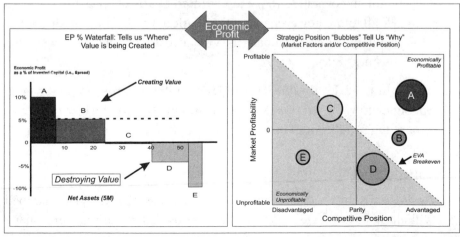

studying to determine if non-value-add costs comprised a significant portion of total costs. If yes, an investment in cutting waste and costs could move them into strong Economic Profit position and capitalize on their already strong competitive position. (In fact, the company did use Value Stream Mapping to identify which activities within operation D were creating the most waste and delay, then applied basic Lean and Six Sigma tools to those areas in priority order.)

- **Invest in making value stream C more competitive.** C was in the opposite position to D: neither creating nor destroying value, but lagging in a market sector that was profitable. The company didn't need to worry as much about removing wastes and costs as in making sure that brand line C was more responsive to the Voice of the Customer. Such VOC input could help them determine whether enhancements to current offerings or additional new offerings would give them competitive advantage. (Approaches for improving customer focus were discussed in Chp 3; also see Chp 14 for a discussion of Design for Lean Six Sigma.)

- **Monitor value streams A and B** for any weakening of their competitive position or market sector. The Voice of the Customer and competitive analyses demonstrated to the company just how important these brand lines were to their financial and market strength. Another way to look at it is that any current *improvement* opportunities in value streams A and B are not as critical to the company overall as those represented by the other brand lines. As we all know, however, market conditions can change rapidly, so the company must maintain its vigilance to protect these valuable business lines.

The right boats for this business unit, in Buffett's words? Applying Lean Six Sigma to value streams D and C would likely have the best chance of generating significant improvement in ROIC and value.

Outcomes of the value stream analysis

As illustrated by the example below, an analysis of the type just described will allow you to focus on the value streams that are in the worst shape (destroying shareholder value). Diving down another level once again, the next step is to continue sharpening your focus.

> ### STOP! Check that list of priorities
>
> The process described in this chapter does not account for strategic initiatives that cannot be easily tied to current bottom line shareholder value, such as the need to improve safety, reduce product liability, address environmental hazards, and so on. Lean Six Sigma methods can be applied equally to such priorities, but since they won't typically surface in an analysis of ROIC and Economic Profit, you'll need to add them to the mix before you decide which value streams to map. In addition, some value streams may have negative EP currently, but strong *future* EP. In this case, you must supplement the use of EP with Net Present Value (NPV) analysis, which is found by comparing the discounted value of future E (see p. 16 for a discussion of "discounted" values).

Stage 3: Prioritizing projects (finding the Time Traps)

Once you have selected the value streams that have the highest value potential, the final step is identifying specific projects within a targeted value stream and prioritize them based on the likely benefit.

If your organization is already using Six Sigma, the temptation will be to simply apply data-driven management and the DMAIC process to make improvements. However, one of the themes of this book is that people working in service functions haven't been trained to identify some of the biggest causes of process opportunities—problems that would be better addressed by adding Lean techniques, the elimination of non-value-add cost, and the reduction of the complexity of the offering. (When was the last time you heard someone say, "we have too much work-in-process" or "I'm concerned about our non-value-add costs" or "lead time is suffering from variation in demand" or "I think we have too much offering complexity"? These are insights that traditional Six Sigma tools did not address.)

So part of the challenge in answering the question of how to improve a value stream is to find a method that will help expose Lean and complexity opportunities that we don't know we have, as well as capture what would be considered Six Sigma opportunities.

Fortunately, there is a universal metric that represents speed, quality, and complexity problems: **time**. Understanding how to analyze how time is spent in a value stream is therefore a crucial skill in completing the final link from corporate strategy to improvement projects.

Time: The universal currency of improvement

Through the analysis discussed earlier in this chapter, you will have narrowed your field of vision to a few value streams that have the biggest negative impact or drain on shareholder value. The next question is, to which of the activities within a selected value stream should you first apply Lean Six Sigma tools? Here are some clues from the various disciplines that integrated into this book:

Clue #1: **Lessons from Little's Law about WIP.** Little's Law, introduced in Chapter 2, clearly demonstrates that if you have lots of work-in-process (WIP), you will have a slow process. (Remember that WIP can mean anything in process, from reports and calls to emails, requests, and even customers.) The more WIP you have, the more:

  – non-value-add cost will punish the income statement
  – invested capital will punish the balance sheet
  – and together they punish ROIC and shareholder value

So we're linking value destruction to WIP and hence to delays in the process. Lean tells us that long setup times, downtime, and poor flow cause delay and WIP... but that's not all.

Clue #2: **Think about the impact of quality on time.** Here's a question for you: assume a process has a 10-day lead time and no quality problems. If it suddenly is plagued by 10% defects, what would be the impact on lead time and the amount of work-in-process? You might think the answer is that lead time would also increase by 10%. But in fact the impact is much worse: lead time will increase by 38% and the number of things-in-process will increase by 54%! Thus we can say that an activity within a process that is producing 10% defects will be the source of enormous downstream time delay and non-value-add cost. Here again, a process problem (in this case poor quality) shows up in time delay.

Clue #3: Don't forget complexity: We'll go into details later in this chapter and in Chapter 5, but the complexity of your offerings (the numbers and varieties of your services/products) generally increases non-value-add cost, number of "things in process" (WIP) and time delay (there's that time word again) more than any other single cause.

In short, almost any process problem you could name—defects, WIP, low productivity, process flow complexity—results in added time delays to a process. Hence time is the universal currency of improvement. The obvious conclusion is that calculating the time delay injected by each activity in a process will lead us to the worst quality, speed, and complexity issues that create non-value-add cost and capital. Making the process less costly and faster can only aid revenue growth and further enhance value.

From Time to Time Traps

You might recall a metric introduced in Chapter 2 called Process Cycle Efficiency (PCE), the ratio of value-add time to total lead time in any process. Experience shows that in any process with a PCE of 10% or less (90% of processing time is spent in delays and non-value-add work) that fewer than 20% of the activities (the **Time Traps**) cause 80% of the delay in lead time.

Time Traps therefore give us a way to use time to focus our improvement efforts. Just as the discussion above indicates, the size of a Time Trap is the result of...

- **Delays due to process inefficiencies**: As we've discussed several times with the Lockheed Martin procurement operation, factors such as the setup time and repeated learning curves can lead to low productivity in output per day per person.

- **Variation in supply and demand**: Some service activities only process one kind of offering, and have no significant setup time or learning curves. An example given in *Lean Six Sigma* is a hotel clerk checking in guests. There is practically no setup time, and only one priority job responsibility (checking in guests). In that example, it became clear that if the clerk could check in the guest in *exactly* 5 minutes, and if guests arrived *exactly* every 7 minutes, there would be no queue time—guests could be checked in immediately without having to wait in line. However, if there is *any* variation in the arrival of guests or difficulty in check-in (as there always is!), queue time delays would start to pile up and guests could end up waiting in line 8 or more minutes to get service. (See sidebar.)

- **Variation in process capacity:** In any unimproved process, capacity likely varies greatly from day to day or even hour to hour due to issues such as downtime (of computers, other equipment), absenteeism, and so on. So a customer order that might speed through a process one day could experience lots of delay at some other time.

How variation affects delay time and WIP

A hotel case study in the original Lean Six Sigma book was based on a situation where a hotel clerk could check in 68% of guests between 3 and 7 minutes (one s around an average of 5 minutes), but where guests usually arrived every 4 to 10 minutes (one s around average of 7 minutes). With this amount of variation, inevitably one or more guests might keep arriving at 4 minute intervals when it's taking the clerk 7 minutes to check in a difficult guest. As a result, on average, guests waited in queue 8.5 minutes before they experienced the 5 minutes of value-add service. (Refer back to Fig 2.13 "Effect of Variation on Queue Time" to see a visual depiction of this situation.)

Surveys have shown that hotel check-in time is a leading cause of customer dissatisfaction. A satisfied customer returns to the hotel chain an average of three times per year, a dissatisfied customer generally never returns... but tells three friends about the experience. There is thus high revenue leverage in satisfied customers, and, more specifically, in improving check-in time. Chapter 2 discussed ways to temporarily increase capacity so that fluctuations in WIP (here, the number of customers waiting to be checked in) didn't adversely affect lead time.

- **Quality-related delays:** As described above, quality problems (defects) have a nonlinear effect on the WIP (number of things in process), non-value-add cost, and delay time.

Focusing on Time Traps is therefore a powerful metric that allows us to **simultaneously pick up problems resulting from poor quality and un-Lean practices.** The challenge is to first identify the Time Traps, then determine whether the cause of the delay is most likely a quality problem (requiring application of Six Sigma tools), a speed problem (requiring Lean), or a complexity problem (requiring complexity-reduction strategies).

Finding the Time Delays: Pinpointing Time Traps for improvement efforts

If only 20% of activities are the Time Traps—the biggest inhibitors of shareholder value—how do we find and eliminate them? There are three schools of thought:

1) **"Blind Hog" theory:** Some Japanese companies (and some Lean consultants in America) use the approach of launching scores or even hundreds of Kaizens (intense improvement events) per year. Eventually, you will hit the "Herbie" or Time Trap (see sidebar), and be able to reduce lead times. In Texas, we have a saying,

   "Even a blind hog can find an acorn if he
   roots around an oak tree long enough."

   Kaizen improvement events can accelerate the DMAIC process, but they are far more effective when directed towards prioritized problems.

2) **Target large concentrations of WIP and apply your intuition:** Eliyahu Goldratt espoused this approach of simply looking for the biggest stacks of WIP in your process (the longest queues) and applying process knowledge to see how to reduce that WIP. But sometimes WIP piles up far downstream from the Time Trap that injected the delay (see *Lean Six Sigma, p. 45,* for an example). In the Lockheed Martin procurement example, the biggest non-value-add cost problem was in the factory's productivity, far downstream from the purchasing department where the shortages that

caused the delays arose (and where the problems were ultimately fixed). So simply attacking the point at which the delay is most visible won't necessarily get you where you want to go.

3) **Time Trap Analysis:** You can take your chances with a Blind Hog approach, hope you get lucky by targeting WIP… or you can actually *calculate* where delays are largest based on demand, processing time, and setup time (see sidebar, below).

Time Traps are not always capacity constraints

In his book *The Goal* (which introduced the Theory of Constraints), Eliyahu Goldratt picturesquely referred to the source of delays in a process (the constraints) as the "Herbies" in reference to a single portly Boy Scout who held up the whole troop. Subsequent advances have led to the distinction between capacity constraints (which limit total output) and Time Traps (which insert the longest delays in the process).

One of the counterintuitive results of Lean analysis is that these two factors—capacity constraints and Time Traps—are not always the same. That is, the biggest source of delays is not in the areas traditionally considered as capacity bottlenecks. Many organizations have added capacity (people and/or machines) in an attempt to reduce lead time. It is true, as shown by Little's Law (see Chp 2), that adding capacity will increase the completion rate and therefore reduce lead time:

$$\text{Lead Time} = \frac{\text{Amount of Work-In-Process}}{\text{Average Completion Rate}}$$

However, adding capacity is expensive. What Little's Law also shows us is that we can get far more leverage by reducing WIP, which requires an investment of intellectual capital rather than financial capital (the ongoing expense of additional people and equipment).

Many companies are satisfied with the second approach described above, but Lean Six Sigma encourages us to a more rigorous use of data to make such important managerial decisions.

That's why the next section of this chapter describes Time Trap Analysis, a process that uses data to go from the ROIC drivers identified in Stage 2 to specific projects that will improve the Time Traps hindering the performance of those drivers. The procedure is to…

1. Create a **complexity value stream map** on the selected value driver to capture the flow of work and quantify waste and delays

2. Pinpoint the biggest **Time Traps**

3. **Identify projects** to eliminate Time Traps (using Lean, Six Sigma, and/or complexity reduction tools)

One word of caution for the math-phobes: some of the calculations described below use algebra (though we've included only simplified versions here). However, it behooves every manager to be familiar with the concepts being applied here even if they don't want to learn the math. You should seriously consider training your Champions and some Black Belts on how to perform the more detailed Time Trap Analysis—otherwise you will be lacking rigor in the final link from strategy to projects. (Any company can access the details of the calculations described below, at www.profisight.com, free of charge.)

Time Trap Analysis Step 1: Create a complexity value stream map

As the name implies, a complexity value stream map (CVSM) is a tool that combines three elements:

1) process flow

2) data on how time is spent

3) data reflecting how many different types of services/products flow through the value stream (the complexity)

A traditional value stream map (VSM) depicts the basic process(es) in a value stream, with activities classified into two or three categories: value-added work, non-value-added work, and business non-value-added work. (See sidebar, next page, for definitions.)

There are several ways to visually separate value- and non-value-added work on the process map that will be the foundation of a complexity value stream map. One method is using color coding; other methods include dividing the page into columns (VA vs. BNVA vs. NVA) and placing the step icons in the appropriate columns.

Distinguishing Value-Added from Non-Value-Added work

It's human nature for all of us who work in managerial, administrative, and professional processes to think that everything we do is "value added." That's why its so difficult for us to see the waste in processes we work on everyday. Use the questions below to help people in your organization to start refining their sensitivity to waste:

(A) Value Add (VA) (also called "Customer Value Add"): the work that contributes what your customers want out of your product or service (and that they would pay for if they knew about it).

- Does the task add a desired function, form, or feature to the product or service?
- Does the task enable a competitive advantage (reduced price, faster delivery, fewer defects)?
- Would the customer be willing to pay for this activity, or prefer us over the competition if he or she knew we were doing this task?

(B) Business Non-Value-Add (BNVA): activities that your customer doesn't want to pay for (it does not add value in their eyes) but that are required for some reason (often for accounting, legal, or regulatory purposes). In addition to customer value add, the business or regulatory agencies may require you to perform some functions which add no value from the customers perspective:

- Is this task required by law or regulation?
- Does this task reduce financial risk?
- Does this task support financial reporting requirements?
- Would the process break down if this task were removed?

(Recognize that the work generating these costs is really non-value-add but you are currently forced to perform. You need to be vigilant in making sure such work really is required, eliminating it as soon as you can; work to minimize costs on any such work you cannot eliminate.)

(C) Non-value-add (NVA): work that adds no value in the eyes of your customers and that they would not want to pay for, nor is it required for BNVA purposes.

- Does the task include any of the following activities: rework, expediting, multiple signatures, counting, handling, inspecting, setup, downtime, transporting, moving, delaying, storing.
- Taking a global view of the Supply Chain, having made these improvements. Will the faster lead time and lower costs create higher revenue and consume existing capacity? If not, the excess capacity is non-value-add and should be eliminated.

Reflecting the complexity in a value stream

Traditional value stream maps evolved as part of the Toyota Production System (which gave rise to all the current Lean techniques used in both service and manufacturing). If you have ever read books about value stream mapping (e.g., *Learning To See*), you know that they just follow the flow of *one* product family through the process. That meant it missed any delays due to product complexity. Further, the environment was "simple" by most standards—dealing with highly repetitive offerings, all following the same path (= little product or process complexity), with less than 10% variation in total demand per month. In contrast, most companies face different realities:

- Significant and growing complexity in their services and products (with no organizational effort to reduce complexity)

- Much more than 10% variation in demand per offering

- Process flows that slow down because of a few activities

Because traditional value stream maps only look at one service/product family, they miss the delays and non-value-add costs caused by the realities listed above:

- the **congestion** where work requests, products, information, etc., from different process flows impinge on a single activity

- queue time caused by **variation** in demand rates and service times

- **complexity** of the offering

The need for looking at the flow of all the services or products can be illustrated graphically. Figure 4.5 shows the flow diagram of just *one* family of offerings flowing through a process.

But this company actually has a number of product families that flow through the same process. Figure 4.6 (next page) shows a random sample of just 15% of these offerings. By showing all of those families on the same diagram, we can find areas of congestion that occur around a few activities, which doesn't show up in Figure 4.5. The new diagram qualitatively indicates that a few activities—the places where all the lines converge—may be major sources of delay, the Time Traps.

Figure 4.5: Traditional Value Stream Map

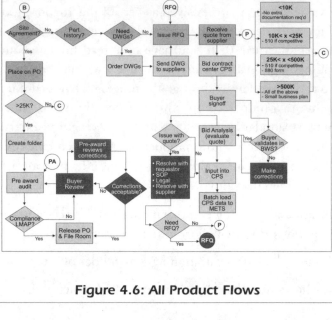

Figure 4.6: All Product Flows

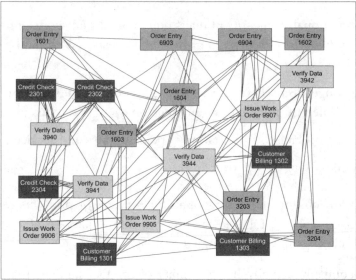

In this example, the Time Traps occur where many products flow through a single step. Such traps can be found only by considering the flow of all the services or products (not just one family, as is done in traditional value stream mapping), as well as variation in demand, and complexity. As you'll see, complexity-value stream data includes variation in demand, the number of different services performed at an activity, and the flows of all products or services in the process.

Creating a Complexity VSM

Creating a complexity value stream map begins the same way as any other process mapping exercise: you need to create a diagram showing the overall flow of work through the processes that comprise the value stream. As in basic flowcharting, it is essential to have employees who work in the process physically follow the work as it flows from activity to activity instead of relying on opinions about how people *think* the processes flow. For each process step, you'll want to collect the following data (including calculations of the average and standard deviation):

1. **Estimated Cost per Activity:** This is the total cost, not the cost-per-offering. (The latter approach is called activity-based costing, ABC, and is quite complicated and time consuming. For the purposes here, the total costs are sufficient because we intend to entirely eliminate any non-value-add activity.)

2. **Process Time (P/T):** Value-add time per unit for each type of service or product.

3. **Change-over time:** Any time that lapses between changing from one service or product to another, including the time it takes someone to get up to full speed after switching tasks (a learning curve cost).

4. **Queue Time:** The time things spend waiting to be processed.

5. **Takt Time:** The **demand rate** of customers for each type of service or product.

6. **Complexity:** Number of different services or products processed at the activity.

7. **Uptime:** Time worked per day minus breaks and interruptions.

8. **Defects** and **rework:** Raw counts (and or percentages) of the time and cost needed to "fix" defective services or products at each activity.

A data form like that shown in Figure 4.7 is helpful in collecting the needed data. It also lists all the offerings being processed at the activity so that the complexity can be quantified as an opportunity for improvement. It includes an estimate of the variation in each average, which is an important driver of queue time.

Figure 4.7: Sample Process Data Collection Form

Activity #	Activity Descrip	Process Descrip	Process #	Time in Queue	# in Queue		Setup Time	Avg Down-Time	Process Time per Task	Date Performed		Hrs Late to Demand	Com-ments
					On Arrival	On Depart				Last	Current		

From this data you are able to compute all the parameters needed to determine which activity (the Time Trap) is causing the longest delay in the process. Moreover, you can determine how much improvement will result from applying a Lean Six Sigma tool or complexity reduction.

Adding this data to the basic flow map results in a diagram like Figure 4.8. From this activity-level data, you can compute process cycle efficiency, lead time, and variation, which in turn will allow you to prioritize the Time Traps, and calculate cost reduction and revenue growth opportunity, as we'll discuss below.

Figure 4.8: Completed Value Stream Map (Excerpt)

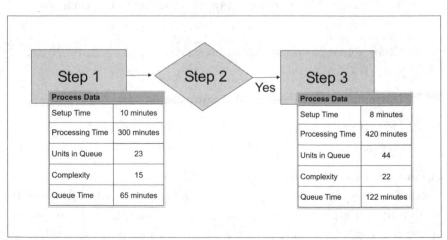

Collect data long enough to cover all product/service flows

Data collection has a special role in value analysis. As noted above, Time Traps are not the same as capacity constraints—and without data, you won't be able to tell the difference. So the core work in Time Trap analysis is having someone record and log sample process data daily for a week or more, long enough to encompass all the various complexities of the targeted area. This eliminates the major shortfall of traditional value stream mapping: only looking at the flow of one offering.

Time Trap Analysis Step 2: Converting CVSM data into information

Even once you have all the data needed to generate a CVSM, you're only part way towards the answers you need. Knowing *where* a Time Trap is doesn't tell you *why*. For example, before Lockheed Martin completed the analysis of their procurement delays (having buyers spend an entire day on one customer before moving on to the next), anything could have been at fault—defects and rework or a host of other problems. In this case it turned out to be primarily Lean-related issues (setup time and learning curves), but they didn't know that up front.

The data you need to pinpoint likely *whys* were collected when you did the complexity value stream map. What you need now is a calculation that can convert that data into information. This is harder than it may sound at first because processes are so complicated: my colleagues and I have invested a great deal of time and energy in coming up with a solution, a simplified version of which is described below. The derivation of this formula and its implications are the subjects of three US patents[2] and over 100 pages of derivation (but as noted above, you can obtain free complexity value stream software from www.profisight.com).

Finding the Cause of Time Traps: Using the Waste Driver Equation

By now, you should know that the delays (and hence waste) in any process are the result of many factors: setup time, rework, absenteeism, offering complexity, etc. That's why the equation used to find the source of delays needs to be complicated. Here what it looks like[2]:

$$\textbf{Waste Driver}_{WIP} = \frac{ëN(S + S_R - PHS_R + PHM + \text{other terms})}{2[1 - X - \lambda PHM + \text{other terms}]} = \frac{\lambda NS}{2[1 - X - \lambda P]}$$

Where... λ=total demand   S=Setup time
              P=Processing Time   H=Human downtime
              M=Machine downtime S_R=setup time to do rework
              X=defect rate

The simplified equation at the right is useful to understand the relative power of the reduction of complexity, setup time, quality etc. The complete equation also takes into account the effect of downtime, absenteeism, variation in service times and demand per offering.

Most people use complexity value stream mapping software, which employs the complete equation, to perform these calcutions. This will allow you to play "what if" simulations of the relative impact on lead time, WIP, and non-value-add cost versus improving quality, reducing setup, and/or reducing complexity (e.g., "if we could reduce delays in order taking, what impact would that have on overall lead time? if we could prevent defects in the application form, what impact would that have?). Later in this chapter and in Chapter 5 we will make the connection between large amounts of WIP to non-value-add cost.

There are two primary outputs from this formula, the first of which is the basis for deriving the Waste Driver equation, and the second of which helps to expose the causes of Time Traps (and the resulting WIP):

1. **Time Delay diagram:** a graph that shows how long it takes someone to cycle through all the tasks associated with a given process

2. **Cost driver analytic:** shows the relative impact of quality vs. Lean problems in your value stream

We'll look at the time delay diagram first (because it helps pinpoint Time Traps) and the cost driver analytic later in this chapter (because it helps uncover the causes of those Time Traps).

Time Delay Diagrams

In any processes where employees can control *when* they work on any individual item—as opposed to customer-facing operations where they cannot keep customers waiting—there will almost always be work in queue. Employees will generally work on one task or activity they deem high priority, switch to another task, and so on. The formula presented above can be used to generate a time delay diagram (first shown in Figure 2.10 and reprinted here), which captures time spent on each task and on the time in between tasks:

Figure 2.10 [Reproduced here]

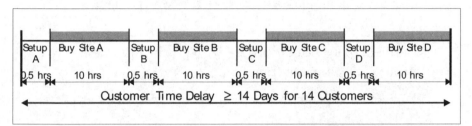

In the Lockheed Martin procurement example discussed previously, the buyers processed all of one site's requests (regardless of urgency) because it was time consuming to switch between computer systems. This caused delays in serving other customers, lots of WIP, and non-value-add costs. In this process, setup was the activity that had the longest turnover time and is the highest priority Time Trap (the 2nd Law of Lean Six Sigma).

Is queue time wasted time?

A value stream map will almost always reveal that the work spends most of its time sitting around waiting to be worked on ("in queue"). Some people argue that it isn't costing the company to have work in queue, so why should it be considered non-value-add cost? There are a couple of reasons: First, if work is in queue, that means there is some end-product or service that can't be delivered—which either causes disruptions internally or delays revenue. Second, generally the work is "in queue" for non-value-add activities—review, rework, wait for approval, etc. So not only is the delay potentially costing you revenue, the things-in-process are waiting for work your customers would not pay for if they had a choice!

By adding together the delay times between activities and sorting the results from largest to smallest, you can generate a Pareto chart of Time Traps (which we'll show later in this chapter).

Time Trap Analysis Step 3: Linking improvement projects to Time Traps

The focusing work associated with going from CEO strategy to Lean Six Sigma projects is now complete: you've identified specific activities (Time Traps) in targeted value streams within a business unit that are most inhibiting shareholder value. The next (and last) step is figuring out what to do about those Time Traps. The two options are:

1) You can bring together people who work on the process and ask them to apply their process knowledge to brainstorm ways to eliminate delays from the Time Trap

2) You can add more rigor by performing a **cost driver analysis**

As before, using the more rigorous approach is preferred because it provides the stronger link between the projects ultimately chosen for implementation and the CEO strategy. And everything you need to do for a cost driver analysis was also capture when you created a CVSM.

Cost Driver Analysis

The Waste Driver equation discussed above is simplified because, for example, it uses *average* demand per product or service when in fact the real formula incorporates *actual* demand, setup, processing time, and quality per offering type. However, even with this simplified version, some interesting deductions follow from the formula:

1. **Setup time** (S) has a linear impact on WIP, as it appears only in the numerator. Cut the setup in half, and you can cut WIP in half!

2. **Quality** is embedded in several factors, including X = defect rate. Quality has a huge impact because as X gets larger, the equation denominator gets smaller, and WIP explodes.[2]

3. **Complexity** is in the numerator, as is setup, but as N (the number of different offerings) increases, the activity is driven up the learn-

ing curve and S, P, X all increase. Thus complexity of the offering may have more impact on WIP and non-value-add cost than all others combined.

These conclusions are even better illustrated on a graph (Figure 4.9). The various lines depict the impact of setup time and learning curves, and the combined effect of all three improvements.

Figure 4.9: Cost Driver Analysis

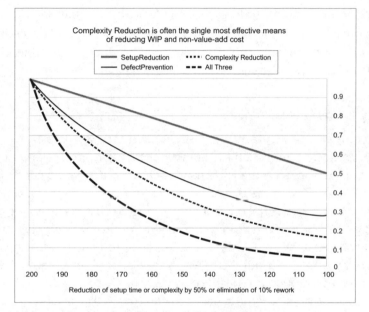

On this chart, the X axis shows the effect of:

1) Making significant Lean gains (reducing all setup times and learning curves by 50%), or
2) Substantially improving quality (reducing rework from 10% to ~0% (i.e., to 6 σ levels), or
3) Reducing offering complexity by 50%. You can see the potentially greater impact of quality problems and the even greater impact of complexity on costs.

Because the waste formula incorporates many sources of delays, we can use the cost driver analysis output to help us decide on an improvement approach, which typically will be some combination of:

- It could be primarily a quality problem (requiring basic Six Sigma process improvements)

- It could be a speed problem (requiring Lean techniques)

- It could be the result of product/service complexity (requiring standardization or optimization, which will be discussed in Chp 5)

Figure 4.10 (next page), for example, shows the Pareto chart that was mentioned but not shown above, where the biggest Time Traps are listed in descending order. Once the cost driver analysis is complete, you can add the suggested improvement approaches for addressing each Time Trap. **Conclusion:** If you dramatially reduce setup time, the WIP and cost of complexity are significantly reduced.

Reality is even more complex

While the equation *illustrates* the relative importance of complexity, it actually understates its impact on the number of things in process and non-value-add cost. When average demand is replaced by real demand, we often find that 80% of the demand is driven through 20% of the offerings. In the rigorous equations, the non-value-add cost generally increases by more than 25%. The reason is that services or products that are infrequently offered either get in the way of, or have to wait behind, the more frequently worked offerings. Moreover, the variation in these quantities is greater for less frequently worked offerings. The equation on page 123 therefore underestimates the amount of WIP. Hence the results of Queuing theory show that non-value-add cost will be further increased. Math-philes who want to learn the details of this fascinating subject are referred to **www.profisight.com** where the technical papers, calculation methods, software aids, and patents reside.

Value Creation Through Acquisitions and Divestitures

In addition to implementing Lean Six Sigma projects targeted at Time Traps, there are other ways for companies to improve shareholder value, such as acquisitions and divestitures. The value analysis procedure outlined above is equally applicable in such situations.

Figure 4.10: Pareto Chart of Time Traps
with suggested improvements

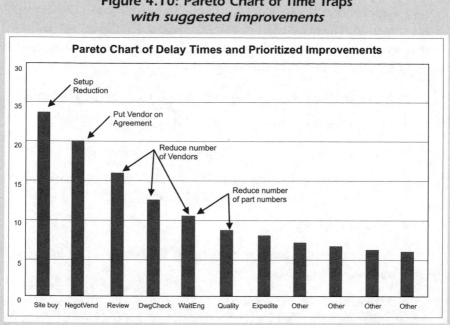

Pareto Chart of Delay Times and Prioritized Improvements

In this case, the Lean Six Sigma tool "setup reduction" was the most important first step in reducing the lead time to place orders (an issue identified as customer Critical-to-Quality). This and the next few steps allowed the removal of several non-value-add steps, reducing process complexity. Reducing the number of vendors and part numbers—used to reduce the complexity of the offering—did not occur until after several Lean-inspired changes were made. (Chapter 5 will have examples where reducing the internal offering complexity through standardization was the highest priority.)

Most corporations will have opportunities to create growth through acquisitions that are synergistic with and strengthen their core business. A survey has shown that most firms who make acquisitions spend 92% of their Due Diligence efforts on legal, accounting, reps and warranties, etc.—non-operational (and largely "service") issues. In fact when acquisitions fail, 85% of the time it is due to operations and management issues. Yet the service functions that comprise M&A departments seldom receive the benefit of any continuous improvement process.

Because Lean Six Sigma staff learn how to perform value diagnostics, they are an ideal complement to traditional due diligence. For example, my firm helped a client with three operational due diligence efforts. Now, with every proposed acquisition, the Due Diligence team autonomously seeks to understand or document...

- How well the company responds to the Voice of the Customer

- The competitive position in the market

- Value creation and estimates of non-value-add costs

- Present state ROIC and future state (based on estimates of the impact of removing non-value-add work/costs)

- Detailed operational synergies

- An estimate of the owner earnings of the business past and next 3 years

- Management team dynamics

The goal of the effort is to understand the real value of the business versus the intrinsic value of the currency offered (stock or cash) and what risks are attendant. This operational due diligence process has never failed to influence the price offered by the M&A officer and the comfort zone of winning and losing. In one case, operational due diligence caused the intrinsic value to be lowered. The seller refused the offer, only to return six months later to accept the price.

Lean Six Sigma value calculations are also useful in the reverse situation, when a company is considering divestiture. As we saw in Figure 4.4, some operations in a business may hold little hope of generating economic profit. The challenge is to extract the highest value from the market. For example, ITT formerly owned a $4 billion automotive division that was earning 9% operating profit, which would seem to be a good margin. However, because the business was so capital intensive, it could not earn an acceptable Economic Profit. Application of Lean Six Sigma helped increase the profits in the division, which was subsequently sold at a favorable price. This allowed ITT to pay down debt and make a number of strategic synergistic acquisitions that generate positive economic profit in an industry with good aggregate economic profit.

Conclusion

Because of its origins in operational improvement, Lean Six Sigma is often perceived as something that happens only in operations. But the principles of customer-focus, defect- and waste-reduction, improving speed, and reducing complexity are applicable at *all* levels of the organization... even the executive suite... and all processes.

The development of a strategic view of shareholder value increase is greatly enhanced by the capabilities, methods, and metrics of Lean Six Sigma. When applied to service applications, Lean Six Sigma allows the reduction of overhead costs that add no value from the perspective of the Voice of the Customer. Lean Six Sigma can also materially aid the strategic functions of acquisition and divestiture in any company.

Endnotes

1. Berkshire-Hathaway Annual Report of 1985
2. This equation is part of a method protected by US Patent 519041. The full derivation of all equations is available from www.profisight.com.

SUCCESS STORY

#3

Fort Wayne, Indiana
From 0 to 60 in nothing flat

The business history of Fort Wayne is revealed in a few simple facts. In 1965 there were 2600 students at Northside High School. Many of the boys planned on working at International Harvester after graduation, just as their fathers and grandfathers did. That plant closed in 1982, a victim of the rust-belt syndrome common in the upper Midwest, and a legacy that cities like Fort Wayne have to work hard to overcome.

Here's another telling fact about Fort Wayne. Take a guess at what the most frequent fire service call is about. Hint: It's not fire. If you answered "medical runs," you'd be right—the post-World War II babies are now booming into middle age and beyond. Fort Wayne's fire stations are so well positioned, geographically, that their staff can reach 911 calls faster than hospital ambulances.

And that's not all, in today's world, firefighters have to be prepared for terrorism, a disaster, hazmat, tanker truck overturning, tornadoes, floods, and there is extensive training that a firefighter ten years ago never got to do.

Mayor Graham Richard is very familiar with this history. He was a state senator before becoming a businessman and entrepreneur in Fort Wayne. A lifelong learner and champion of continuous improvement, in the early 1990s he helped found the TQM Network, an organization that helps businesses in northeast Indiana pool their resources to provide training and education in quality improvement. He later adopted and led Six Sigma efforts in his own companies.

When Richard was elected mayor in the fall of 1999, he had a clear vision: he wanted to help create a safer city, a city with more good jobs, a city that provides excellent service to its citizens. Part of this vision is what he calls e-City. "What we need is people who see themselves as 'e-mayors,' " he says. "Our definition of 'e' is not just the classic electronic commerce. I see it as a pursuit of the extraordinary, the pursuit of excellence, that a city needs to have very, very clear-cut shared goals that you will strive to meet in education, in the environment, in engaging citizens."

His plan for achieving this vision was clear—by bringing business techniques and business philosophies to the way city government was run.

Rollout

Take a look at the background of the other people interviewed in the company profiles, and you'll see a common theme. Karen Rago of Stanford Hospital and Clinics, for example, was there when TQM was first introduced, and was part of its transformation into Stanford's Operations Improvement. Myles Burke of Lockheed Martin can recall a time when SPC was the accepted *modus operandi* of manufacturing improvement. His colleague Mike Joyce learned about Lean manufacturing from some of the Japanese experts who invented and refined it. Roger Hirt spent much of his career at GE, living through quality circles, SPC, and ISO certifications.

In short, just by being involved in business over the past decade-and-a-half, these people have all been exposed to and involved with quality improvement.

The same cannot be said of employees in the public sector. None of the previous quality methodologies have infiltrated public agencies to any degree. So in February 2000, when Fort Wayne's newly elected mayor, Graham Richard, announced to his staff that he wanted the city to start using Six Sigma, few people knew what he was talking about.

The upside of having a green field in terms of improvement meant there was little of the "been there, done that" attitude that causes experienced employees in the private sector to dismiss yet another quality initiative.

On the downside, to achieve any success with Six Sigma, Fort Wayne's employees would have to be ramped up from 0 to 60 in nothing flat. There is very little use of data in government agencies; little awareness of process flow, customer needs, and variation—which means that even once they were trained, there weren't many resources they could turn to for support.

Yet just three years into the new way of doing city business, Fort Wayne has saved or avoided the need to spend nearly $3 million and has made numerous other changes that have meant better service for city residents. Here's how they've done it:

The official rollout began in February 2000 in a rapid series of actions…

- Richard set up an executive council that would serve as a deployment team for the city. The council included himself, several of his appointees, Roger Hirt, and Dale Siegelin from the TQM Network. This council laid out a plan about how to get the new methods deployed into city government: how many Black Belts they wanted to have trained, the kind of projects these Black Belts should work on, what departments they would come from, and so on.

- The division managers (all appointees) and other departmental leaders went through a two-day training session about what Six Sigma is, why it was being deployed into the city government, and what their role would be.

Fort Wayne's experience with Lean and Six Sigma is told here by Graham Richard, Mayor of Fort Wayne, and Roger Hirt, a former MBB at GE who now serves on the executive team guiding deployment at Fort Wayne, and Michele Hill, the city's first Black Belt.

Fort Wayne is a city of about 220,000 in northeastern Indiana. Like many Midwestern cities, its economy has suffered from the rust-belt syndrome: the steady and occasionally dramatic loss of well-paying manufacturing jobs.

As in many city governments, the "CEO" is an elected position; direct reports to the mayor are all appointed and change with each change in leadership. The remaining 1800 employees are civil service, typically people who have held their jobs for a long time and will continue to do so no matter what happens at the top of the organization.

- Mayor Richard created a Quality Enhancement Manager position for the city, selecting Michele Hill for the job. She is the first person to become a Black Belt for the city. (In all likelihood, Michele is the first person in the country to be trained and certified as Black Belt while a city government employee.)

- The second wave of city employees were sent to Black Belt training (there were five people in the second class).

- Roger Hirt agreed to serve as a coach and mentor for the new Black Belts and to start developing Green Belt training.

Initially, the projects and team leaders were selected by the executive council; now that more people are trained and each department has more experience with Six Sigma, the choice of projects is sometimes left up to the department managers in consultation with their Green Belts. Potential projects continue to be identified based on criteria such as…

- What things are bothering each department the most, and where they are falling short on current goals. This helps the executive council focus on barriers that would prevent departments from meeting the Mayor's goals.

- Are all areas of the city receiving the same services? Each department has strategies that may be working in some quadrants that either don't work or aren't currently being used in others.

- Customer/citizen complaints: what services do citizens and other customers complain about the most?

- Will the project either save money or avoid future costs?

Each potential project is evaluated based on its potential impact on customers and citizens, and its impact on internal effectiveness or efficiency. Whenever appropriate, the council would choose a project that impacts citizens over one that improves internal operations.

To staff the projects, Fort Wayne began training city employees. In fact, because the educational gaps were so great, much of the effort in the first year was devoted to training three waves of Black Belts, where each participant had to successfully complete a project as part of their training.

In the second year, the city began doing Green Belt training as a way to populate more agencies with people who could participate in projects and support the Black Belts.

Interestingly, neither the Black Belts nor Green Belts are full-time, dedicated resources: Black Belts are expected to spend 20% of their time on projects; Green Belts 10–20%. This is partly because city governments face a restriction not encountered in the private sector: every city employee has a job description that has to be approved by the city council—and "Black Belt" is not one of those descriptions. Roger Hirt admits it would be nice to have at least one or two full-time Black Belts who could be deployed anywhere in the city and work cross-functionally, but he admires how much the city has accomplished with only part-time resources. One advantage of the city model: their Black Belts are usually process owners, so they benefit directly from improvements, and also have a vested interest in seeing that process changes are maintained.

Walking the Talk

By all accounts, Mayor Richard is a leader who walks the talk of Six Sigma. He is a strong advocate of team building, applies DMAIC in his own thinking and approach, adapts his behavior to accommodate different learning styles, and asks people for data: "What are your measurements, how are you going to develop your measurements?" He also regularly sets aside a few hours on his calendar to meet individually with the Black Belts and Green Belts to discuss their projects.

Results

In the first three years of deployment, Fort Wayne trained more than 20 Black Belts and about 40 Green Belts. (They have since lost one Black Belt who was hired away into the private sector. In typical fashion, Mayor Richard remarked, "Won't it be great when businesses come to city government for employees?")

They also launched 60 projects, resulting in direct savings (or avoidance of expected costs) totaling nearly $3 million and many less-tangible improvements:

- One of the first city projects was started in support of Mayor Richard's goal of creating a safer city. A Fire Department team studied the fire code reinspection process. By eliminating variation (a Six Sigma strategy) and reducing bottlenecks (a Lean approach), they can now perform 23% more reinspections each year without any increase in staffing. The length of time between reinspection, which was running in the hundreds of days at times, was reduced to an average of 34 days.

- Street pothole complaints response time was ranging up to 80 hours from notification to repair, with 77% of the reported potholes repaired within 24 hours. With the completion of the project, 98% are now repaired within 24 hours (with mean time at 10 hours).

- Not long ago, 35% of transportation engineering projects varied from their cost estimates by more than 10%—resulting in cash shortages when the costs ran higher, and unnecessarily tied-up cash when the estimates were too high (dollars allocated to over-estimated projects are held in an account until the project costs are finalized). After improvement, only 14% of such projects exceed their final estimates by more than 10%, resulting in an increased freed up cash flow of $150,000 over the first six months following the completion of this project.

- A Parks Department Black Belt project addressed citizen complaints about the degree and frequency of tree trimming. The project included a designed experiment to determine the optimum communication methods. At last count, the rate of complaint calls had been reduced by 33%.

Roger Hirt can also cite a number of as-yet intangible gains that may pay off in the future. For example, in initial discussions about how the Fire Department could contribute to the Mayor's vision of a "safer city," no one could answer the question because questions like "what would you measure" had never arisen before. People all over the city are starting to get more attuned to thinking about what customers and citizens want, how they measure the performance of their work units and improvement efforts, and about ways to eliminate waste.

Another perk from the improvement efforts? "People can't blame the bureaucracy as much," says Mayor Richard. He goes on to cite one example: "One of the things we learned was that many of the reasons why we were losing cycle time in our building permitting process was because the architect or engineer would have 30 or 40 different projects going on. So it was really easy for them to tell the owner that they could not get their permits from the city. And everybody would accept that explanation—'It's over in right-of-way... Oh, goodness, the city utilities didn't do their work... The storm water permit is not done.... The county highway department didn't give you the cut.'

"By doing what we have done with our process improvement and our new tracking system, it's all online, and our cycle time has dropped... they can't blame someone in the city anymore."

> Response time—or "lead time" in Lean speak—is a critical metric in city government, because oftentimes the problem is a safety concern. That also involves developing the ability to make priorities clear. "It's clear that having a street light go out in front of somebody's home isn't as high a priority as fixing a traffic signal that's out," says Mayor Richard.

Lessons Learned

Fort Wayne is still on the steep slope of its learning curve, but they've already learned a number of lessons...

- **Public sector organizations should expect to have a long learning curve at first.** Because none of the city staff had any history with prior quality movements, it took a lot longer for the process to get started than it does in other sectors. Besides training the Black Belts, almost nothing else happened the entire first year except a lot of communication—getting people introduced to the language, helping them get comfortable with basic improvement concepts (what it means to measure, what data means, where data comes from), and so on. Once the first few waves of training were completed, awareness and understanding proliferated much faster.

- **Being persistent to overcome long-held patterns of behavior.** "Just think of a permit approval process where you have 14 different agencies, all under different jurisdictions. Then people look at me and say, 'Change that,'" says Mayor Richard. "What they don't understand, which I understood because I was a state senator and I had been involved in government since the 1970s, is that the siloing of govern-ment has been going for 50 or 60 years with no profit or bottom line reasons for changing. The levels of expectation in the public are so low—people think the words "government" and "bureaucracy" are the same."

Roger Hirt ran into that history recently. He recalls telling one admin-istrative assistant that it was okay to implement changes identified in a particular project. He later found out that she made four phone calls to get four more approvals before taking action. Can anyone really blame her? For all of her career up to that point, she probably would have been reprimanded had she NOT had multiple approvals for every action. It will take leadership consistency and persistence to convince people that life really has changed inside city government.

- **A lot can be gained from simple tools.** Two tools that really paid off and got people excited in Fort Wayne are:

  - **Process maps**… because they forced people to understand what's really going on in their operations. No one had ever had the desire or tools to do that before. Hirt found that most people really strug-gle with doing even simple maps at first, but when the maps are done, they know a lot more about their processes.

  - **Failure Modes and Effects Analysis.** FMEA is a tool that helps people prevent problems before they happen. When city engineers were asked to define "control factors" that would help them mon-itor and judge city projects, they were at a loss. Why? Because no one had ever asked them to define specifications in the first place, nor to think about the various ways in which something could go wrong.

- **It's vital to have a deployment team and plans for internal and exter-nal communication.** Having the deployment efforts coordinated at the top has proven critical in maintaining commitment and consistency in the implementation efforts. While the city has done a lot of Six Sigma communication internally, Roger Hirt says the message hasn't yet reached the public.

- **Praise and recognition are the strongest motivators.** "In government, praise is the most important thing you have got, because we can't as easily use money," says Mayor Richard. "Recognition is very, very critical, because most people go into government for public service, and they want to be praised for that."

The Most Important Praise

One contractor recently told Mayor Richard, "I have been building commercial buildings for 20 years either for others or for myself, and then I rent them out. I quit building in the city of Fort Wayne about five years ago. Since you have been mayor, there has been a 200 percent increase in the effectiveness of getting permits, and it's now just about as easy to do one in Fort Wayne as it is in any of the other cities that I work in. So I am now going to start building again in Fort Wayne."

- **It's important to have frontline people and union representatives on projects.** Fort Wayne has tried to make sure that there are frontline people in each of the Six Sigma projects—the people who touch the problem most. If the project is going to be one that's perceived to be in any way controversial, before they scope the project they will have union representatives involved in the scoping. If it's not a controversial area, they will typically work through the department head, who will then select the team members.

Conclusion: Is it really sustainable?

"I think it would be very difficult for any politician to undo some of the things that we have put in place," says Mayor Graham Richard. "Some are structural, such as merging different units of government together to make it less complex. Some of it uses technology."

CHAPTER 5

The Value in
Conquering Complexity

It all started innocently enough. About four years ago, a few of Bank One's Wholesale Lockbox customers asked if they could use overnight delivery and get their deposits—sometimes as much as $1 million—credited quickly the following day. Bank One naturally said "No problem. We'll give you a four-hour turnaround time. And there won't be any charge for the service."

And, at first, it wasn't a problem. They'd receive a few overnight deliveries, each containing one or two items at most. But very quickly, the overnight business mushroomed. Now, many of the Wholesale Lockbox customers use this service, which may range from a single deposit to multiple deposits, and may contain anywhere from 1 to 500 checks, representing up to 200 invoices. Not only that, but a large majority of the customers wanted Bank One to follow customized procedures unique to them for processing their checks. Some of these procedures included data entry, data keying, imaging items, stapling in the left hand corner, or the right hand corner, or using paper clips, clipping sets of invoices together, and so on.

All in all, Bank One estimates its "single" overnight service actually comprised several hundred different pathways—which explains why the "four-hour delivery" promise was operationally challenging to accomplish. The complexity of the offering, and the resulting complexity of the processes, made it certain that Bank One would fail some customers eventually. They also realized that most of their competitors were charging for this premium service, but how could they consider doing that when it was difficult for them to approach 100% of their service commitments?

The solution to Bank One's problem was multilayered. Part of the answer lie in applying some of the basic Lean principles to streamline their own internal processes. They could attempt to reduce setup times between different tasks (like the Lockheed Martin buyers), they could triage the work, etc. Making such changes allowed them to reduce WIP (the number of deposits waiting to be made), which helped improve internal process problems by reducing waste, cost, and lead time. This reduced the number of non-value-add activities, and reduced process complexity to an extent. But in the face of such a broad offering, there is a limit to how much you can reduce non-value-add costs by internal improvements in flexibility...

Thus there is another element they must attack: the *complexity of the product or service offering* itself. As shown in Chapter 4, such **external complexity** (the variety of products and services) that is often thrown at a process creates even more things-in-process (WIP) and hence non-value-add cost than do internal process problems (e.g., setup time).

The Lockbox group at Bank One is well on its way towards their ideal solution. Improving their processes, and understanding exactly what service levels they could commit to, has made it possible for them to convert this overhead-consuming service into one that generates revenue and consistently satisfies customer expectations. The process is now performing to industry standards and is improving every month. There is still a lot of complexity with the services subsumed under the Lockbox system, but now they understand the source and impact of that complexity, and are able to charge variable fees accordingly. And the group has embarked on an initiative to create cellular/modular processing—a "platform" approach to complexity reduction in services discussed later in this chapter. (You can also find more details of this case in Chp 13.)

The purpose of this chapter is to expose the insidious nature of complexity, and arm you with the knowledge you need to make rational strategic decisions that will allow your organization to still differentiate itself in the market without being consumed by non-value-add complexity costs.

Many of the examples in this chapter come from manufacturing companies because complexity reduction inside service companies is in its infancy. But the principles involved apply equally whether your company is making widgets or providing a service. (And, in fact, if you read closely, you'll see that the source of product complexity from the manufacturing companies we'll cover are the result of services inside those companies—especially marketing and product development.) Whatever your business, the payoffs of eliminating unnecessary complexity often dwarf those of Lean and Six Sigma taken separately.

Face-to-Face with the Cost of Complexity

My intense interest in reducing, and specifically computing, the cost of complexity is borne of experience that was bought, not taught. I was formerly the CEO of International Power Machines (IPM), which I founded, took public, and subsequently sold to a division of Rolls-Royce. The company designed and produced Uninterruptible Power Supplies (UPS) that protect critical computers and instrumentation from AC power failures. Our systems protected the computers of the NYSE, Depository Trust, Merrill-Lynch, and nuclear power plants, to name but a few applications.

IPM began with just one product offering, a 5 kilowatt unit. Then, like most companies in this market, we started developing additional power units (10kw, 20kw… and ultimately 300kw) to satisfy the needs of customers. Over the years, this drive to grow our power ratings had resulted in seven separate mechanical and electrical designs in just the 10–80kw range, with virtually no parts in common between different power ratings. Being able to satisfy the needs of customers requiring different power ratings is *value-add complexity;* needing seven sets of electrical designs each with unique components to do it is *non-value-add complexity* (also known as "transparent complexity"). Our customers derived no particular value out of the variety of parts such as "bus bars" or "heat sinks" that were used. Because of complexity, any effort that engineering and manufacturing applied to one rating created very little learning that could be applied to another rating. Our manufacturing processes were also complex (and expensive), dominated by the assembly of a vast profusion of subassemblies going into an unlimited number of final assemblies.

We tried in vain to find a "vital few" causes that would explain our high costs, quality problems, and long lead times, but the Pareto charts were flat. The company was flirting with insolvency and had massive quality problems in the field, unhappy customers, and little revenue growth.

Product Development's Role in Complexity Reduction

The units from 10–80 kilowatts generated 15% Gross Profit Margin and a negative return on capital. As the company grew, overhead costs grew in proportion to volume. We had to increase our invested capital by borrowing.

> "Depend upon it, when a man knows he is going to be hung within a month, it concentrates the mind wondrufly"
>
> Dr. Samuel Johnson

In desperation, I went to the public library and read, among other things, about Toyota's drive to make many different customer-facing products and option "packages" out of a small number of standardized subassemblies. The cost-benefits reported were amazing. But I also read of the disaster caused by the "look alike" cars that GM was producing, as their approach to cost reduction. Clearly the best approach was to standardize internal processes yet satisfy a variety of customer needs at low cost.

What options did we have? There were two paths. We could attack the complexity directly through **standardization** using Design for Lean Six Sigma (DFLSS) tools in service/product development (with no impact on the customer), or we could try to improve our process quality by applying the Lean Six Sigma tool, with the goal of becoming more flexible and efficient despite our internal non-value-add complexity.

Our internal manufacturing processes were primarily assembly, with small setup times. So there didn't seem to be much potential in applying Lean Six Sigma to the manufacturing application. And our main quality defects—mis-wiring or mis-assembly of products—were related to the huge number of different products we offered (i.e., product complexity). Therefore it seemed that complexity reduction was our best path, as depicted in Figure 5.1 (next page).

**Figure 5.1: Standardization Reduces NVA Costs
Far More Than Lean or Six Sigma**

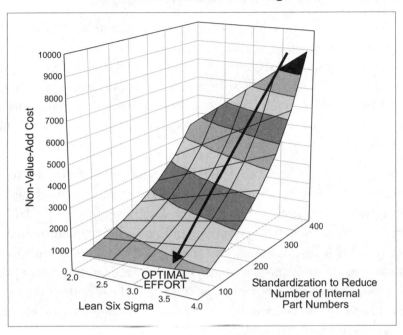

One of the author's previous companies faced the same situation that Stanford faced: they could achieve greater reductions in cost and improvement in speed by reducing complexity than by simply trying to improve the processes in their current state.

In our cases, standardization—and, more precisely, platform standardization—meant developing a common mechanical and electrical design across a range of power ratings. In fact, we reached a point where more than 80% of the components, subassemblies, and wiring were common to *all* products.

Other changes ensued. For example, we concluded that the systems for nuclear plants—which were entirely custom made—had complexity costs hidden from accounting, and we withdrew from that market. Production lead times, originally in a range of 6 to 12 weeks, fell to less than 2 weeks. The quality of the product improved dramatically—an unexpected benefit. (Any improvement efforts attempted prior to standardization would likely have proven ineffective since they'd be diffused over many designs. But post-standardization, we could focus our efforts like a laser on one mechanical design.)

With common wiring tables, the units would go into the lab and come up and run immediately, greatly reducing testing, documentation, and engineering costs. Reliability in the field showed similar improvement, which reduced warranty costs. In fact, we used our improved reliability as a competitive weapon: customers were promised their money back if they didn't like the performance. At the time, nobody else dared make that offer.

Moving to platform standardization also opened up new markets for us. Because of the unreliability of foreign power, our quality problems, and tariff duties, we'd had limited sales abroad. However, the standardized product was so simple to assemble and so well-documented that we exported the high-value-add subassemblies, licensing local firms to add local content transformers, cabinets, etc., to reduce tariffs. It was a proud moment when these subassemblies, shipped halfway around the world, also started up and ran perfectly. In the midst of all our past quality problems, this had been my goal.

I had recalled a passage from Ernest Hemingway's *For Whom the Bell Tolls*:

> "His eyes, watching the planes coming were very proud...and he watched their steady, stately, roaring advance... They had come, crated on ships, from the Black Sea, through the Straits of Marmora, through the Dardanelles, through the Mediterranean and to here, unloaded lovingly at Alicante, assembled ably, tested, and found perfect!...his eyes were hard and proud...this was how it could be!"

And this is how it became. Marketing productivity grew with our reputation, as we won a larger percentage of opportunities. By suitable redesign, all mechanical designs were combined into one all the way to 200kw. This eliminated the costs associated with WIP, the learning curves and related non-value-add costs, which resulted in an increase in Gross Profit Margin from 15% to 37% (see Table 5.1 and Figure 5.2). ROIC was driven from –6% to +30%, and the company was eventually sold to a division of Rolls Royce for 7.2 times book value. This gave me the resources and time to finally visit Toyota and other Japanese firms, and subsequently to found the George Group.

In short, we discovered that the service functions that created complexity were marketing strategy and product development execution. Manufacturing and Testing were simply the innocent victims that got the blame.

Table 5.1: IPM's results from Complexity Reduction

Year	1	2	3	4
Gross Profit*	18%	25%	31%	37%
Operating Profit*	-3%	6%	17%	20%
(* as % of revenue; ref. SEC Registration 2-68861).				

Figure 5.2: Standardization Improves Profit Margin

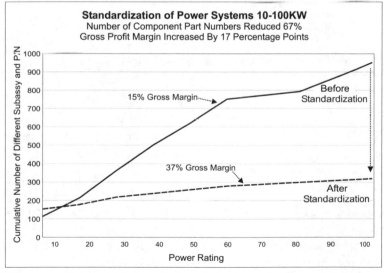

The upper line on this graph shows the huge impact of the cumulative effect of multiple options and unique designs for each power rating. Once the internal components were standardized, the cumulative number of parts dropped, and gross margin more than doubled.

The concept of complexity reduction is depicted graphically in Figure 5.3 (below).

Figure 5.3: The Path to Complexity Reduction

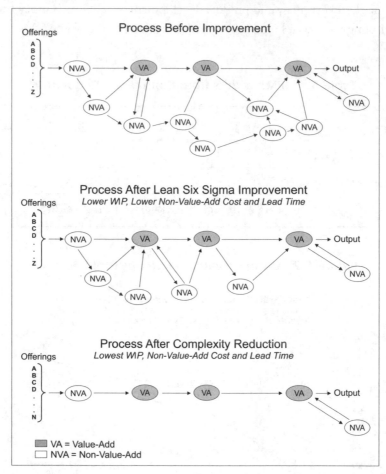

The first panel shows an unimproved process. The second panel shows the application of all the traditional Lean Six Sigma DMAIC tools, such as Pull systems, setup reduction, process control, designed experiments, etc. Note that the number on non-value-add activities in the process has been reduced by nearly 50%, as has the work-in-process (WIP) and lead time. However, by cutting the number of different tasks that each activity must perform, further dramatic reduction in non-value-add activities, WIP, and lead time can be achieved. The method of calculating the benefits of complexity reduction has long been one of our goals, and one that is discussed later in this chapter.

The Forces Driving Increased Service/Product Complexity

For the past 80 years, the operating thesis in business has been that you have to offer customers any options they want (= high offering complexity) as the path to differentiated product/service lines, and hence to high profits. The origins of this premise—and the strong belief in the value of complexity—lie in the industrial struggles of the early 20th century, as exemplified by the classic story of the demise of the Model T.

In 1921, the Ford Model T commanded over 60% of the low-cost market and appeared impregnable. In his book *My Years with General Motors,* Alfred Sloane recalls that dark time, as GM teetered on the brink of bankruptcy:

> *"To compete head on with Ford would have required the resources of the U.S. Treasury."*

But as Sloane saw it, the Model T had served the early market's need for utility transportation. Available in only one style and color, the T defined the extreme limit of mass production and was the antithesis of product complexity. Soon, this utilitarian need would be furnished by the rising tide of *used* Model Ts. Sloane reasoned that the strength of the economy in the 1920s would lead many owners of the Model T to want to buy a *better* car, priced slightly higher, but available in different colors, offering a better ride, more power, etc. To meet this projected demand, all effort was focused on correcting Chevrolet's quality problems—to the exclusion of other development efforts (such as developing the type of air-cooled engine that would later bring Porsche fame)—and on creating an offering with many desirable options.

In other words, GM was differentiating the company in the market **by offering a wider variety of choices to consumers**. By 1925, the strategy was working, writes Sloane—*"Ford's precious volume, upon which all depended, started falling"*—and by 1928 the Model T was driven from the market.

The concept of a single product with no options justifiably entered the dustbin of history, and the unfettered pursuit of differentiation began.

The result? Fast forward 80 years. The costs of product and offering complexity are generally unknown *inside* a company, let alone shared with the outside… unless a catastrophic market change forces action. We have had such a rare event in the airline industry. American Airlines has been "mired near the bottom of air transport ratings for three years," falling short on Critical-to-Quality needs such as on-time departure. Ralph Richardi, VP of Operations Planning remarked: *"We studied every departure delay by city, by time and we didn't find one thing that was causing the delay. It was tough to figure out. Well what was it?"*

The answer, American says, wasn't in its scheduling or staffing of flights. The underlying problem was its *complexity*. American had been trying to **build a differentiated service offering** by customizing its aircraft configurations into 30 "subfleets" to separately service each market and optimize costs. They were up to 14 different types of airplanes, including some 757s with life rafts (for overseas flights), some without; some MD80s with 20 First Class seats, others with only 14; Fokker F-100s, and so on.

Was that complexity really serving American and its customers well? Judge for yourself: They had to train mechanics in maintenance and repairs on 14 types of aircraft, with the associated "learning curve cost" (people have a harder time remembering and getting good at tasks they perform infrequently). Having to stock spare parts for 14 different types of planes not only increased inventory overhead and capital investment, but meant that they were far more likely to encounter shortages, which created delays.

What happened to the air-cooled engine?

Porsche was in difficult straits in the 1990s. Dr. Ferdinand Porsche had been the first to develop the type of robust air-cooled engine that GM had abandoned in the 1920s, creating the early Porsche mystique of high performance. However, Porsche also manufactured a line of super-high performance water-cooled models. The company had so many different models that a frontal attack (using Lean tools) on such a broad front would have a very slow rate of improvement of cost. A fateful decision was made: Porsche would abandon the air cooled engine. (A similar emotional wrench would occur if, say, Xerox got out of copiers.) This difficult decision, resulting in less complexity and focused improvement efforts, contributed to the renewed financial health of the company.

The realization of all the costs associated with American's market differentiation strategy and resulting complexity lead its president, Gerard Arpey, to remark: "The cost of complexity isn't offset by what you can charge. Complexity creates opportunities for you to fail your customer."

American then reduced the number of different types of aircraft from 14 to 7, moved mechanics closer to the planes, and made a host of other changes that contributed to better flow. On-time performance ranking improved from fifth to second, and customer complaints were cut in half in just 18 months. But is this enough? Southwest, with one aircraft type, shows the cost dominance conveyed by low complexity.

Companies must balance two opposing forces: the **Force of the Market**, which drives complexity up through pressure to introduce new services/products and broadening of the offering; and the **Force of Complexity**, which mandates a simplification of the offering and associated internal complexity due to cost pressures. The optimal point is the one that maximizes EP. As companies allow levels of complexity to become too great, they risk becoming non-competitive on cost. But if they simplify their offerings excessively, they risk sudden loss of market share as customer demands shift (because they are non-diversified).

The benefits of conquering complexity hit both revenues and costs: Value optimizing the portfolio enables higher focus and sales force effectiveness, and it removes the cost associated with low-EP products. Internal standardization impacts cost by increasing the productivity of labor with a faster learning curve, as well as lowering unit costs in areas such as warehousing, purchasing, etc.

Impact of Complexity on Revenue Growth

But cost is not the only lever. **Excessive complexity in your offering can also be a barrier to growth.** Look at any high-complexity company, and you'll often hear its customers saying, "They're hard to do business with." This reaction can be the result of several things:

- **Customers having to negotiate through your complexity.** If your company has a lot of different service/product offerings, each with lots of options, that complexity is transferred to customers, who are forced to navigate their way through bloated processes, reams of non-value-add offerings, etc., to find the one or two key products or services that meet their specifications. (This is an application of Little's Law applied to customers: Customer Decision Period = Decisions in Process/Completion rate.) Reasonable people tend to want to give at least a modicum of attention to every decision; thereby transferring complexity to the customer selection process is burdening them with a bloated decision period—and lengthening the time period (before close) during which they might change their mind!

- Ineffective sales processes. The second impact on growth is played out internally. It boils down to this: Focus. And it is best demonstrated through the example of a client's sales force. We saw an example of this in the triaging of the marketing quotation process in Chapter 2. Effectively, opportunities in which the company was competitively disadvantaged, had a poor GPM, and were very difficult to quote moved to the bottom of the queue in Figure 2.4, and effectively were never input to marketing. This is a Darwinian approach to reduction of offering complexity. The same result can be achieved far faster and more effectively by the complexity value stream analysis process.

Impact of Complexity on Organizational Effectiveness

As the discussion above has shown, complexity impacts both the top and bottom line. And it also impacts management effectiveness. In fact, the greater the complexity, the less focused management is, and the less likely they are to be in a position to understand, let alone conquer, complexity. A vicious cycle! The way to break this is by understanding the key cost drivers of complexity and focusing resources using the Pareto principle.

The examples given in this chapter and in Chapter 4 have shown how complexity is a driver of non-value-add cost. In fact, complexity is often the greatest single determinant in this category of cost. Removing "excessive" offerings that do not meet their cost of capital will carve out far greater savings than simply optimizing the process for delivering these offerings. Standardizing the "subcomponents" via standardization and modularization—whether the offering be mortgage applications, widgets, or consulting services—has a similar effect without impacting what the customer sees. In both cases, reducing the complexity can improve the cost competitiveness of an organization by a magnitude.

How Can We Conquer Complexity?

As described above, from 1908-1921, Ford's single mass market product met the Voice of the Customer. Sloan's "product for every purse" met the VOC for 1922-1929 while avoiding the excess complexity and cost of the "fancy class" (e.g., Pierce Arrow) with positive consequences for economic profit.

Financial services is an industry that has evolved to meet complex customer needs and wants from the early days of individual savings accounts to the complex financial instruments available today. The big winners in today's financial services markets are those that can optimize the degree of complexity to align with customer tastes. For example, a major commercial and investment bank that for decades operated as a "universal bank" in its home market—offering all things to all people—over the last decade found that countless competitors were cherrypicking the most profitable customers and segments, leaving this bank with the most unprofitable customers and segments and high overhead cost.

But many companies, like American Airlines, are suffering from too much complexity. At some point in their histories, advanced technology companies like 3M, HP, and IBM have all stressed differentiation and created a corporate culture that put a premium on a high velocity of new product introductions. Annual reports would proclaim that "30% of our revenue comes from products that did not exist three years ago" without any discussion of standardization, or of elimination of slow moving offerings. Things aren't any better in the service sector. How many different service options does your telephone or wireless provider offer that weren't available five years ago? How many more services does your financial services company offer now compared to ten years ago?

The problem, as both Bank One and American Airlines discovered, is twofold:

- First, differentiation dramatically increased their non-value-add costs.

- Second, because they were internally overwhelmed in dealing with their service complexity, neither of them really succeeded in achieving market differentiation. They never created a franchise; at best, it allowed them to stay even with the competition.

In addition, they are in immense strategic risk when faced by a less-complex competitor.

These lessons put businesses in a tough spot. On the one hand, they can't ignore the need to constantly add new services and products into the market to create competitive advantage. And to the extent that new products are needed to meet the Voice of the Customer and earn adequate ROIC, there is no disagreement. But if no corresponding effort is made to reduce complexity of offerings which do not meet these criteria, the benefits of new products or services may never see the bottom line.

Strategies for Reducing Complexity

The IPM case told above illustrated the first of two approaches to reducing complexity; here's a quick overview of them both:

1. **Standardization**: Standardizing and modularizing the internal tasks and components of an offering so that a fewer number of them can be assembled into many different services/products that respond to the Voice of the Customer

2. **Optimization**: Eliminating those offerings that generate sustained negative economic profit, particularly where you are strategically disadvantaged or in a declining market

Strategy #1. Standardization: Market responsiveness at low cost

The two functions that have the biggest impact on your costs of service/product complexity are marketing and R&D (or any comparable service/product development department). While a lot of complexity is related to the historical evolution of an offering, trying to redesign services or products is an expensive business.

Math is a good thing, arm waving is not

You have all read arm-waving discussions about the evils of complexity and the benefits of a narrow service/product line. But in fact restricting yourself to a narrow service/product line cuts off revenue growth opportunities. The waste equation introduced in Chapter 4 (and repeated below) is what lets us add some rigor to the argument.

$$\text{Waste Driver}_{WIP} = \frac{\ddot{e}N(S + S_R - PHS_R + PHM + \text{other terms})}{2[1 - X - \lambda PHM + \text{other terms}]} = \frac{\lambda NS}{2[1 - X - \lambda P]}$$

If you haven't had to analyze equations anytime recently, you may not readily pick up on the key features of this equation. For thing, a complex offering (meaning "N" in the equation is large) is indeed very bad if you do not reduce setup time between tasks by...

- Standardizing different internal tasks. Think of this as trying to create a Lego™-like service or product, where basic components can be combined to create a cornucopia of final offerings.

- Reducing setup time between the (now-fewer number of) standardized tasks to near zero, as in the procurement example. Since your employees will now have fewer different tasks to remember, they can get more proficient at the remaining "Lego" components.

Both of these subjects are discussed at length in this chapter.

Also, as setup time (S) is reduced to zero, the WIP and effective cost of complexity falls to zero. This is absolutely true in service applications, and approximately true in manufacturing.

Thirdly, the defect percentage (x) enters insidiously into the denominator. That means as x increases, (1-x) will decrease and the work-in-process will explode. I don't want to underestimate the challenges of standardization and setup time reduction, and defect prevention, etc. But the complexity value stream mapping process introduced in Chapter 4 turns arm-waving arguments into a rational means of making investments. So on the subject of complexity, and for the same reason, we agree with Napoleon:

> "He took eagerly to mathematics, here was a discipline
> congenial to his demand for clarity and exactness,
> something beyond prejudice and argument."

The principle of standardization is illustrated by the IPM experience described previously: we reduced non-value-add (transparent) complexity by condensing eight separate engineering designs into one design. The new single design is called a **platform**. Standardization has the merit of making breakthrough cost reductions without eliminating any customer facing products or services.

What is a platform? Any offering, be it a product or service, generally consists of different parts—physical subcomponents of manufactured goods, or different subprocesses in a service. (In service applications, the issue is often shared web pages, training, common software applications, and so on.) The goal is to standardize these components and the processes used to deliver them. The component platforms can then be added together to make a vast profusion of offerings for the marketplace at low cost. (In training, this principle is demonstrated by asking participants to build a number of final products using either custom parts created for different purposes or using standardized Lego™ blocks. Though the latter come in only a limited number of shapes and sizes, they can be combined in countless ways.)

The first step is to reduce the number of internal tasks to the minimum by standardization, then to reduce the setup time between these tasks to the minimum (using the Four Step Rapid Setup method, described in Chapter 11), eliminate defects, and so on.

In many cases, the total number of tasks can be reduced to one task, eliminating all setups. The benefits of this form of standardization were also illustrated by the example from Stanford Hospital and Clinics described in Chapter 1. As you may recall, they had a lot of non-value-add costs in their coronary artery bypass graft (CABG) surgery because each of six surgeons had his/her own special tray of instruments for different types of surgeries. After one afternoon of discussion among all the surgeons, they were able to settle on two basic surgical trays, which dramatically cut material costs. (In Lean terms, the two types of trays became the platforms.)

Clearly, standardization of the trays had a lot more impact than trying to train the nurses to more efficiently prepare 12 different types of trays. This is depicted by the Complexity Value Stream calculations that are graphed in Figure 5.4.

Figure 5.4: Complexity Reduction at Stanford Hospital

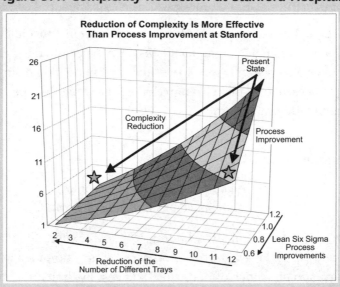

Reduction of Complexity Is More Effective
Than Process Improvement at Stanford

Stanford could have chosen to simply improve the quality of its
"surgical tray preparation process," but that would not have generated as much cost savings as reducing the number of trays.

This chart was prepared based on data from Stanford Hospital and Clinics.
Initially, they had 12 different types of surgical trays to prepare (counting
different trays for different surgeons and different surgeries). One option
would have been for Stanford to simply use basic process improvement
techniques to improve procedures for prepping all 12 trays. The alternative
was complexity reduction: getting the surgeons to agree on standard trays.
As you can see, complexity reduction had a much greater impact on reducing costs than process improvements alone could have accomplished.

There's another part to the story that wasn't covered in Chapter 1:
Originally, Stanford had as many as *eight* vendors for various supplies,
including surgical instruments. Led by their supplies manager, Stanford
was able to settle on just *two* vendors for everything from defibrillators
and pacemakers to sutures. From 2001 to 2002, this change saved them
over $25 million. The key factors in their savings were:

- **Standardizing the surgical tray options.** They now purchase much
  higher volumes (about a six-fold increase) of far fewer parts.

- **Compressing the supply base** to two suppliers per part (which further increases volumes purchased at each supplier).

- **Reducing labor costs**. After standardization, hospital staff were preparing higher volumes of just two types of trays, rather than having to switch trays all the time, check individual surgeon preferences, and so on. This moves the processing time per unit down and reduces "learning curve" delays.

Prevention of Non-Value-Add Cost

"An ounce of platform prevention
is worth a pound of standardization cure"

We have spent a lot of time finding, classifying, and *eliminating* non-value-add cost. The goal of this process is to transition managers and all employees to *prevention* of non-value-add cost by designing future offerings from standardized "Lego"™ tasks with zero setup time between tasks. But to make this transition, we first build capability by tackling an existing process which has high value potential. The reason that standardization has received so little investment is that managers:

1. Underestimated the benefits (which the complexity value stream calculations address)

2. Worried about the expense and disruptions of trying to standardize existing product/service lines

The first of these issues was addressed in Chapter 4: reducing complexity can often provide a greater increase in ROIC than applying Lean or Six Sigma tools to improve existing processes. The second issue has to be acknowledged and dealt with: it's true that if you want to standardize a product or service, you will have to define a cutover date for the change and coordinate with customers well in advance of the change.

The best way to address the cost of redevelopment is to avoid it altogether—that is, incorporate standardization (platform thinking) into your development and marketing decisions as a new product or service is being designed, long before it affects what the rest of the organization does and what customers expect.

The standardization process achieves low cost without the market penalties that an optimization strategy (i.e., having to eliminate existing products or services) may suffer. You should be aware there is a certain amount of extra cost required to conceive and establish a platform strategy, so it clearly doesn't work if you are only going to build one product or offer one type of service. But if you have more than one product/service in a family, the economics of the platform strategy quickly become a critical success factor (see Figure 5.5).

Figure 5.5: The Benefit of Platform Standardization

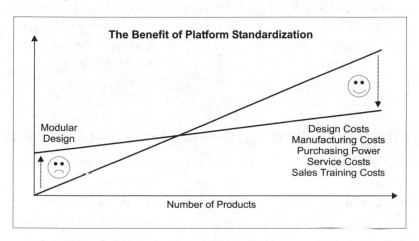

As in Figure 5.2, the costs of complexity soar as the variety of offerings increases. Standardizing the components used to delivery those offerings—platform standardization—can allow a company to maintain its offering complexity but reduce the associated costs.

By increasing the number of commodities on purchase agreement, Lockheed Martin effectively standardized the task of placing purchase orders to "point and click" for most items. The *number* of different items didn't change—the internal clients could still get the products they wanted—but the process of placing orders was made identical across more products. The large variation in the time it took to place an order was reduced, with important reductions in queue time and hence WIP.

Standardization and the accidental invention of the microprocessor

In 1969, Intel was approached by a Japanese calculator company to produce a dozen special-purpose chips. Because Intel's resources were so slender, they decided to build a general-purpose chip that could perform all 12 functions, and be produced in 12 times the volume at lower cost. Out of this intelligent effort to reduce complexity was born the 4000 Series microprocessor, the first ever produced worldwide. This is an example of the "platform" concept discussed above, and what a boon this "accidental empire " has been to the world! Indeed, as Andy Grove pointed out in his book Only the Paranoid Survive, Intel would have been destroyed if it had not abandoned its primary business (memory chips) and made the leap to microprocessors. Yet they agonized over this decision for a year, fearing customer reaction. When the event happened, the customers by and large were only surprised it had taken so long!

Strategy #2. Product/Service Line Optimization

Despite the best attempts to reduce costs, your organization will likely have some services or products that are unlikely to ever earn an ROIC greater than the cost of capital (as discussed with the 5-brand-line company depicted in Figure 4.3). These services/products should be removed from the offering or re-priced to attain an adequate return. This **optimization** may result in short-term loss of revenue and is often resisted, but can be very effective in lowering costs and providing customers with a higher value product or service. The fact is that these products and services, with allowance for overhead absorption, are destroying value in the business. They either have to be improved in cost or eliminated in a way that will not create customer hostility.

Complexity standardization that simply eliminates *non-value-add* complexity can be executed once the costs and values are known. But products and services whose features and functions are *desired by the customer*, i.e., non-transparent, require thoughtful consideration before they can be cut from the offering. The elimination of products or services which do not add to shareholder value must be balanced against customer relationships, the company strategy, the impact on internal processes, and the improvement in economic profit. The goal is to identify a desired "future state" fixed cost position and create a supporting strategy and Lean Six Sigma implementation to achieve it.

The strategy of the company may require the optimization (removal) of certain services/products, and thus enable a more intense focus on standardization and process improvement to improve performance of the remaining offerings. The board of one company was faced with just such a decision: exit a large product market where it was disadvantaged, or attack with standardization and process improvement. In this case, they were able to radically improve their competitive cost position through standardization alone.

Application: Marketing's role in reducing the cost of complexity

In every company, service or manufacturing, marketing rightly views its role as growing revenue. The natural assumption is that if you're applying good Six Sigma thinking, and listening to the Voice of the Customer, you should be OK in the market. However, a company ought to calculate ROIC by customer. If you are not earning your cost of capital from a customer or customer segment, and can't formulate a strategy to do so, you need to gracefully withdraw. As noted above, by withdrawing some offerings, you are able to focus Lean Six Sigma efforts on a smaller range of offerings with much greater impact.

Historically, there was no such check on marketing or product development plans. In fact, the slow rate of improvement in reducing manufacturing overhead cost is often due to excess complexity inflicted by marketing.

As an example, a former division of United Technologies Automotive produced coupled hose and fittings for brakes and air conditioners. The division was barely earning its cost of capital. It produced 168 different types of coupled hose products principally for Ford and Chrysler, with smaller production for Toyota and International Truck. Opportunities at Ford and Chrysler abounded if the company could reduce lead times from 12 days to 3 days. The earnings on sales from Toyota and International were running below its cost of capital and no credible plan could be devised to make them into value creators, so they were removed from the product line. This removed two very demanding clients from the backlog who had defocused both engineering and manufacturing engineering improvement.

Though this example deals with product complexity, it is *not a manufacturing issue; it requires management and marketing to take the initiative to reduce the costs imposed by offering complexity.* Complexity reduction is definitely a strategic and cross-functional endeavor.

Thus the initial reduction of complexity in the product line enabled a focused Lean Six Sigma effort. Internal product complexity on products for Ford and Chrysler was relatively fixed by the qualification testing requirements. Redesign to standardize components thus required a long and costly cycle time. So a Lean Six Sigma assault was launched on the optimized product lines. Because they could deliver within three days (= reduce lead time), the company more than doubled sales to Ford, doubling company revenue. The principal sources of non-value-add cost, manufacturing overhead and quality cost, were reduced by 22%. This is an example where a diagnostic would have revealed that the major ROIC opportunity lay in Lean Six Sigma process improvement if the company could be freed from complexity. The results of application of Lean Six Sigma was quite dramatic (see Table 5.2).[1]

Often, the right answer is to pursue standardization and/or optimization and then pursue process improvement. Data from one company that used optimization to reduce the number of its offerings was used to generate Figure 5.6 [next page]; this company went on to use process improvement to lower costs in its remaining offerings.

Sometimes, all the standardization or process improvements in the world can't help service or product lines become profitable. In the situation shown here, this company realized that they would be better off eliminating several service lines ("optimization") then focusing its improvement efforts in the remaining areas.

Calculating the Cost of Complexity

Complexity adds cost on many levels, but the two major drivers are related to the amount of work-in-process (WIP) and the lower productivity that complexity creates. We can estimate these figures using data

Continued on p. 166

Table 5.2: Results of Optimization

Operating margin	From 5.4% to 13.8%		Capital turnover	From 2.8 to 3.7
ROIC	From 10% to 33%		Enterprise value	Increased 225%
EBITDA	Increased 300%		Economic Profit	From −2% to 21%
Lead time	From 14 days to 8 days		On-time delivery	From 80% to >99%
Quality performance	From 3σ to 6σ			

Optimizing it's product line—eliminating some under-performing products—allowed this company to focus it simprovement efforts on higher-value offerings. The company increased its shareholder value, and having been sold at book value once was sold at 3.6 times book just 26 months later.

Figure 5.6: Using Optimization to Reduce Product Breadth, then Lean Six Sigma for Process Improvement

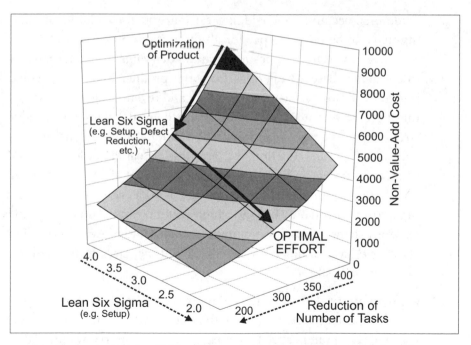

As demonstrated by Table 5.2 and this figure, the optimal path to increasing ROIC is to sometimes eliminate offerings, then attack the remaining services/processes with traditional Lean Six Sigma tools.

taken from the Waste Driver equation calculations described in Chapter 4 (where it was used to generate a complexity value stream map). The output from those calculations will reveal:

Excess WIP: A fundamental Lean principal is that long setup time creates large amounts of work- or things- in-process (WIP), and that large WIP creates non-value-add cost activities such as rework, lost customers, expediting, etc. As the formula on page 157 and Figure 4.11 show, complexity of the offering actually increases WIP more than does setup time. Let's say that you offered three product families and had 1500 things-in-process. If the total volume transactions was constant but now those three only accounted for 80% of demand, there were, say, 13 other offerings that accounted for the remaining 20% of demand, how much would the WIP increase? 300%! Non-value-add cost is a log function of WIP, the proportionality factors are determined during complexity value stream mapping.

Traditional accounting would suggest that those 13 additional offerings have to be priced to pay for all the increase in cost, or else they will have low ROIC and destroy shareholder value. The alternative is to eliminate these 13 offerings from the product line, which could lead to major loss of customer goodwill and revenue. However, knowing the cost of complexity as determined by the complexity value stream map, managers can now make rational investments in standardization, setup reduction, etc., to preserve variety at low cost and positive economic profit. The equations show that, if you preserved all 16 offerings, but reduced the setup time by 67%, you would have the same cost as if you only had the 3 high volume parts! And if you could standardize the 13 to a lesser number, costs would be even lower. (For clarity, we have assumed no defects, downtime, etc., in this analysis, but they are easily added.)[2]

Low productivity: The more the complexity, the less frequently a given task is repeated, and the higher the value-add activities are on the learning curve (and hence higher cost). In addition to low cumulative volume, people's knowledge of how to perform the task decays the longer the period between repetitions. Both of these factors drive higher cost. As we have seen, standardization is the key antidote to low productivity.

Both of these costs can be estimated from the Waste equation, which provides a rational foundation for making an investment in complexity reduction.

Complexity reduction effectively reduces costs related to work-in-process and low productivity. A graph of the United Technologies, shown below, illustrates the logarithmic relation of WIP to non-value-add cost. (See Figure 5.7) Lead time (and WIP) should be reduced to low levels to eliminate non-value-add costs. (Interestingly, that level is generally far lower than what is demanded by the customer.)

Figure 5.7: Impact of WIP on Non-Value-Add Costs

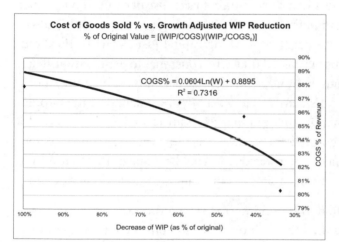

The relationship between WIP and non-value-add costs is logarithmic, not linear. That is, the *rate* at which non-value-add costs drop increases with incremental reductions in WIP. This chart actually focuses on the reverse situation: as WIP is cut from its original level (the 100% value, left side of graph) there is a much greater drop in non-value-add cost. The costs really dive down when WIP is cut to 30% of its original value because many costs are quantized, and a lot of WIP has to be eliminated before these costs can be reduced. Reductions also depend on management decisions, and the opportunity to move non-value-add and personnel to value-add jobs.

Conclusion

For most companies, the hidden cost of complexity represents a hidden profit pool that provides an important new avenue for value creation. The cost of complexity can be conquered first by internal standardization, and then by application of Lean Six Sigma tools such as setup reduction and defect prevention on the reduced number of tasks. Ultimately, some offerings cannot be transformed into positive economic profit contributors to shareholder value, and must be optimized out of the offering. Sometimes optimization is the strategy.

You can experience the power of complexity reduction through optimization simply by walking into any Wal-Mart or Sam's Club. Just compare the number of types of toothpaste at Sam's to your local supermarket or drug store, and you'll see how they are using optimization as a competitive strategy. Sam's is able to drive enormous volume through a few SKUs (Stock Keeping Units). This gives them huge buying power over their suppliers, much lower store space cost per unit, lower labor cost to stock, etc. Suppliers are not paid until the goods are sold, allowing Sam to work with negative working capital just as Henry Ford did. Much of Sam's savings is passed on to the consumer to gain market share, to "preserve precious volume on which all depends." But unlike Ford, Sam's products are satisfactory to at least 68% (= 1 sigma) of the population as a whole. Within this population, Sam has effectively created a franchise—people go to Sam's because it is often the only source of low-cost goods that meet their needs. It can be argued that Sam's and Southwest Airlines' whole strategy is built upon complexity reduction.

Complexity reduction, through internal standardization, Lean Six Sigma improvements, and then through optimization offers enormous competitive advantage. Think of complexity reduction as a new competitive weapon and a potent tool to increase shareholder value.

Endnotes

1. See www.profisight.com for calculations.
2. Ibid.

SUCCESS STORY

#4

Stanford Hospital and Clinics:
At the forefront
of the quality revolution

Stanford Hospital and Clinics (Stanford) was applying the basic elements of Lean and Six Sigma long before those terms were invented. Their use of quality and process principles began in the mid-1980s, when changes in Medicare reimbursements and the advent of HMOs meant that healthcare providers had to start balancing fiscal concerns with their primary mission of providing high-quality patient care.

The pressures that sparked Stanford to adopt what was then Total Quality Management (TQM) have continued to intensify. For one thing, changes in technology have made medicine an increasingly capital-intensive enterprise. At the same time, revenue sources continue to tighten. California is a particularly competitive healthcare market, with large HMOs and employer groups exerting enormous pressure to keep costs down. Many hospitals in California began accepting contracts that were not covering their costs, a path that Stanford was reluctant to follow. The pragmatists argued, "No margin, no mission."

Details on the Stanford Hospital and Clinics come to us through Karen Rago who worked there from 1977 to 2002, rising through the ranks from staff nurse to nurse manager to the Vice President of Program and Service Line Development. Stanford is a private, not-for-profit academic medical center and 650-bed hospital affiliated with Stanford University. They have a long history of fostering innovation, including the first heart transplant in the United States and the first successful heart/lung transplant in the world.

By the late 1990s, many of Stanford's clinical specialties, like cardiac care, started to see patient volumes dwindling, a fact that alarmed both physicians and administrators alike. Like most healthcare providers, they needed more profit to sustain operations, revitalize reserves, and refund the capital budget. The solution they found was to ramp up their already existing improvement efforts to look for even greater improvements in speed and quality. Here's their story.

The Business

Every business feels pressure to cut costs, but those pressures are exacerbated in healthcare. In fact, its business model is very different from what most people learn in their MBA programs.

For one thing, healthcare organizations cannot fully control their fixed costs. In California, for example, there are even laws mandating nurse staffing levels. For example, if there are 26 patients in the cardiac "step-down" unit (where patients go after leaving ICU), California says you should be using 8 nurses to care for those patients. A hospital can be cited for not maintaining the mandated levels. So even if Stanford figured out a way to provide high-quality care with only 6 nurses, they would be unable to take advantage of those changes.

The situation gets worse: as we all know, the growing influence of HMOs means healthcare organizations have less and less control of revenues. They can charge whatever they like for a service, but whether or not Medicare or insurance will pay that price or allow the patient to pay is an entirely different matter. For example, as Karen Rago explains, "Most contracts spell out how much they will pay per day per hospitalized patient. It doesn't matter what we do for patients, what care they require, we only get that per diem. If a short-stay patient requires an expensive surgical procedure, we would take care of that patient even though we may never recoup those costs."

Stanford worked with their managed care contracting group to get additional "carve outs" for special procedures and implantable devices (such as heart valve implants), so they stand a better chance of getting paid what it costs to provide many of their services, but the market forces that determine what they get paid are unlike those in other business environments.

Lessons #1 and #2: Ownership and Integration

To address the need to substantially cut costs, Stanford's first foray into quality improvement in the mid-1980s was a short-lived effort called Service Improvement. It failed miserably because it encompassed ideas and approaches very alien to the staff. Stanford soon followed up by implementing Total Quality Management, which fared much better partly because of its emphasis on working in teams. This had two big advantages as Rago recalls: "I'd worked at Stanford long enough to know that nothing could get anywhere unless we got everyone to agree. And working in teams was one way to get people to come to agreement." The other advantage, she adds, was that TQM got Stanford started down a path of involving operational people in the improvement work. These people had the knowledge needed to understand the situation, and they were part of deciding what changes would be made," says Rago, "so changes were more likely to stick."

But even the TQM efforts fell short of the organization's needs. That's when Stanford's leadership decided to develop their own unique program called Operations Improvement (OI), which began in the late 1980s. The key change was that Operations Improvement took the place of the annual budgeting process—that is, the push to find improvements was tied in with the development of annual plans and budgets. Stanford didn't simply mandate across-the-board percentages or arbitrarily cut out some functions. Rather, they looked at their operations, identified waste or excess, and applied what we would now call Lean and Six Sigma thinking and tools to eliminate that waste.

Development of OI addressed two key issues:

- **The benefits of embedding quality initiatives into the culture** of the organization. Though Operations Improvement drew on concepts and tools used in TQM and Lean, it was something unique to and owned by Stanford.

- **The need to integrate "improvement" with "business goals."** To characterize even Stanford's early efforts as simply "quality improvement" is somewhat misleading. The purpose was always to help reduce operating costs while maintaining or improving patient care. So improvement was never something done in addition to their regular work or done solely for the purpose of improving quality; it was how Stanford was going to achieve its business goals. Incorporating improvement thinking and efforts into annual planning and budgeting achieved this integration.

Preparation and Rollout

When OI began, the initial focus was on having individual departments identify savings opportunities (revenue enhancements were also considered, but the primary thrust has always been, and continues to be, on ways to cut costs or achieve other efficiencies). Several years into OI, however, it was expanded to include a cross-functional assessment of clinical care, taking a broad look at everything patients experience while they're at the hospital.

To implement this broader view of OI, Stanford first trained a group of people within the organization to be full-time trainers, a move taken so that employees would be trained by people they knew. (Credibility is a big issue among professional staff, which is most of Stanford's employee base.)

Stanford then looked around the organization and chose managers they thought would make good team leaders as participants in the first official wave of training. The pioneer class got a basic introduction to TQM (remember, this was in the late '80s) in a three-day course that covered everything from fishbone diagrams to facilitation. In the first training session 100 staff and managers were trained to be team leaders or facilitators; by the end, approximately 1500 staff and managers had been trained in quality and Lean principles—about 30% of the employees.

Every year since OI was begun, the trained facilitators have run and/or coached between 10 and 16 cross-departmental teams. The official OI budgeting/improvement cycle begins in January when the teams come together. Prior to the OI kickoff, department managers solicit improvement ideas from their staff. The first two OI meetings are then spent brainstorming, sharing these staff-contributed ideas, and generating even more ideas. The teams continue meeting weekly through April to analyze and implement ideas, then the leaders of those teams meet with the CEO, CFO, and COO to report on ideas and projects. The executive team then completes the hospitals' plans and targets in time for the beginning of their fiscal year in September.

From the start, these teams have known that the OI process means finding ways to cut costs, but there was an additional incentive to make their participation worthwhile: if they could identify improvement ideas that could provide a return on investment in three years or less, they could get capital and operating dollars outside the normal capital budget process. This incentive helped create pull for OI initiatives by convincing people that it was also an opportunity for gain, not something they were going to lose. "For example," says Rago, "sometimes departments could add a new FTE nurse because they were accomplishing savings which more than paid for adding that position."

As mentioned above, these cross-departmental teams originally existed only from January through April to come up with ideas and plans for the next fiscal year. Later, they were often maintained throughout the year as a mechanism for monitoring performance and identifying further opportunities. The teams would continue to meet monthly, share data (volume of patients, cost per case, reimbursements, etc.), and discuss any issues that needed immediate attention.

Results

Stanford's Operations Improvement strategy has been in place since the late 1980s, so it is difficult to represent the full scope of their achievements. Most managers can pull out documentation on dozens of projects that illustrate Lean Six Sigma principles ranging from eliminating medication errors (reducing defects) to redefining procedures by eliminating non-value-added work. Here are just a few benchmarks from the areas that Karen Rago knows best, cardiology and cardiac surgery:

ICU hours of care per patient day: Dropped from a starting point of 29.6 hours in the 1980s to 20.5 hours by 1995 and 19 hours by 2001

Material cost saved: $25 million per year (cash flow impact based on the reduction of supply expense per adjusted patient day indicators)

Cardiac surgery cost savings: $1.1 to $2.6 million saved per year

Cardiology cost savings: $4.4 million

Cardiac Bypass Graft Surgery savings: $2400+ per case

Where did all these gains come from? Projects focused on complexity reduction were described in previous chapters. But here's one other example of the kinds of changes that made a big impact on cost: Until recently, all of Stanford's supplies were kept in a huge basement stock room, which represented an enormous capital investment. When nurses needed supplies, they would either call down to the center and explain what they wanted to someone who may or may not be familiar with medical terminology. If it was a night shift, nurses could have ended up going down to the basement themselves to root for what they needed.

Then Nick Gaich, the Vice President of Materials Management and Customer Service, implemented a new process built around the Lean ideals of minimizing work-in-process and mistake-proofing work by eliminating the chances for human error. The new procedure was built around a computerized system that allows nearly just-in-time stocking of "service centers," small supply rooms located throughout the facility. Each service center stocks a three-day supply of material for three to five specific hospital units. A nurse or a support services person enters requests into the computer, and the needed material is delivered to an appropriate mailbox in the unit within five minutes of order entry. The computer systems also communicates directly with the appropriate supplier(s), and the used material is replenished usually within the same day.

Now, the nurses (being paid $30-$40 an hour) can spend more time on patient care and less time running around gathering supplies. Support staff, trained in the materials system, perform the majority of the work. The huge basement stockroom, representing huge wasted capital, has been replaced by many smaller stockrooms that, in total, consume far less capital investment.

Lessons Learned

Over the nearly 25 years that Karen Rago spent at Stanford, four lessons stick out in her mind:

1 Moving to cross-departmental teams

The change to cross-departmental teams was critical, says Rago, because it eventually brought with it a very strong focus on entire service lines (known as "value streams" in Lean parlance). "When we reached the point of having service line teams, we would look at patient care from beginning to end, not just from each individual department budget," she says. In effect, she adds, they were changing the process of care. The cardiac care team that Rago led included:

- The chair of the surgery group as a co-leader (what they called a "physician Champion")

- The nurse managers from the units that cared for the cardiac surgery patients

- The operating room manager for the operating rooms where they did cardiothoracic surgery

It saves money on self-stick notes, too!

Karen Rago remembers that it used to be a common sight to see nurses with rows of self-stick labels stuck to their name badges as a way to remember what supplies they needed to charge to patients. Going to a just-in-time electronic ordering system has not only eliminated the $60K/yr budget her unit had for lost material and supplies (the sticky label system was somewhat unreliable) but also reduced the hospital investment of inventory in excess of $250,000. It also enhanced net revenue by interfacing (real time) with the Hospital Billing system, so the patient charges are now more accurate and complete. The sticky label system was eliminated.

- A clinical nurse specialist representing units that handled cardiac patients

- A pharmacist, respiratory therapist, and physical therapist who cared for those patients

- Social workers, case managers

In short the team included representatives from everyone who dealt with patients as they "flowed" through the value stream. This allowed Stanford to break down barriers and work toward common customer-centered goals.

> "A key thing we did is have physicians co-lead the teams with a manager. That was the only way we had any credibility with other physicians and nurses."
>
> —Karen Rago

One rule set down at the very beginning was spawned by the kind of systems thinking incorporated into Six Sigma: no team could make a change that affected another department unless they had buy-in from that department. This wasn't as onerous as it might sound at first: remember, they were using cross-functional teams, so it was likely that a representative from the affected department was in the room.

Rago recalls an example from the early days of a project aimed at getting wheelchairs to where they need them (which turns out to be a huge logistical challenge for many hospitals). The first time that a team came together to attack this issue, the changes didn't stick. Results came only when the problem was attacked a second time by a cross-departmental team. "Instead of having the nursing director pointing fingers at supplies management, a supplies management representative was there at the table. So they understood how their department affected others. And they dug in there to help fix it," says Rago. A side-effect of this collaboration, she notes, was that people were no longer constantly complaining about the same problem over and over again.

2. Increasing the availability and use of data

During the initial implementation efforts, it was difficult for people to get the data they needed. They even had to bring in an outside group to hand-count patient charts to determine, for example, how many of each kind of lab test was performed. Such data is essential for making decisions about whether procedures could be changed to reduce patients' hospital stays without doing them any harm. Soon after the Operations Improvement program became operative, Stanford invested in a cost-accounting system that made such data much easier to gather. Rago also helped shape a group of staffers within the service line structure who were available to provide quick support to the OI teams.

At a fundamental level, having easy access to good data helped improve each team's decision making. It was also critical because of the population that Rago was dealing with: "Physicians want to see data," she says. "They aren't going to be convinced otherwise." Also, one of the biggest implementation challenges Stanford faced was when non-physician clinical staff identified changes to physician practices. "Getting physicians to change their practices is very difficult, and you have to have compelling arguments and data to support any recommendations," says Rago.

Lastly, having "after" data was important in being able to show people what they had accomplished and provide a morale boost for continued improvement efforts.

3. Adapting the process to staff needs and working styles

As the head of the cardiac care units at Stanford, Rago spent her time working with both cardiology physicians and cardiac surgeons. She discovered early on that these two groups had very different approaches, and she had to adapt her approach to fit the audience: cardiologists, who spent their time in the clinics, liked to think in terms of process and teams. They would willingly attend weekly meetings and talk through their ideas. The cardiac surgeons, on the other hand, were much more independent and outcome oriented. Initially they were not prone to working collaboratively with other surgeons, and wanted to quickly reach decisions and move on. By accommodating these styles, Rago was able to get more accomplished.

4. Benchmarking

Every business faces questions around where to set its targets: How fast is fast? What kind of quality levels are possible? What helped Stanford identify priority areas for improvement and set realistic targets was their affiliation with the University Health Systems Consortium (UHSC), which started doing clinical benchmarking projects. Each member organization had to submit 30 cases related to a number of practice areas (such as hip replacements and coronary bypass grafts). UHSC evaluated all the cases and benchmarked the members against each other. They also identified which members exhibited best practices in each area, and shared those practices among the membership. Rago says it helped Stanford see where it was best-in-class already, and where they could learn from others.

Creating a Matrixed Organization

By the late 1990s, Stanford had become a fully matrixed organization. As Rago describes it, "What changed the most was that I and everyone like me went from being insular department managers to collaborating with our peers. In the early years, I would not have normally done a whole lot of problem solving with other managers. If I was having a problem with the lab, and 10 other units were having problems with the lab, then we had 11 problems with the lab. It wasn't until we started working together across boundaries that we could recognize and start to fix major system problems."

Rago credits Stanford's leadership, and especially previous CEO Malinda Mitchell, with embracing the changes early on and carrying that commitment for many years. "It needed to be the way we functioned, not in addition to our other work," she says. "Even though at first it meant some extra meetings, eventually our OI efforts started changing the mindset for how we thought and functioned. That's when we started seeing the big gains."

Part II

Deploying Lean Six Sigma in Service Organizations

> "If people have something to do they believe is worthwhile, they have a purpose, they can make a difference in a very defined and measurable way. If they make that difference, and they're rewarded, they get energized and motivated and want to come to work and make a difference. And if you can do that for people, that's the magic."
>
> —Geoff Turk, Corporate 6σ Champion, Caterpillar

With Max Isaac

Special credits for Part II

Special thanks go to **Lou Giuliano**, CEO of ITT, and **Geoff Turk**, the Corporate Six Sigma Champion at Caterpillar. Both have been involved in leading highly successful deployments of Lean Six Sigma in both the service and manufacturing functions of their organizations. Their thoughts on how to make Lean Six Sigma deployment work are much appreciated.

Also thanks to **Max Isaac** for being the coauthor of these chapters. With over 30 years of general management and consulting experience in North America and Europe, Max is a leading expert in the field of leadership and organizational behavior. His knowledge of how to weave change initiatives into the fabric of an organization provides an under-appreciated complement to the standard discussion of how to launch Six Sigma.

INTRODUCTION

The CEO of a midsized retail chain[1] was excited. He'd just been to an Executive Roundtable on Lean Six Sigma and thought it sounded like the answer to his prayers. His company was suffering from a steady drop in sales—he'd already had three bad quarters in a row and couldn't afford many more. He was a little skeptical of claims that other companies were seeing net benefits of $500,000 or more of increased operating profit per Black Belt, but even half that would be significant to a company like his.

After a little more research, the CEO called together the senior management team and spoke enthusiastically of Lean Six Sigma and how it could help their organization bridge the gap between their current promises to the "street" and what they could reasonably expect to deliver. He appointed the VP of operations to be in charge of getting Lean Six Sigma up and running. He was most emphatic about the need to see results within the fiscal year and sooner if possible, telling the VP, "Judging from what I hear we should only need a dozen Black Belts out there and we'll make our fiscal targets. This is your baby. Just give me monthly updates."

If you had to guess, what odds would you give for this company ending up as a stellar example of Lean Six Sigma deployment?

Lean Six Sigma's supporters emphasize how much more effective it is than predecessors such as continuous improvement and TQM: better tied to customer priorities, easier to track throughout the company, much more linked to business strategies. And we all know the companies—like Bank of America, GE Capital, Starwood, ITT—who have used Six Sigma to drive customer satisfaction, improve quality, and generate impressive financial payback. Yet for each of these success stories there are many other companies like the one above who stand to achieve only a fraction of the full Lean Six Sigma potential.

The question is what makes the difference between the successful deployments and those that end up as a program-du-jour, an initiative forgotten or ignored at executive levels, living on only in the work of a few passionate, frustrated zealots?

An article in *Fortune* from June 21, 1999, called "Why CEOs Fail," provides a crucial clue. Authors Ram Charan and Geoffrey Colvin comment, "In the majority of cases—we estimate 70%—the real problem isn't the high-concept boners the boffins love to talk about... It's bad execution."

For anyone struggling with the execution of strategy, Charan and Colvin's article is a wake-up call. For years, the experts have told us that the most critical leadership skill was mobilizing the troops around a clear vision and winning strategy. A leader's job was to clearly communicate where she or he wanted to go, then trust employees to find a way to get there.

As Charan and Colvin point out, it's becoming increasingly clear that we need to put as much or more emphasis on implementation. And they are far from alone in their belief. Pushing that idea even deeper, consultant Tom Curren described a two-year research effort by McKinsey and Company that identified nine mistakes responsible for 80% of the failures of significant change efforts.[2]

1. No performance focus
2. Lack of winning strategy
3. Failure to make a compelling and urgent case for change
4. Not distinguishing between decision-driven and behavior-dependent change
5. Failure to mobilize and engage pivotal groups
6. Over-reliance on structure and systems to change behavior
7. Lack of skills and resources
8. Leaders' inability or unwillingness to confront how they and their roles must change
9. Inability to integrate and align all the initiatives

Notice that having the right strategy is only one of these factors; the remaining eight relate to implementation: either poor execution or a lack of attention paid to interactional issues (engaging people in shaping and supporting the deployment).

For an organization considering (or already involved in) Lean Six Sigma, this means the biggest challenges will most likely arise in...

Execution barriers...

- Attaining CEO and P&L management engagement

- Resource dedication: Achieving 1% (or more) of employees as full-time Black Belts assigned to continuous improvement efforts

- Project selection: Choosing improvement projects based on strategic goals/needs prioritized to increased value (ROIC)

- Developing "Lean" eyes: Recognizing the need to eliminate process waste and delays (in terms of work and/or costs)—not just improve quality—to achieve their operational goals

- Data-driven management: Using process knowledge and data to make decisions

Interactional issues...

- Creating alignment and understanding of strategy, especially among those who wield the most influence (formal or informal) within the organization and those who execute projects

- Fostering a collaborative mentality—between coaches and teams, between departments, between managers—as a means for leveraging efforts

The companies profiled in Part I of this book come from very different sectors and face very different competitive pressures. They don't all use the term "Lean Six Sigma" to describe what they're doing (though it forms the substance of their improvement efforts), nor have they chosen identical pathways through execution and interaction. But the fundamental consistencies in their approach far outweigh the superficial differences. At the most basic level, they are all working to avoid the implementation barriers by **integrating** Lean Six Sigma into the everyday business of running and improving the organization.

To achieve such integration in your own organization, it helps to think of deployment as occurring in four phases:

1. **Readiness:** Identifying all the factors that should be considered when structuring how Lean Six Sigma will be used to more effectively execute your organization's strategy (such as your organization's ability to implement major change)

2. **Engagement:** Getting people excited about (and asking for) Lean Six Sigma by demonstrating its role in helping them achieve their annual and quarterly goals

3. **Mobilization:** Establishing the infrastructure and getting other elements in place for deployment

4. **Performance and Control:** Implementing deployment plans, establishing control measures and processes to ensure that Lean Six Sigma improvements endure and that efforts remain closely aligned with business strategies

For the purposes of this book, we've devoted separate chapters to each of these phases. But it's important to realize that these stages overlap: The way in which you do a readiness assessment will influence whether people want to become engaged in the effort; work on building engagement will continue long after you've begun erecting the formal infrastructure and launching projects; control measures will be layered over ongoing performance activities.

In reality, the separation between phases will not be as neat as that described in the following chapters. Many of the lessons you'll see in these chapters are summarized in a master list of success factors in Chapter 9 (p. 255). But keep in mind that what is appropriate at one company may not be for yours, so any interpretation of the guidelines should be tempered by your own judgment and experience about what works in your environment.

Endnotes

1.All cases in Part II are based on real companies and people, but some identities of some companies and their employees have been disguised to protect confidentiality.
2. See www.topteamalignment.com/whyfail.html

CHAPTER 6

Phase 1: Readiness
Assessment

Almost two years into its Six Sigma initiative, a *Fortune* 500 company with over 10,000 employees was at a crossroads. Some initial projects had generated up to $750,000 per project, and incremental operating profit per Black Belt per year had originally been in excess of $500,000. But now the project pipeline was drying up and the fiscal return per project had dropped below $100,000. Project duration had been a problem from the outset: on average, projects had taken 6 months or longer to complete. Most current projects were not related to strategic objectives because individual managers or Black Belts were allowed to select their own projects without a formal process to evaluate the selections against corporate priorities.

Throughout the organization, there was a growing resentment of the special treatment afforded the Black Belts, and growing frustration with the lack of alignment with the rest of the organization. Where once the best and brightest competed for Six Sigma positions, trained Black Belts were now requesting transfers back to their old jobs.

The CEO and executive leadership faced a critical decision: Could they revive the initiative and achieve the significant gains that had convinced them to adopt Six Sigma, or was it time to drop it altogether and invest their time and money in something else?

Given their initial success, the executive team at this company conducted an in-depth diagnostic of what had gone wrong with their initiative. Here's what they uncovered:

1) **They had not structured the deployment correctly.** On the one hand, all the executives from the CEO on down believed that Six Sigma

needed to be an integral part of the company in order for it to succeed, and a capable executive had been put in charge of coordinating the effort as corporate Champion. But other elements of their deployment plans were inherently flawed. For example, P&L managers had been unevenly trained. Many regarded Six Sigma as an additional task rather than a process to surpass "my numbers." The Black Belts, Master Black Belts, and projects had no official relationship with any of the executives, division presidents, or other P&L managers. That automatically set up the Six Sigma effort *in competition* with the everyday work of the company.

2) **They hadn't selected the right kind of person to oversee deployment.** True, the corporate Champion had spent most of his career in process improvement and problem solving, and was widely acknowledged as one of the best in those areas. However, he lacked similar expertise in the art of leadership, and was unable to wield his influence effectively. Also, he did not report to the CEO and his voice wasn't part of the executive team.

3) **They had not prepared the organization to be receptive to and supportive of such a major change.** The people directly involved with the Six Sigma implementation had received extensive training and support, but there was little communication with or training of others not directly involved in Six Sigma projects.

If it seems odd that a chapter on readiness assessment starts out with an example of mid-deployment woes, that's because this Six Sigma initiative ran into trouble as a consequence of decisions made long before the first Black Belt was trained. The company had gone into Six Sigma without fully understanding what it would take to make it work.

This example explains why the first step when planning a Lean Six Sigma initiative should be an environmental scan or **readiness assessment**, a gathering of information to uncover all the critical issues that may impact how you design and implement your program. At Bank One, for instance, they've learned what will and won't work in their environment:

> Darryl Greene, now a Senior VP at Bank One, spent part of his career at GE. He's learned that you can't just copy what some other organization is doing. "The GE environment trains you very

well to execute within a robust infrastructure," says Greene. "But if you go into an environment where you don't have that infrastructure, and try to use the same approach… it just doesn't work. At GE, 40 percent of managers' incentive compensation was tied to Six Sigma, so obviously they'll run with it as far and as fast as they can! At companies that are new to this, that infrastructure doesn't exist and people's familiarity with collecting data, understanding gaps, and closing gaps in a repeatable and consistent manner varies."

There are many approaches to doing a readiness assessment. Here's a typical sequence; the steps are described in detail below:

1. Select the Lean Six Sigma Champion

2. Establish a baseline snapshot of the organization

3. Interview top management

4. Engage key influencers (those who wield formal or informal power in the organization) through focus groups and interviews

5. Assess the impact of what you've discovered

Before reviewing these steps in more depth, here's one tip: The way you conduct the assessment will set the tone for what people expect out of Lean Six Sigma. By including a wide range of people in the assessment you can create a lot of positive feelings towards the initiative, especially if you go in with an open mind and "listen" more than you "tell."

Readiness Step 1: Select the Champion

The reason for selecting or designating a corporate Lean Six Sigma Champion first is simple: he or she should lead the rest of the work involved in preparing for and rolling out the initiative. Having the Champion involved early on and reporting directly to the CEO is important because:

- Regular communication between the corporate leader and Champion will help ensure consistency in the messages being sent to the organization

- The Champion is more likely to feel a stronger sense of ownership in something she or he has helped shape

- The Champion will be more effective if he or she can speak with authority about the reasons why the organization is undertaking Lean Six Sigma

All of this early work associated with deploying Lean Six Sigma revolves around building alliances and becoming connected with management's priorities. That's why an effective Champion needs to have a combination of top-notch people skills coupled with the ability to understand the business—not to mention planning and deployment skills, knowledge of Lean Six Sigma, and so on.

Readiness Step 2: Establish a baseline snapshot of the organization

The first step in any plan is knowing what you're starting with. The Champion, working in conjunction with the executive team, should compile basic information on two fronts: the business status of the company overall and its major subdivisions (much like the competitive assessment described in Chapter 4), and existing knowledge/attitudes towards change in general and Lean Six Sigma in particular.

Though the executive team should be up to speed about the organization's overall status, it helps to document some basic information up front to make sure that the decision makers are all starting from the same point. Think of it like an annual physical: you just want to compile data on how the organization and its major subdivisions are doing fiscally, where people are currently deployed, and so on. Include any existing information on customer satisfaction.

What also helps here is benchmarking: visiting other companies who are involved in Six Sigma or Lean Six Sigma to see what has worked or not worked for them, see how they adapted the initiative to their work style, culture, business needs, and so on.

Readiness Step 3:
Interviews with top management

Typically, the Champion and/or outside experts will meet the CEO and his/her direct reports in one-on-one interviews. The purpose of these interviews is to identify critical elements of success for the business as a whole (what will it take to increase ROIC? market share?) and for the Lean Six Sigma initiative itself (what do we need to pay attention to make sure Lean Six Sigma is a tool we use to drive corporate strategy? what could stand in the way?).

Since the purpose is to uncover factors that will shape deployment plans, the topics covered typically include:

- Experiences with change initiatives from the past (are they still in place? why or why not? have they made people enthusiastic or cynical?).

- Understanding of corporate strategy and priorities:
    - Key competitive selling points of the organization and its products/services
    - Key barriers that may hinder or derail deployment of strategy (such as whether people think they can afford to dedicate 1% of the workforce as full-time Black Belts)

- Current attitude towards Lean Six Sigma (do they see it as a means for accomplishing their goals? as a necessary evil?).

- How decisions are made, how conflict is resolved. Styles of decision-making, commitment to a team decision once made, support for divergent views, the level at which decision making occurs.

- What people consider key to their personal success within the organization; how strategic planning and individual goals are aligned in performance evaluations.

Why the questions about decisions and communication?

How authority is exercised and how conflict resolved are issues that coalesce around decision making. Exploring how decisions are made can therefore reveal important dynamics that will influence plans and tactics for deployment.

- How work gets done (collaboration vs. silos).

- The organization's and these individuals' understanding of and experience with any element of Lean Six Sigma (processes, data collection, cycle time reduction, best practice sharing, etc.).

- Training history: what training has the company provided in the past? what skills have been emphasized? how well has it worked?

- Union issues: To what extent will unions be a factor in the Lean Six Sigma implementation?

- How strategies, goals, success measurements, and targets are cascaded throughout the organization. What structures and processes exist that determine improvement priorities? How is progress monitored and who participates in the processes?

- Teamwork/collaboration (or the lack thereof) within the organization; turf wars.

- Openness to new approaches. How prevalent is the "not invented here syndrome"?

Asking the above questions of all top managers will reveal the extent to which executing strategy is an issue. A skilled interviewer will be able to gain the confidence of interviewees and pick up on inconsistencies in the interpretation of roles and strategy. Because many major Lean Six Sigma opportunities lie in the "white space" between functions or in processes that cross traditional boundaries, you'll need to know how willingly different parts of the organization will come together and support cross-functional goals that may not directly benefit their organization.

Readiness Step 4:
Engage key influencers through focus groups and interviews

One organization that was embarking on a Lean Six Sigma initiative had a frontline employee who also happened to be a part-time pastor, and who, not incidentally, had presided at the weddings of half the company. He was looked up to by most *employees, and his opinions were always sought out. Unfortunately, no one bothered to talk to this employee or involve him in any aspect of the Lean Six Sigma planning or launch. It is widely acknowledged at this company that this oversight was one of the biggest reasons why the initiative encountered major resistance from many parts of the organization.*

In any organization, there is a core group of perhaps 5% to 10% of the employees who have a bigger effect on what does and doesn't get done than do their coworkers. Everybody knows who they are. As shown by the story above, these **key influencers** can be anywhere in the organization from the board room to the reception desk. Their influence can arise from formal authority or from a number of any other factors (personality, longevity, connections). Anyone with formal P&L responsibility, and often their direct reports, should be included in these lists.

This concentration of influence is fortunate to those of us trying to implement change because it means we can get enormous leverage by focusing our initial efforts on a relatively small percentage of the organization rather than trying to directly engage every single employee. If you get these high-leverage people involved in and excited about the initiative, then deployment, dissemination, and sustainability will come much more smoothly.

The one caveat is that you have to be diligent in finding all the people who fall into this category. If Joe is the "go to" guy in IT, you'd better talk to Joe. If Maria knows the ins-and-outs of accounting better than anyone else in the department, you'd better talk to Maria. The more of the key influencers you

> **The leverage of key influencers**
>
> Key influencers can come from anywhere in the organization. This notion is incredibly powerful. Why? As a Champion at one otherwise successful example of Lean Six Sigma discovered, many of the richest opportunities are cross-functional. But addressing those opportunities was impossible when individual silo leaders or key influencers didn't appreciate how Lean Six Sigma could help them and their staff. In fact, results in one division of that company are marginal because a key influencer keeps saying, "I don't need this." You can avoid this situation by following the engagement guidelines given in the next chapter.

include, the greater the chances that the deployment will progress smoothly and receive support.

From a practical standpoint, the contact can occur either one-on-one or in focus groups depending on how the logistics work out for your assessment, but the key point is to have face-to-face contact with as many of these influencers as possible. Though you should let the discussions go in any direction that these people want to cover, it helps if there is at least some overlap with the topics discussed with top management (see list of topics/questions, above)—that way you can compare perceptions at different levels of the organization.

Readiness Step 5: Assessing the impact of what you've learned

The information from top management and key influencers is usually synthesized into a leadership training course that outlines the critical issues that will impact the Lean Six Sigma strategy and unique challenges faced by the company regarding deployment, training, and infrastructure.

You will likely find patterns that indicate some areas of your company will be more receptive to Lean Six Sigma than others. If the less-receptive areas are involved with value streams that are critical to your business, you won't have any choice but to include them in the deployment, though you will have to do more communication and education up front to convince people that Lean Six Sigma can help them.

Though every organization is unique, there are some general patterns often seen in service organizations that have predictable effects on how a deployment should be structured. Here are a few of the most common issues:

1. Retaining and building human capital is needed for competitive advantage

2. Little history with improvement; little or no process orientation, little use of data

3. Strong people orientation; little technical orientation

4. "We're already overworked"

5. Big payback from standardization

1. The need to retain and build human capital for its competitive advantage

Service organizations are essentially big "people machines," where having a high level of turnover is just as deadly as if a manufacturer was constantly asked to change machine parts. The issue is true both for the business as a whole and especially for deployment of Lean Six Sigma: It can be challenging to establish and impossible to maintain momentum if the people you train one week are out the door the next week. This problem is especially critical for the people you put through extensive training: Champions, Black Belts, Master Black Belts. If they leave a few months into your deployment, all the knowledge you just paid for is lost with them, and you'll need to invest more in training a new wave. These people are most likely to leave because of a lack of management. The same is true for project team members: high turnover can mean less resident knowledge to tap into at a grass roots level.

Organizations that can retain employees, including their Lean Six Sigma resources, will be at an advantage compared to their competitors. Reaching this state requires attention to a lot of the guidelines given in this and the following chapters, such as selecting Black Belt candidates based on their leadership skills, maintaining high visibility of Lean Six Sigma in the organization, demonstrating at every turn that Lean Six Sigma is critical to success, and so on. Using that path means your best people will be "lost" through promotion, not through departure.

2. Little history with improvement; little or no process orientation, little use of data

Think for a moment about the four organizations profiled in Part I: Most of the ancestor organizations of Lockheed Martin had *some* experience with improvement, knowledge that is of great benefit to the supporting functions. Similarly, experience with quality improvement is also relatively more common in the healthcare field (such as Stanford Hospital and Clinics), largely because of the long-standing incorporation of quality principles into accreditation. But at both Bank One and the City of Fort Wayne, the general employee populations had little experience with quality improvement.

In organizations with a history of quality improvement, Lean Six Sigma is best viewed as a unifying framework that incorporates everything that has gone before plus adds in some new elements. You'll be better off subsuming previous initiatives into Lean Six Sigma than positioning it as a replacement. Those with little or no history don't have to worry about supplanting methods that may be near-and-dear to people's hearts, but they should expect to do more upfront awareness training so that people understand the goals of Lean Six Sigma and how it can help the organization.

Most service organizations have not used data to make decisions because it didn't exist. Rather, problems were ascribed to a "cause" based on hunches or intuition. This led to solutions that, if implemented, were doomed for failure.

3. Strong people orientation; little technical orientation

Though it is a stereotype to some extent, people who have worked with both manufacturing and service organizations consistently find that the former are more technically oriented and the latter are more people oriented. These differences often emerge as recognizable patterns throughout the organizations:

- Technically oriented people are usually relatively skilled at structuring work, using more sophisticated analytical tools, and developing the discipline needed to come to decisions quickly based on logical analysis. They are likely to be correspondingly relatively weak on resolving conflict and balancing advocacy and inquiry.

- Those from people-dependent functions (i.e., service processes) typically exhibit the opposite skills. They've learned to value collaboration skills because the best way for them to get anything done is *through* other people; but their ability to impose discipline on a team and employ structured problem-solving processes are often noticeably lacking. While quick to pick up on process analysis tools, they may shy away from the tools that require mathematical computations.

Effective implementation of Lean Six Sigma takes a combination of technical and people skills, so if you observe either of these patterns, it helps to adapt your training plans accordingly. If you find people in your organization are less technically oriented, you'll need to be more sensitive to avoiding jargon or to using statistically sophisticated techniques where simpler ones might do as well.

4. "We're already overworked"

In many service functions today, especially those in sectors that have recently gone through downsizing, you'll find some resistance to Lean Six Sigma based more on the general principle that people are already overworked than any specific objection to Lean Six Sigma itself. These feelings can pop up anywhere, in any type of organization, and you'll need to overcome the perception that Lean Six Sigma will just be bureaucratic work piled on top of already impossible workloads.

There are several ways to work through resistance arising from this objection. George Sanders, a Director of Sourcing at Lockheed Martin, for example, has found that the "overworked" syndrome can be a powerful motive for change, especially once people realize that much of the 10 or 12 hours in their days is spent on non-value-add work. Using Lean Six Sigma to eliminate waste creates buy-in by giving people back their 8-hour days!

Also, you can establish a sustainable foothold in "overworked" areas if you go out of your way to make sure that Lean Six Sigma is tied in with the real, everyday work and business priorities of managers and staff in this situation. Going for quick, incremental improvements at first that free up even a small portion of someone's time will give you a lot of leverage for taking the next (bigger) steps.

Bottom line: if you believe that Lean Six Sigma is worthwhile, implementing it in areas that are "overworked" simply becomes a matter of leadership and priorities.

5. Big payback from standardization

If you owned a chain of hotels, it wouldn't do you much good to give five-star service in one hotel if every other location fell into a two-star category, just as it doesn't help your organization if customers get excellent service one day and poor service the next. The axiom that "variation is evil" is never more applicable than when it comes to providing services to internal or external customers. To stay competitive, you need to be able to provide *consistently* high quality services.

The impact of this reality is that service deployments of Lean Six Sigma have to have a strong component of best practices sharing, establishing common practices at every location, every process, where customers are met face-to-face or phone-to-phone. By standardizing subprocesses across staff, shifts, and locations, a company can dramatically improve cost, quality, and lead time. Lean Six Sigma therefore becomes a potent competitive advantage as customers get more uniform, higher quality service levels regardless of location or shift or operator.

Conclusion

When speaking to a group of American consultants, Dr. Noriaki Kano, one of the premier thinkers and shapers of the Japanese quality movement, once described the biggest barrier to successful implementation of any change strategy this way: "Too many managers act as if they are starting with a blank canvas. They introduce change without understanding what has come before. They have to start recognizing that every canvas in their organization has been painted already... usually several times over." The purpose of a readiness assessment is to learn what's on your canvas, so you can make better decisions about how to structure and deploy Lean Six Sigma.

CHAPTER 7

Phase 2: Engagement (Creating Pull)

If you ask the leaders at many companies what they've done to make sure their improvement efforts feed into strategic priorities and contribute to key financial goals—and that these links are visible within the organization—you'll see light bulbs going off. "We haven't really done anything like that."

One of the fundamental secrets of success is publicizing the link of Lean Six Sigma to business strategy because doing so...

- Gives people—especially P&L managers—a compelling personal reason to support the Lean Six Sigma initiative (the "**What's In It For Me**" factor, or **WIIFM**)

- Removes reasons for them to actively *resist* Lean Six Sigma, or worse, simply comply

- Shows the link between shareholder value and Lean Six Sigma projects

Not all firms have coupled Six Sigma to strategic objectives:

Trying to survive in a market where customer needs change quickly, one company decided to use Six Sigma as part of its core business strategy. They hired a Champion who had extensive experience with Six Sigma, trained several waves of Black Belts, launched a number of critical-to-quality projects. But still the results weren't what they hoped it would be.

Two years into the effort, they did a diagnostic review, including interviews with key decision makers throughout the organization.

One of the more revealing interviews came from the VP of Product Development—a key role in this organization.

First, this VP said, he had not been invited to attend any Six Sigma training, nor had any Champions or Black Belts sought him out to understand his priorities. Second, he and his staff were keenly aware of the money and effort being devoted to the Black Belts, especially now that the company had created performance incentives based on the Black Belt's average return per project. "Don't these people realize that what we do here in Product Development has a much greater impact on our customers and our financials than anything the Black Belts do?," said the VP. "Why don't my engineers receive bonuses when they develop a really great product?"

This VP and his employees had absolutely no reason to actively support Six Sigma, and instead had grown to view it with some resentment. By ignoring the importance of their commitment and support, the organization missed a prime opportunity to capitalize on all its resources. The product development staff were very comfortable with several key pieces of Six Sigma, including the scientific method and data analysis, and could have worked well on project teams. Some also had the people skills necessary to make effective Black Belts. Getting these people involved could have been accomplished rather easily in the beginning of the deployment; now, it would take a huge amount of effort to overcome the built-up skepticism and even antagonism towards Lean Six Sigma. (This process was accelerating through use of Design for Lean Six Sigma, which will be discussed in Chapter 14.)

Like most companies, this one spent nearly all its improvement budget on the people directly involved in deployment, the newly formed cadre of Champions and Black Belts. Only a small fraction of time and effort was spent communicating with others and explaining the what, why, and "what's in it for me" (WIIFM) to those not directly involved. This strategy essentially ignores the fact that any changes made as a result of Lean Six Sigma would have to be sustained by those who live with that job every day, and who aren't part of the Lean Six Sigma infrastructure. A *sustainable* Lean Six Sigma initiative needs to engage *both* those directly involved and non-direct resources in the effort.

By narrowly defining who it designated as "involved" in the Lean Six Sigma initiative, the company described above limited what it could achieve—and overlooked some resources that could have made valuable contributions. Companies who follow this path often have some initial success, emanating from projects that represent low-hanging fruit or that are supported by a small but vocal minority. But results typically tail off quickly and are hard to revive.

If your P&L managers don't identify with Lean Six Sigma, if they view it as taking *away* from their resources rather than adding capability and helping them be more successful in achieving their goals, as eating up vital budgetary allotments rather than investing in what will soon be significant financial payback and activities that help them achieve their goals, they will never fully support your Six Sigma efforts.

This ain't your grandfather's change management

Traditional approaches to introducing Lean Six Sigma or other initiatives have stressed a traditional form of "change management." You're supposed to identify everyone involved in or affected by an effort and classify them as a resistor or supporter, or something in-between... then come up with strategies to "overcome resistance." The approach to change management described in these chapters is very different. While no change of any significance is going to be implemented without any resistance, you can avoid much of the resistance that occurs when changes are implemented from the top by

- Fully understanding your organization (through the readiness assessment)

- Engaging people in shaping the initiative in ways that support their personal goals (as well as those of your organization)

- Making sure Lean Six Sigma resources are devoted to priority problems

- Positioning Lean Six Sigma resources (Black Belts, etc.) as support for line management

- Recognizing that resistance to change is a way that people defend current good performance; what Lean Six Sigma offers is the opportunity for great performance

- Training all top managers, creating enthusiasm rather than compliance

The same is true at other levels of the organization. There are numerous studies showing the positive effect of employee satisfaction on both job satisfaction and retention—with the critical "by-product" being the ability to deliver recognizably superior customer service. Employees who feel ownership by being part of your Lean Six Sigma deployment will be empowered to make many other self-directed small improvements daily without making every thing a project.

Examples of Engagement Strategies

For Lean Six Sigma to become the way you do business, the majority of key influencers must truly believe Lean Six Sigma will help them in the portion of corporate strategy that they are held personally accountable for—in other words, they must have a clear answer to the WIIFM question ("what's in it for me?"). As the companies described in Part I demonstrated, there are a lot of different ways to engage key influencers, to help them discover their own WIIFM:

- **Bank One's NEO division** is using a *one-year demonstration phase* where internal consultants guide Focus 2.0 improvement events on target areas selected by management (see their Story in Part I). This approach puts minimal demand on employees (no prior training required) but brings substantial results. As senior VP Mike Fischbach puts it, "Nobody [was] going to pay attention until [we] had proved success with real examples, with real gains."

- **Lockheed Martin** and the **City of Fort Wayne** are using a more traditional approach of relying on a more formal infrastructure to create engagement in their initiatives. At Lockheed Martin, the widespread leadership education has created a large group of managers who understand Lean Six Sigma and how it can be used effectively to push their agendas and make their numbers. Frontline staff in Fort Wayne are seeing how becoming educated in Lean and Six Sigma gives them more power in performing and improving their jobs and work processes. In both organizations, strong leadership at the top is key. Lockheed Martin's Vance

Coffman has not only stated but also demonstrated his support of the LM21 initiative. Fort Wayne Mayor Graham Richard is famed for practicing what he preaches; asking for data, reviewing projects, emphasizing a customer-oriented mindset, and using data-based thinking.

- Stanford Hospital and Clinics integrated improvement into their annual planning and budgeting process. Given their competitive environment, managers knew they would be given budget cuts every year—what was in it for them in participating in the process was a chance to control where those cuts occurred and even gain additional resources in key areas by making improvements in others. Key leaders also worked hard to engage others in creating a new vision for the organization.

Convincing with Evidence

Mike Fischbach of Bank One's NEO group says, "In our group, our focus is on operational efficiency. We are striving to drive every last penny out of the unit costs that we can.

"Firsthand experience is important to us. We're not a conceptual group that will draw conclusions based on concepts somebody puts on the table; we draw conclusions based on experience. When a question comes up, people say, 'Do I have experience with this?' So we must create the experience.

"For us to tell people that we're going to send everybody through five days of training... it's just not feasible. At least not until we've created momentum and people are saying 'I want to get involved now.' They have to recognize that they're better off with Lean Six Sigma as part of the culture."

What does it take to convince people to get involved? "The pilot effort is the proof of concept," says Darryl Greene. "For example, we've done several projects in the areas run by Doug Hartsema (senior VP of Remittance and Information Processing), who sits on our leadership team. Whenever someone brings up the subject of Lean, he can sit there and say with confidence, 'This stuff works, guys.' That's a lot more effective than just asking them to trust me."

Education, Communication, and Involvement: How to use key influencers to your advantage

Knowing who your key influencers are is a good first step, but how can you leverage their influence to build support for Lean Six Sigma? Timing is critical. You have a short window of opportunity to proactively shape people's perceptions. If you leave communication up to word-of-mouth, you lose a once-and-for-all opportunity to shape the perception of (and ultimate outcomes of) Lean Six Sigma.

As noted in Chapter 6, you can start building key influencers' engagement from the first interviews or other contact you have with them, if you make it clear by deed and word that Lean Six Sigma is being used to support their business goals. It will continue in how you frame required training or education for managers and other key influencers. Such training should be structured to build towards true internalization of Lean Six Sigma, not just an intellectual understanding of principles or concepts.

For senior management and other key influencers to use Lean Six Sigma as a powerful performance engine, they must be familiar with its basic precepts, tools, and requirements. Only then will they be able to effectively guide Lean Six Sigma efforts and allocate sufficient resources to guarantee a reasonable chance of success. As Lou Giuliano puts it, "If the executive team doesn't understand the language, doesn't understand the potential and what could happen, it doesn't work very well."

Hearing a presentation is a good first step *if* the presenter is seen as credible (such as a CEO who is actively practicing Lean Six Sigma), but a deeper understanding of what Lean Six Sigma can and cannot do is essential. Every management member also participates in a three- to four-day Lean Six Sigma training course that includes a simulation (or other "live experience" in application), and participates in chartering a project. Such an approach immerses these key influencers in project discovery and selection, and creates an emotional connection with Lean Six Sigma that will carry them far into deployment. Richard Sullivan of Xerox once said, "When I participated in the Lean Six Sigma simulation, the lights went on… I could see I could use this."

Rules of Engagement

Much of the information throughout this book will help you truly engage key influencers (and others) in shaping and deploying Lean Six Sigma in your organization. But here are three rules of engagement to provide you with a starting point.

Rule #1: You need a clear "burning platform"
(aka "You can't ask people to commit to something whose purpose you can't explain")

Every successful deployment is based on a "burning platform," some major challenge or risk which, if overcome, will push the organization towards greatness. One of the commonalities in the organizations profiled in this book is their clarity on *why* they are adopting strategies based on Lean Six Sigma principles. At the National Enterprise Operations division of Bank One, the initial directive was to bring the chaos under control. In Fort Wayne, the Mayor clearly articulated the need to use Six Sigma to support his goals of creating a safer city, a city with more good jobs, a city that provides excellent service to its citizen. Lockheed Martin saw the need not just for a common company identity and culture (after the major defense industry consolidations) but a tool to become more competitive. At Stanford, everyone was aware of the changing environment of healthcare and the need to really push cost savings while improving patient care. Having a clear strategy that is well-communicated allows people to guide their own actions: "Will doing this support or detract from our goals?"

Above all else, the CEO and other executives must speak with one voice about the burning platform for their business. It could be a need to regain competitiveness in the market, a need to introduce new services, attract new customers, retain existing customers, or simply improve profitability.

Whatever the platform, it is often articulated in one or more 2- to 5-year goals. These goals must be specific to your company, and should be driven by your corporate value creation strategy. The issue here is to make sure that goals reflect the types of gains you need to get from your Lean Six Sigma effort—not what you can safely achieve using the same systems you have in place today. Here are some examples of typical multi-year stretch goals and financial performance:

- Improve gross margin 5–10%

- Increase ROIC by 5–15%

- Increase revenue growth to 10% per year

- Gain 4% in market share each year

- Win 12 new major clients/customers

- Increase capacity 12–18%

- Reduce the number of overhead employees by 12%

- Cut time-to-market and redesign in half

- Generate an average return of $500,000 per Black Belt per year (judged in operating profit)

- Generate 80% of our capital needs from operating profits

Once the CEO and P&L executives understand the power of Lean Six Sigma, they will be in a position to select a set of goals appropriate to the business and market conditions. The actual process of refining and achieving these goals will require the contribution of many minds, which are usually formed into a Design/Deployment Team described in Chapter 8.

Rule #2: Create a concrete picture of how people's lives will be different

One reason that people often resist change is because they can't envision how they will operate under a new set of rules. The key influencers in an organization can help overcome this obstacle by demonstrating the new way of thinking and acting in their own professional lives. For example, Roger Hirt, the Master Black Belt with the City of Fort Wayne who "came of age" in an improvement sense while he was with GE, has noticed a big

Building partnerships with key influencers

"Part of it is coming up with a strategic vision of a highly delivered pro-gram," says Nick Gaich, the Vice President of Materials Management and Customer Service at Stanford Hospital and Clinics. "With the vision in front of you, it's essential that you establish a very personal relationship with key stakeholders who (1) are receptive to the vision, and (2) help con-tribute to the vision by bringing their team to the table. That's where I spent some time. It's not so much about how things are done today, but more importantly—if you take a look at it from an optimistic perspective—what would it look like if given the opportunity to create a world class program."

difference in how leaders act before and after their exposure to Lean Six Sigma. "Before, emotion carries a lot of weight in people's evaluation of a situation," he says. "They look at something, remember what happened before, and the results they got. And if it worked, once, they'll try it again.

"What changes," continues Hirt, "is that people start separating their emotional responses from what the *data* is telling them." He can see a big difference in the questions that managers start asking: "Yes, I feel like that's the right thing, but what data do we have? Is there any information that could indicate this is the correct thing to do? How are we going to measure it? What's going to change?"

Such changes are pervasive as a manager's mindset changes from "protect my turf" to "do everything possible to serve our customers better." The more a manager learns about and experiences Lean Six Sigma, the more data-driven and self-confident their responses and ques-tions become. When presented with an idea or suggestion or even com-plaint, the first questions out of a Lean Six Sigma manager's mouth are usually "What do our customers say?" or "What does the data tell us?"

When faced with a new problem, they'll delve into whether it is caused by special or common cause variation ("does the data show that some-thing like this happens all the time, or is something special going on?"). Simply asking those questions helps managers avoid one of the most deadly of all managerial sins: overreacting to common cause variation—

or "tampering" as it was called by Dr. W. Edwards Deming. Tampering usually *increases* variation and makes the problem worse than it was originally.

When walking through a work area, a Lean Six Sigma manager looks for evidence of process management and Lean techniques: process flow-charts, data on process speed and defects, visual management tools, and so on. As much as possible, demonstrate these skills through your own behavior, and give people a safe environment in which to practice them on their own.

Changes in the daily life of an organization

For most of its 100+ year history, Caterpillar was a very structured, very buttoned-down organization. To demonstrate that the old ways were changed, CEO Glenn Barton appeared at their Six Sigma kickoff meeting dressed in Karate uniform and accompanied by several world-class Karate experts. Geoff Turk, the 6σ Corporate Deployment Champion, describes a host of other changes: "We've got Black Belts talking to the CEO about their storyboards. We've got line managers who had built a facade over the years of 'I don't make mistakes' who are now open to discuss the data and facts about how things could really be better. The interaction of people, the common language, removing the emotion, basing most decisions on data and facts—all of this has done wonderful things for the development of our people."

Rule #3: Change your management meeting agendas

There's another truism of business that has a big influence on whether your Lean Six Sigma initiative will be successful: what gets covered in management meetings gets paid attention to. Take a look at your management team agendas. If Lean Six Sigma projects and results aren't a big part of those agendas, then either you've got the wrong agendas or the wrong focus for Lean Six Sigma.

Mayor Richard of Fort Wayne carves out time on his agenda to meet with project team leaders. Manny Zulueta, Vice President of Lockheed

Martin's MAC-MAR procurement operations, has a standing, weekly one-hour staff meeting dedicated to Lean Six Sigma for team reviews, project completion status, and re-alignment planning. You can bet that people in these organizations view Lean Six Sigma (or their version of it) as important to their personal success.

Placing Lean Six Sigma work front-and-center in management's eyes is a way to increase visibility of the effort and reinforce to all the key influencers how important it is.

Conclusion:
Starting off on the right foot

Lean Six Sigma will reach its full potential only when all key influencers (and eventually the rest of the organization) view Lean Six Sigma as a vehicle for them to achieve personal success in their roles. But, as human beings, we tend not to change entrenched patterns of behavior unless we see that where we're standing right now is going to get a lot more uncomfortable than where we'll be if we change. The purpose of engagement is to help make it easier for people to change than to stay the same, to generate support by finding ways to make sure Lean Six Sigma is seen as an asset—that is what's going to create the pull. As Lou Giuliano says, "I spent a lot of time and energy trying to convince people this wasn't just some Machiavellian trick to try to cheat everybody out of their bonus, and that this really was a serious effort to try to change the way we do things, and if we were successful we'd all have higher bonuses." And that is what happened.

CHAPTER 8

Phase 3: Mobilization

Y ou've read this mantra several times in this book already: a business initiative like Lean Six Sigma can reach its full potential in terms of both business results and resource deployment only when it is fully integrated into the regular management structures and business flow of an organization. If not, it will eventually become isolated into silos or programs-du-jour that fade away.

There are hundreds of decisions you'll face in shaping your Lean Six Sigma deployment that will influence its ultimate fate, including everything from selecting and training Black Belts to corporate-wide communication. Covering them all is beyond the scope of this book. Instead, this chapter highlights some decisions that are most critical in making sure that Lean Six Sigma will become the new way that business is done in your organization. The mobilization goals covered here are to:

1. Commission an executive team to oversee deployment

2. Set up an infrastructure of line management and dedicated resources

3. Design and develop appropriate training

4. Identify and charter first-wave projects

5. Reach consensus on common metrics

Mobilization Goal #1: Commission an executive team to oversee deployment

The launch of Lean Six Sigma represents a major directional change for most companies, and will affect every corner of the business. Part of leadership engagement in Lean Six Sigma is to undertake the responsibility to define and oversee what Lean Six Sigma will look like in the organization, and how the need and benefits of this effort should be communicated to others. In most cases, the CEO assigns these responsibilities to a **Design/ Deployment Team** responsible for developing the business case and detailed plan for the first 100 days of implementation.

The charter of the Design/Deployment Team is to create the vision, establish the goals and budgets, and make policy and infrastructure decisions that ensure linkage to the CEO's strategy. This initial design team may be able to develop a preliminary design and business case in anywhere from 2 weeks to 2 months depending on the size and complexity of the company, and the need for tailoring the initiative. In fact, one company was so committed that they began rolling out the process the very first week after they made the decision to go forward. They based their design on a template provided by a consulting firm (giving them a leg up on the learning curve) and created a concurrent process to modify and adapt it if needed as they went along. This accelerated approach is made possible because of lessons learned from the large number of companies

---

Look for "fire in the belly"

Geoff Turk, the 6s Corporate Champion at Caterpillar, advises companies that the people leading a Lean Six Sigma deployment should have a "fire in the belly."

"It's not an easy job," says Turk. There will be tough decisions to make and a lot of pressure to perform. There's going to be pushback; there's going to be all kind of resistance: Hidden resistance, quiet resistance, apparent buy-in with no real action and follow-through. He adds, "Management must lead it visibly and be in front of it."

that have already trod the path. This process is not for every company but it accelerated the time to results for them by at least two months.

Documenting the business case and developing the preliminary proposal

The Design Team is initially charged by the CEO and executive team to...

- Determine the gaps between current and desired performance

- Determine how Lean Six Sigma can close the gap

- Develop a preliminary design for the implementation of Lean Six Sigma

- Benchmark performance against other firms (if this wasn't done in the Readiness phase)

Timing of the Design/Deployment Team creation

The issue of establishing a Design/Deployment team has been delayed until the Mobilization phase based on the assumption that a company may want to select a Champion, do a readiness assessment, and begin building engagement before deciding which executives to assign to the team. However, some companies may find it works better for them to establish such a team back in the readiness phase so the executives can partner with the Champion from the start in overseeing deployment.

Establishing the difference between current and desired performance is important in giving your leadership a gut-level feeling about the magnitude of change required. You can make the initial gap analysis as complex or simple as you want, Minimally, it typically includes:

- You should have some data on your current performance, though it may take some effort to get reliable figures "Desired performance" will derive from long-term goals, though you may want to reframe some of them in customer-focused terms. Closing the gap between the current and desired performance should be part of the CEO's agenda. For example, how much better would you have to get at delighting your customers in order to grow revenues by 10%? to drive ROIC from 10% to 15%?

- Many companies find it beneficial to do benchmarking here, if they haven't done so already. Talking to other firms involved in Lean Six Sigma and understanding their challenges and results helps calibrate the gap established by internal figures and plans.

Once your Design team has completed the gap analysis (which establishes the business case for change), it needs to develop a preliminary design of the program, analyze the costs and benefits, and outline its implementation. Detailed plans around infrastructure and launch will happen in the next Phase; the purpose here is to sketch out the implementation framework. The design should include:

- The general organizational structure and staffing needed to support a Lean Six Sigma effort.

- Implementation targets and plans (general timelines for launch, numbers of people who will be dedicated, types of training, etc.).

- Financial metrics and their targets (both costs and benefits) linked to strategic goals. The benefits were most likely defined in your long-term goals. By far the largest investment is usually in the salary cost of the Black Belts and Champions, followed by the cost of training, hiring external consultants, etc.

- Estimated costs in terms of productivity loss and any decline in customer service that results from taking team members off their jobs to attend team meetings and work on improvements. (Do not underestimate this factor!)

This initial plan for the program will ensure that the management team understands Lean Six Sigma and its operational and financial benefits to the business. Sufficient depth of analysis is required such that the management team and, if necessary, the Board of Directors will understand the investment necessary and any risks involved.

At the end of these efforts, the Design team will report their findings about the applicability of Lean Six Sigma to your business, present a preliminary proposal for discussion, and recommend any needed outside assistance. A major component of this plan will be deciding how quickly and how extensively to deploy Lean Six Sigma:

- At Bank One, Mike Fischbach and his group decided that a well-supported demonstration phase that achieved significant, visible improvements was the best way to go.

- Caterpillar took the opposite approach, training 750 Black Belts per year based on their belief that "density drives cultural change." As Caterpillar's Geoff Turk explains, "In a large, distributed organization [like ours], in our culture... if you move slowly, your chances of success are pretty low. Snipers will pick off the guys who are doing it, and you'll never really get to the endpoint. Speed was our ally; we moved forward with a passionate, global tsunami that blanketed the entire organization around the globe all at once."

Mobilization Goal #2: Create the infrastructure

A Lean Six Sigma initiative will not succeed if it becomes just another silo in the company, a program conducted by people who have no connections to real work or business priorities (that was the unnecessary fate of TQM). Another failure mode is to expect that Lean Six Sigma can be done well by people who have other full-time jobs and responsibilities in the organization.

The way to avoid these pitfalls is to have a Lean Six Sigma infrastructure that weaves together people whose primary allegiance is the everyday work of the organization and people who have the improvement expertise and the time to inject Lean Six Sigma into that everyday work. The main types of role in each category are:

A. Positions with primary line responsibilities

- CEO

- Business unit/P&L managers

- Line managers (sponsors)

- Green Belts/White Belts/Team members

B. Positions with Lean Six Sigma responsibility

- Champions

- Black Belts

- Master Black Belts

A. Infrastructure Positions with Line Responsibilities

It's not just the people who will be working on Lean Six Sigma full-time who need to be educated and trained. Constantly expanding awareness of Lean Six Sigma and reinforcing its importance among anyone who will be guiding or supporting the efforts will be critical to success.

1) CEO/President

Besides being the person who ultimately determines whether the company will adopt Lean Six Sigma, the CEO also performs a role in infrastructure processes by…

- Consistently reinforcing the links between Lean Six Sigma and corporate strategy to direct reports (both unit managers and the company Champion, for example), employees, and shareholders (in his last letter to shareholders, Jack Welch mentioned Six Sigma fourteen times).

- Following up communication with action by focusing his/her attention on Lean Six Sigma issues with both direct reports (by monitoring detailed planning, informally inquiring about progress, etc.) and to the organization as a whole (through memos, presentations, etc.). Anne Mulcahy, the CEO of Xerox, led the way by attending a 3-day Lean Six Sigma training session with all her direct reports, as did CEO Vance Coffman of Lockheed Martin, and *all* of their managers.

- Monitoring the rolled-up results versus plan and taking corrective action.

- Making Lean Six Sigma nomenclature part of the warp and woof of management reviews.

The CEOs role in creating visibility

"I specifically ask for and try to create visibility around the Value-Based Six Sigma projects. We track the savings and we talk about that. I have Black Belt teams come in at a management site or a review and talk about their projects. When I have corporate-level reviews, I expect the management company presidents to talk about how [their VBSS efforts are] doing, what's working, what's not working, where the problems are, how they're doing against their plan. Each time they send me a monthly report they've got to highlight at least one key Black Belt project. At the corporate headquarters, on a weekly basis, we send out a corporate-wide e-mail on a project of the week. What that's done is share the best practices and trigger ideas."

—Lou Giuliano, CEO, ITT

2) Business Unit (P&I) managers

The Business Unit managers work with the Champion to clearly articulate the unit's strategy, which becomes the criteria by which the value streams and projects will be selected. The final decisions about which value streams to select and which projects to execute, and in which order, belong to the Business Unit manager. This integration continues as the Business Unit manager works with the Champion to…

- Use Lean Six Sigma to solve the most pressing problems in the business

- Create a Lean Six Sigma deployment plan for their unit

- Identify Black Belt candidates

- Develop and support Black Belts and other resources in their project work

- Make it a priority to provide the time to review team progress and hold line managers accountable for success to engage the workforce

3) Line managers/sponsors

Line managers are the people who own the processes that will be improved by Lean Six Sigma. They are often referred to as process owners and are responsible for the largest number of people in the processes. Most importantly, they are the people who must sustain and increase the benefit after a project is completed and the Black Belt moves on to a different project. The line managers' responsibilities include...

- Lead the way by educating themselves about Lean Six Sigma (often through joint training sessions with other line managers &/or direct reports)

- Aid in project selection within the value stream by using their intimate knowledge of the process, its customers and suppliers

- Help select Black Belts based on their knowledge of the candidates' capabilities

- Create an environment for project success

- Make implementation of the team recommendations a priority

- Work with the Unit Champion and Black Belts to help provide data and insight on the projects that the teams are working on

- Monitor the progress of the project by conducting DMAIC stage gate reviews

- Sustain the improvements and financial gains after the Black Belt has moved on to the next project

- Work with the Black Belt to select team members

4) Green Belts (Team Members)

A Green Belt works on a Lean Six Sigma project part-time, on a specific process in which he or she generally possesses knowledge important to the success of the project. The Green Belt will typically receive two weeks of training (often from the Black Belt) and will learn to apply the specific DMAIC skills that relate to the project at hand. In addition to assisting the Black Belt, a Green Belt may be assigned specific projects for independent execution. Green Belts have regular duties assigned by their line managers,

The critical role of sponsor

Next to having strong CEO support, perhaps the most pivotal point of contact between Lean Six Sigma and the rest of the organization occurs in the role of sponsor. A project sponsor is, by definition, a manager with P&L or other line responsibility; they control the resources needed to conduct a project, and are accountable for results. That makes them, also by definition, key influencers in our terminology. Here's what some of our contributors have to say about sponsors:

"In most cases you want a sponsor who's a process owner, someone who's going to own the outcome of the project once it's complete, and will be able to ensure that it's being sustained. When you don't have a process owner involved, and you make a change... when you go back a month or so later things will be back to the way they used to be because the owner wasn't involved in making that change."

—James Isaac, Director, Procurement Excellence,
Lockheed Martin SIBA MAC-MAR

"The reason why [sponsor involvement] is so critical, though, is the implementation component. If they're not hearing and understanding what changes are being asked of them by the team, then they're not going to buy into the process."

—Darryl Greene, Senior VP, Bank One

but usually they regard the Green Belt position as an opportunity to excel and gain valuable tools and experience. A growing number of companies are encouraging project sponsors to become Green Belts.

5) White (or the company color) Belts

White Belts are another part-time resource that some organizations use to expand the pool of people who have some understanding of Lean Six Sigma goals and tools. White Belts receive 2–4 hours of awareness training through classroom, distance learning, books and/or articles. Project participation is generally NOT required for White Belts. Another approach is to exploit "teachable moments" where a resident Black Belt (or other expert) provides just-in-time training on specific concepts or tools helpful in solving a problem or answering a question that people are facing on the job. The White Belt may take the initiative to join a team as a potential Green Belt resource and make a contribution to the continuous improvement process.

> **Driving cultural change**
>
> "If Six Sigma's going to become not only the unusual way you do unusual work—the stuff you kind of do on the side to improve the day-to-day operations—but more and more the way you do all your work, you've got to keep driving the density of trained employees."
>
> —Geoff Turk, 6σ Corporate Deployment Champion, Caterpillar

B. New Infrastructure Positions with Specific Lean Six Sigma Responsibilities

There are two categories of dedicated Lean Six Sigma resources, familiar to anyone who knows about Six Sigma: Champions and Black Belts.

1) Champions

In any major initiative, there will be just a few people (or roles) that have a bigger influence on success or failure than practically everyone else combined. Champions fall into that category. The qualities those people have are key to their success.

> Brian is a highly regarded Champion in one of the premier organizations using Lean Six Sigma. Ironically, he credits his ability to work outside the Lean Six Sigma infrastructure for his success. He learned how to "sell" his ideas. His skills in using tools such as style flex (being able to adapt his working style to various situations and individuals), understanding team roles, and understanding leadership styles helped him navigate through a corporate jungle and be successful. It really boiled down to influence management.

In discussions with successful Champions like Brian, most state that their ability to effectively manage people—to connect with individuals or groups within their sphere of influence—was even more important than their knowledge of Six Sigma's tools.

A corporate Champion should report directly to the CEO or President, as applicable (this direct reporting relationship is critical); divisional or business unit Champions should report directly to the person in charge of that unit. A corporate Champion's *primary responsibility* is to ensure that the rest of the company executes a consistent, rapid deployment. Because of this requirement and the need to be able to address major barriers that will arise, the corporate Champion must be a strong and respected manager and leader. Other responsibilities include:

> **Layers of Champions**
>
> Larger organizations will typically have multiple layers of Champions to correspond to their business structure. The corporate Champion has company-wide responsibility and should report directly to the CEO. Business-unit Champions will typically report directly to their business unit head, and have dotted line responsibility to the corporate Champion. This type of arrangement reinforces the notion that Lean Six Sigma is there to support line managers, not to become a parallel structure in the organization.

- Work with the P&L managers to select the projects and value streams that have the largest potential for value creation

- Develop the Lean Six Sigma schedule and deployment plans for the unit (in conjunction with the unit manager and corporate Design/Deployment team)

- Oversee the deployment of Lean Six Sigma (either corporate-wide or in their business unit, depending on their level of accountability)

- Ensure that 1% of the employee population becomes Black Belts (except in operations that are very capital-intensive relative to the number of employees, in which case a rule of 1 Black Belt per $20 million in revenue is used)

- Manage the project queue and restock the pipeline as needed with high-potential projects: monitor and adjust the number of projects in process as appropriate to control lead time to results (by applying Little's Law, see p. 30), track project status, track project completion rate, compile results

- Identify and, with the Business Unit manager, remove barriers to deployment
  - Lead the process for proper selection of high value projects based on strategic fit, ROIC, Revenue Growth, and hence shareholder value (see Chp 4)
  - Present projects derived from a value analysis to P&L managers for approval and integration into strategic results
  - Provide mentorship, management, and performance review
  - Intervene when teams are stuck

- Provide communication (up and down)
  - Keep the Unit Manager informed of team progress
  - Ensure that best practices are widely shared
  - Compile and track Lean Six Sigma results for presentation to the CEO and executive team

- Work to achieve business unit engagement, not compliance

- Work with the unit's Controller to validate the bottom line impact of each improvement

- Provide integration for cross-business-unit processes and across silos to make sure the Voice of the Customer is represented and avoid suboptimization related to both project scope and utilization of Black Belts

- Resolve conflicts in any aspect of deployment (Black Belt non-performance, lack of support by sponsors, etc.)

2) *Black Belts & Master Black Belts*

Black Belts are full-time positions responsible for leading project teams. (Some organizations have chosen to not have full-time Black Belts even though there are some risks involved. This issue is discussed below.) They are responsible for delivering the value and benefits that were determined for each project during the selection process. Specific Black Belt responsibilities include...

- Achieving the goals of the project (which should be viewed as a contract with management)

- Working with the project sponsor (line manager) and unit Champion to formulate and implement improvement projects and select team members

- Training Green Belts in the DMAIC process (as anyone who has ever served as an instructor knows, you learn much more about a subject when you have to teach it to someone else)

- Bringing a standard approach to solving a problem

- Keeping teams on track relative to what they're trying to achieve within the agreed-on time frame

- Enforcing a process discipline

- Coaching and mentoring Green Belts and team members as needed

Black Belt candidates receive extensive training, usually at least a five-week course built around the Lean Six Sigma improvement process, tools, and leadership skills. To become "certified" by their organization, they must also complete a training project and one or two additional projects with total annualized hard benefits of at least $500,000 per year on average, and must have conducted Green Belt training.

Master Black Belts are internal expert consultants to Black Belts and their teams. As such, the Master Black Belts must be experienced in successfully managing improvement teams to reach goals using improvement tools and skilled leadership. In fact, a typical Master Black Belt will

"You don't need everybody in the company to be a Black Belt. You would like as many people as possible to be Green Belt trained so they have a basic level of knowledge, but don't have to be considered experts. A mature Lean Six Sigma organization will have institutionalized Lean Six Sigma to where Green Belts run the majority of projects with guidance from a Black Belt, leaving Black Belts to concentrate on strategic cross-functional projects."

—James Isaac, Director Procurement Excellence,
Lockheed Martin, SIBA MAC-MAR

have worked as a Black Belt and completed 5 to 10 projects with annualized benefits of $1 million per year.

The education and grooming of Master Black Belts is an important process in the organization. During early implementation, few organizations have people with the proper expertise, which is why external consultants often fill this role. Eventually, as Black Belts get more hands-on experience with teams, they can be certified as Master Black Belts once they gain training experience and additional education in their specialty area. (After completing their own training, Master Black Belt candidates become certified by co-teaching a five-week Black Belt training cycle, then leading a second cycle on their own except for a Master Black Belt who will approve the certification.)

C. Selecting Candidates to Fill the Infrastructure Roles

Here's another area where experienced practitioners of Six Sigma all agree: the companies who have been the most successful in deploying Lean Six Sigma have selected Black Belts and Champions with the view that they are future leaders of the organization. As a result of their Six Sigma experience, these people will have demonstrated their leadership skills, their problem-solving and process improvement skills, and an ability to make a difference in the organization. They will also have become attuned to opportunities to create shareholder value. Who else would you pick as leader?

For this reason, candidates are typically chosen based as much or more on their innate leadership than on their technical or problem-solving skills. The latter will come quickly: being full-time, dedicated resources, they will receive extensive training and cycle through numerous projects even if they are only in the position for a few years.

There are two practical issues you have to deal with here:

- First, how you will select and choose the candidates to be sent to training

- Second, how you will deal with the vacancies created when those selected leave their positions

Selection processes vary widely. Some organizations treat the Black Belt, Master Black Belt, and Champion positions as they would any other: developing and refining job descriptions, asking for candidates to submit their names, going through a formal review, and so on. Others hand-pick the people they think will be good candidates. Some decide to hire new people into these positions (particularly Master Black Belts and Champions, positions where there's no substitute for experience); others decide to solely promote from within (with the concomitant commitment to rapid, extensive training of the MBBs and Champions). Whichever method you use, the ultimate decision should be based on the individuals' leadership potential.

At ITT, they asked for volunteers. Why? "Think about who might volunteer to do something like this," says CEO Lou Giuliano. "The only people who would sign up for something like this were people who thought there needed to be a change, who were willing to take a risk, and who wanted to have an impact on the organization. Those are exactly the types of people that we're looking for." By making Black Belt selection a hallmark assignment, says Giuliano, the people they got, particularly in the first round, have turned out to be key players in the organization.

Afraid of losing your Black Belts?

Some companies fear that their reward for investing in training Black Belts will be seeing those people depart to competitors. Experience has shown that the number one cause of Black Belt "loss" is through promotion (a good thing!). Running a distant second is having them resign their positions due to frustration or lack of support.

Similarly, decisions about how to deal with vacancies vary. Most organizations choose not to replace those who move into Lean Six Sigma positions for a multitude of reasons, some symbolic (having managers demonstrate commitment by "giving up" an employee) and some practical (gains made from early improvements will eliminate a lot of non-value-add work and you may find you don't need as many employees anymore). Remember that the goal is to use 1% of the organizations staff as full-time resources to generate far more than a 1% return on that investment!

D. Balancing the Roles: The RACI chart

In setting up a Lean Six Sigma infrastructure, you also set up many potential conflicts in authority and responsibility. Being clear about the responsibilities of both the P&L and Lean Six Sigma roles will help you avoid innumerable conflicts.

A **RACI** (pronounced ra-see) format that helps people sort out and clarify responsibilities is a useful tool for this situation. The letters stand for different levels of expectation:

- **Responsibility**, people who are expected to actively participate in the activity and contribute to the best of their abilities

- **Accountability**, the person who is ultimately held responsible for the results

- **Consultation**, people who either have a particular expertise they can contribute to specific decisions (i.e., their advice will be sought) or who must be consulted with for some other reason *before* a final decision is made (e.g., finance is often in a consultation role to projects)

- **Inform**, people who are affected by the activity/decision and therefore need to be kept informed, but do not participate in the effort (they are notified *after* the final decisions are made)

The principles in making RACI decisions are captured in Table 8.1, along with the risks you run if you choose a different alternative.

The guidelines in Table 8.1 are just that; general principles that work in most circumstances for most organizations. However, every organization is unique, and you'll have to find a balance between sticking with the principles (which are known to work) and accommodating special circumstances in your organization (especially if ignoring those circumstances will generate resistance).

Because each organization will divide roles and responsibilities differently, RACI is not a "one size fits all" model; Table 8.2 shows an example of how you can document the way you would like roles and responsibilities to work, but the specifics may vary for your organization.

Table 8.1: RACI Principles

Design Principle	Risk if Violated
Accountability for project results rests with the process owner or P&L manager	Resources may not be committed and/or results will not be sustained.
Black Belts subordinate to the business	If Black Belts are held accountable for results, their agendas may replace that of the P&L managers they are supposed to support. Eventually, they will be perceived as elite specialists and resented. Six Sigma can become isolated and eventually ineffective.
Program governance & resource allocation authority must be concentrated in one person / role (the corporate deployment Champion)	If there is no single, executive-level person held accountable for overseeing Lean Six Sigma, constantly managing the project pipeline, and making the required judgment calls when conflicts arise, you'll end up with suboptimization of an effort, weak accountability for program results, and a depleted project pipeline after the initial rush.
The key influencers must participate in direction setting for the Lean Six Sigma program (project selection, Black Belt selection, resource contribution, and how to address organizational barriers)	As discussed in Chapter 7, it's critical to have full engagement of the organization in Lean Six Sigma, beginning with key influencers and then cascading out from there. If that doesn't happen, if people not directly involved with Lean Six Sigma are kept in the dark, you'll end up with compliance, not commitment, to the Lean Six Sigma philosophy. Ultimately, the link between strategy and execution will also break down.
Accountability should be pushed down as low as possible	If the organization's executives hold onto all or most of the accountability, employees will continue looking upward for approval / permission—resulting in gridlock, and reinforcing the notion that nothing has truly changed. You may also end up with poor decisions because those at the top lack the local knowledge held by the people who work with the processes every day.
RACI must be published publicly and discussed with all those affected	Going through the exercise of developing a RACI chart will gain meaning only when the outcomes are acted upon. (Otherwise, you will have wasted time on something that winds up being a non-implemented planning tool.)

Table 8.2: The RACI Method
for Clarifying Lean Six Sigma Roles

Activity=> Task	Own the LSS Deployment	Identify Projects	Select Projects	Project Results	Project Execution	Team Support	Sustain Changes
Exec Team	**A**	**R**	**A**				
Champion	**R**	**A**	**R**			**R**	
P&L Management		**I**		**A**		**R**	**R**
Process Owner		**C**		**R**	**R**	**R**	**A**
Black Belt		**C**		**R**	**R**	**A**	
Tm Leader/Green Belt				**R**	**R**		
ETC							

This excerpt of a RACI table shows how it can clarify roles (their level of participation). List only one "A" [accountability] for each activity. The division between "responsibility" and "accountability" is often not clear, and most organizations discuss the issues at length to reach consensus. For example, since Black Belts are positioned as support for teams, they cannot be held accountable for team results—though they can be held accountable for providing expert support. (The project sponsor usually has the "A" for project results.)

There are a number of key decisions you'll face as you complete a RACI chart. One of them will be the balance of power between Black Belts and teams. Black Belts are put in a delicate situation: On the one hand, they have a lot of knowledge that teams and line management can use to make the project a success. On the other hand, if they impose their knowledge on those they are supposedly helping, they're sending the message that Lean Six Sigma means "do it my way." As a rule, Black Belts should be positioned in the role of support staff, not decision makers, because they are not experts in, nor do they have any ongoing responsibility for, the work. (There's more discussion on this issue in Chp 10.)

E. Decisions Surrounding Infrastructure

Think of creating the Lean Six Sigma infrastructure the same way as you would starting a new company division from scratch. There are dozens of decisions to make; we'll focus here on three that are particularly important or contentious:

1. Whether the resources will be full-time or part-time

2. Reporting relationships among the Lean Six Sigma resources and between them and line management

3. Compensation tied to project results

1) Full-time or part-time resources

Ask anyone who's been involved in Six Sigma deployments, and they'll tell you that results come more quickly when Lean Six Sigma Black Belts are full-time because they can:

- Concentrate their attention

- Simultaneously coach a number of teams (which means improvement proceeds faster)

- Spend their time applying tools to investigate the root causes of quality and speed problems (which is a challenge for team members who have only a fraction of a Black Belt's training and can only devote some of their attention to the problem)

- Quickly gain a lot of experience with improvement

- Serve as neutral resources since they have no other current job affiliation (and therefore are the perfect type of coach for cross-functional teams)

- Get results faster

Yet some service organizations balk at adopting a traditional Six Sigma infrastructure because they can't afford to pull people out of their regular jobs to be full-time Black Belts. In fact, only one of the organizations profiled in Part I (Bank One) had their Black Belts (which they call internal consultants) working full-time from the beginning of their deployment; the others used part-time resources initially, but have already or are moving towards making at least some of them full-time.

"The risk of using part-time instead of full-time Black Belts is that their managers have no skin in the game and can more easily pull them back into their old jobs," says Mike Joyce of Lockheed Martin. "We have found that this does not happen if the manager [understands] how Lean Six Sigma is solving his or her biggest problems."

Another risk, pointed out by Roger Hirt of Fort Wayne, is that part-time Black Belts usually work on projects within their work area—which means you lose the "outside eye" that happens when full-time Black Belts are brought into an unfamiliar area. "When you're working on a process that's self-contained within one organization or function, it always makes good sense to have someone who does not really have a stake in the process and may not even be an expert come in and shake up the dynamics a little bit," says Hirt. "They can ask questions that sometimes may seem like dumb questions, and they may see things that are not real obvious to folks that are the experts because they don't have any stake in the existing process."

That said, it must be acknowledged that the organizations profiled in this book don't see the lack of full-time Black Belts as an excuse to not move forward—and have proven that a lot can be done with part-time resources. At Lockheed Martin's Naval Electronics Surveillance System's group in Moorestown, New Jersey, for example, all the Black Belts were part-time at first. They have started moving some of these people into full-time Black Belt positions as a result of the gains achieved, which have provided not only a strong financial incentive for focusing more on Lean Six Sigma, but also greater flexibility in staffing (currently, 9 of their 65 Black Belts are full time) with most reporting to their functional organizations. At the end of 2002, Fort Wayne had no full-time Black Belts; all of their Black Belts spent only 10-20% of their time on projects. As Roger Hirt will tell you, results come a lot slower... but you do get results and you do get started. Stanford had full-time trainers and coaches only in the first few years of its quality initiative; in later years, managerial staff often served as team facilitators in addition to their regular jobs.

These decisions also impact your expectations about how much work a Black Belt could or should handle. Obviously, a full-time Black Belt could be expected to support more projects than a part-time Black Belt; or you can still assign them to only one or two projects and shorten the time frame of when you expect results.

Bottom-line: Having full-time Champions and Black Belts sends a strong message that leadership is truly committed to making Lean Six Sigma work. More importantly, full-time Black Belts and Champions will pay for themselves more quickly than those who are part-time. You should work to convince your P&L managers that they are not "losing" their employees who move into full-time Lean Six Sigma positions. Rather—and generally for the first time—these resources are being used to create a critical mass of trained resources who will help achieve P&L goals by working on the value streams with the greatest potential for creating value.

2) Reporting relationships

The caveat in creating roles whose primary responsibility is Lean Six Sigma implementation is to make sure they don't lose sight of the business's strategic goals and start pushing the *method* over the *goal*. Another silo-bound path is having line management perceive that Lean Six Sigma projects are draining away resources and attention needed to achieve their annual goals. If that happens, Lean Six Sigma resources will quickly become marginalized to trivial projects and denied the support *they* need to complete projects on time and in budget.

That's why it's important to push connections between line positions and Lean Six Sigma positions in any way that you can. At Caterpillar, this problem was resolved by having Black Belts report directly to the P&L manager. In this way, the managers were intimately involved in project selection and weren't "losing" resources to efforts they deemed irrelevant to their business unit. It also helps increase Black Belt commitment to the results of their projects.

On the other hand, you don't want Black Belts and Champions to feel isolated from each other. There's a lot to be said for fostering close connections among these resources: they can discuss problems or challenges with others who understand their situation, find guidance, learn from each other, and thus progress more quickly. So you also need to avoid the extreme of having Black Belts or Champions connect *only* to line management. Minimally, therefore, you might want to also create "dotted line" responsibilities between the dedicated Lean Six Sigma positions. (Some companies have performed quite well even in switching the relationships: direct reporting of Black Belts to Champions; dotted line to P&L management.)

Also, there is one reporting relationship that should be non-negotiable: Ultimately, the CEO or its equivalent is the chief steward of customer needs and shareholder value. The job of the corporate Champion is to provide him or her with the input needed to make decisions about whether Lean Six Sigma is contributing to or detracting from those goals. Having the Champion report directly to the CEO helps position Lean Six Sigma as strategically important and allows the two to act in confidence of fully understanding the organization's needs.

3) *Compensation tied to project results*

Compensation has never been an easy issue, and it doesn't get any easier when dealing with Lean Six Sigma resources. On the one hand, you hope these people represent future leaders of the company, and they will likely be held to high performance expectations, so they need to be compensated accordingly. But does that mean that they should receive bonuses of some sort based on gains from their projects? Before you say yes, consider what happens to the other team members—do they share, too? And what happens to employees not on the team but who picked up extra work so that others could be. Don't they deserve some recognition?

Each company has to make these decisions for itself, but it will be important for your deployment team to wrestle with these issues *before* people are put into Lean Six Sigma positions. What will help is having the deployment team define criteria for their decision, such as whether it must be more likely to foster teamwork than resentment, whether it must be consistent with existing compensation standards or establish a new pattern, whether there should be some reward for exceeding expectations, and so on.

Because the variability in approaches is so great, we suggest you do some benchmarking with other companies that are using a variety of approaches to help establish your own guidelines. These will vary from no additional compensation to Black Belts, to team compensation, to detailed project-by-project compensation.

Mobilization Goal #3: Develop training

Six Sigma is not a "feel good" process like Quality Circles of the 1980s. You are training people to produce bottom line measurable results on the highest ROIC projects. To use your training effectively, tailor the content, duration, and approach to the various audiences.

- Executives attend a three-day overview that includes an introduction to Six Sigma principles, a simulation of the DMAIC process, and leadership training.

- Process owners (e.g., P&L managers), who will be using Six Sigma to drive their individual and departmental goals, benefit from more extensive training, usually a one-week course that covers everything the executives got but in more detail.

- The people who will directly coach and guide teams (Black Belts, Champions) receive 4 to 6 weeks of training (see sidebar).

- Green Belts receive one to two weeks of training and support, customized to the projects they are working on.

- The balance of the company should ultimately receive some level of Six Sigma orientation.

As you can see, there is a lot to cover in training people to become adept at DMAIC and its tools. Use the time effectively by...

1) **Focusing the curriculum on relevant tools.** Early Six Sigma-only curricula often focused a lot of time on the more sophisticated statistical tools. One course allocated 25% of the instructional time to Design of Experiments, for example. Yet data gathered via web-based tracking software on what tools were actually being used at

several companies revealed that only about 5% of projects used DOE; 40% needed Lean. The solution that many companies have adopted is to keep the general Black Belt training focused on tools and skills that they know their teams will need (including leadership and teamwork skills, not just statistical tools).

2) **Incorporating a lot of project work.** The usual pattern in Black Belt training is to have 1 week of course work followed by 2 to 4 weeks of application, where they work real-time on one or more projects. There should be plenty of time allotted during the training sessions

---

Black Belt Training

A well-rounded Black Belt training program includes:

- 4 to 6 weeks of classroom training, starting with 1 week of leadership training. The remaining 3 to 5 weeks are spread out and interspersed with project work. A Black Belt attends a week of training, returns to project work for a few weeks, comes back for the second week of training, and so on.

- Diverse instructional techniques: demonstration, simulation, student practice, exercises.

- A curriculum that includes Lean, Six Sigma, and complexity reduction tools (see Fig 11.1 in Chp 11). Presenting both Lean and Six Sigma simultaneously shows the trainees that they are complementary, not competing, methods, and equips them to attack *any* problem. The course should also cover project management skills (planning, action tracking, critical path).

- Expert coaching (opportunities for one-on-one or small group interactions centered around project needs) to increase the socialization process and accelerate internalization (typically 5-10 days across the overall training cycle).

- Individual testing to provide feedback on the effectiveness of learning.

- Application of new methods on real projects so participants can internalize new skills.

- Access to training materials, case studies, and other resources through both printed and electronic means.

---

for the Black Belts to share what they're doing with their peers and get guidance/advice.

3) **Tailoring the level to the competencies of the average student.** In my own company's experience participants in the "service" version of our Black Belt training are typically less numerate than their manufacturing counterparts. The courses must therefore be adjusted in terms of both the number and complexity of the statistical tools, with emphasis made on service applications. For example, more emphasis is placed on complexity value stream mapping and data collection.

For all of these reasons, you will also want to develop separate deep skill enrichment courses on topics like DOE and even separate advanced curricula on Lean and other statistical topics that could be offered to Black Belts or Master Black Belts. Lessons from companies who have been through such training before include:

- Leadership skills are essential for all dedicated Lean Six Sigma resources. Even if your Champion and Black Belts already have some leadership experience—and especially if they don't—it's essential to include leadership training as part of your curriculum. (It can also help your experienced managers work together more effectively, so should be considered for training your executives, P&L managers, and sponsors/process owners.)

- Champion and Black Belt training should overlap but typically are not identical. Black Belts need much more depth on the tools; Champions need additional skills such as project selection based on ROIC and project tracking.

The emphasis on leadership skills should come as no surprise. Black Belts and Champions alike have to be able to deal with people who are uncomfortable with or even threatened by the change (perhaps they fear losing their job). They've got to be able to explain to the organization why Lean Six Sigma is good for the organization, why they need everyone's help, what's going to change, what's going to be the result.

You can avoid many problems by funding training out of a centralized corporate budget (as Lou Giuliano says, "If I think this is important, I've got to demonstrate that I believe it's important. So I'm going to pay for the training.") If you want to charge the P&L centers, initiate this charge after they have outstanding results, and they'll cheerfully pay.

The Champion as VOC Guard Dog

An important role of a Champion is to prioritize project selection based on value, making sure there is a balance between identifying projects that are manageable but also significant to customers. Keep in mind that external customers don't see the results of any individual process in your organization; they only experience the results of the entire value stream. As you get more experience in project management and process improvement, start thinking in terms of "value stream" improvement, not "process improvement." That might mean, for example, that you work several different projects simulta-neously with multiple teams or even multiple Black Belts on an entire value stream to try to effect a change that the customer actually sees and is willing to pay for.

Mobilization Goal #4: Select and charter first-wave projects

Lean Six Sigma lives and dies with project discovery, prioritization, and selection. The traditional approach has often allowed Black Belts to pick projects, sometimes with input from Champions and process owners. This seldom led to projects that were related to corporate strategy or prioritized around ROIC. Often, too many projects were launched, leading to long lead times to results (as you would predict from Little's Law). Black Belts sometimes competed for resources. Over the past few years, a growing number of companies have based project selection and prioritization on shareholder value as covered in Chapter 4:

Step 1: Identifying the burning platform for the organization as a whole and for each business unit

Step 2: Completing a complexity value stream map to pinpoint the Time Traps

Step 3: Determining what approach to use on the targeted Time Traps

The purpose of this process is to make sure that projects support business needs. Management must know how to use properly structured processes to select projects. Involving key managers in this project selection creates an instantaneous link between line management and the Lean Six Sigma team, which preempts the possibility of a Lean Six Sigma silo developing.

Project chartering

The objective of a project charter is to commission a project that has a clear scope and ties to financial and strategic objectives. The charter should include a product/service description, business case, project goals, project scope, a high-level project plan, and list team members. The charter should be sufficiently detailed so that the business objectives and the scope are clear to both the team and the management. The Black Belt and the project team receive a draft of the charter from the Leadership Team. Projects should only be launched that have been through a rigorous prioritization and selection process.

It is important to view the charter as a contract between all the people associated with a project: the sponsoring P&L manager, the Champion, the Black Belt, Green Belt, and other team members. It represents a two-way commitment: management will commit a certain level of resources (time, people, equipment, etc.) and capital to a project, and in return the team will deliver results in a certain time frame. You'll find more detail on chartering projects in Chapter 11.

Mobilization Goal #5:
Reach consensus on common metrics

Anyone experienced with corporate life knows that what gets *measured* gets *done*. Measuring Lean Six Sigma results and making sure there is the projected bottom line impact is an important element in managing your deployment. Inspect what you expect.

A word of warning: reaching consensus on *common* metrics is seldom easy, and you'd best be prepared to spend a fair amount of time up front...

- Deciding what it is you want to know.

- Identifying which existing systems generate the kind of information you need (and making sure those systems are reliable and used consistently across the organization).

- Developing new systems to fill in the gaps.

- Really digging for the "critical Xs that drive the final "Y" results. One dynamic that Lean Six Sigma tends to remedy in many organizations is the tendency to focus on final results rather than the critical factors that drive those results. Choosing the correct input, process, and output variables to measure is a vital component of making Lean Six Sigma a sustainable part of the organizations culture.

Typical metric systems include ways to measure both hard savings (dollar impact on the bottom line) and soft savings (improvements that result in cost avoidance, that delight customers, that remove a lot of hassle in the workplace, etc., but that are difficult to track to the bottom line and translate into dollar figures). Often times, it's difficult or impossible to make a one-to-one correlation between your project results and what the P&L statement says, especially in today's environment where changes in pricing and other changes in the organization are happening faster and faster. Savings from projects can get eaten up in other ways. "But I also know, because I have some history with these operations, that we wouldn't be improving margins in flattened-down markets if something else wasn't happening that was making a positive difference," says Lou Giuliano.

As with any metric system, you should include both indicators of results (the Ys) and the process itself (or Xs). Typical measures are listed in Figure 8.1.

Figure 8.1: Typical Indicators to Track For Lean Six Sigma

Financial results	**Scope of effort**
Project return on investment [1, 2]	# of Black Belts/Green Belts trained [1]
Avg return per Black Belt or per project [2]	# of projects completed [1]
	Average time to certify Black Belts [2]
Before/after project results...	**Project duration**
Process cycle time [2]	Overall time to completion [2]
Defect levels [3]	Avg time spent in each phase of DMAIC [2]
Customer satisfaction ratings [2,3]	# of projects per Black Belt per year [2]
Waste/scrap [3]	
Rework [3]	

1 = single data point (or time plot of periodic measures)
2 = histograms (frequency plots) showing average and mean
3 = time plot(s) or control chart(s) for each process or metric

Conclusion

The people who have contributed to this book all use terms like "significant" or "huge" or "substantial" to describe the amount of work needed to successfully mobilize resources throughout their organizations. In short, it's hard work. And the impact of the decisions described in this chapter, and all of those we didn't have space to address, are truly important—meaning the choices you make have a significant impact on whether Lean Six Sigma becomes THE best way for your employees to achieve their business goals or whether it will be here-and-gone like so many of its predecessors.

> "The biggest single difference in this part of the journey from all the other continuous improvement efforts that I've made is having dedicated resources."
>
> —Lou Giuliano, CEO, ITT

The main weakness in those predecessors, as Giuliano indicates, was that they lacked infrastructure. There was no way to coordinate the results of diverse projects, to standardize methodologies in order to accelerate learning and improvement, to compare value-creation potential across diverse sections of your organization. Few people worked on improvement full-time, and any efforts were diluted by the everyday pressures to get the job done. (This is why we express caution in relation to part-time Black Belts.)

The good news is that you don't have to invent the infrastructure wheel. There are hundreds of companies out there deploying Six Sigma or Lean Six Sigma, some of which are likely similar to yours, and all of which you can learn from. Use their lessons—whether they've succeeded or failed—to better inform your own decisions and jump start your own learning curve.

CHAPTER 9

Phase 4:
Performance and Control

Y ou've identified, selected, and trained Champions and Black Belts. You've communicated with the organization about what Lean Six Sigma is and how it will be used strategically. You've developed project charters and sent teams off on their journeys. What comes next? Let's hear again from Lou Giuliano, someone quoted often in this part of the book because he has such excellent advice:

> What it takes is **constant attention**. Every time I visit units we talk about this, in our business reviews we talk about these efforts. I go to the training classes, I go to the Best Practices symposiums, and I get other people talking about it.... You've got to have some other people in the organization who can pay attention to what's really happening, figuring out who's getting it and who's not getting it, figuring out who's backsliding and deciding, 'Well, I'll send people to training but I won't let them work full-time,' and go out and confront those issues and get the process working.
>
> —Lou Giuliano, CEO, ITT

That's what this chapter is about: how you pay attention to your Lean Six Sigma deployment, and what you should be paying attention to.

Planning Ahead: What will happen when you start getting results?

Throughout this book, we've said that even though Lean means "cutting costs," you shouldn't equate that with "cutting people," though there have been some companies who have had to use it for that purpose. To truly get to excellence, you have to capture the hearts and minds of every employee, as well as their hands. If you have to lay off people, do it before Lean Six Sigma is deployed. People will have to work harder and longer to compensate for the staff reductions, but finding they can often cut out 20–40% of their work (the non-value-add portion) is a great incentive for adopting Lean Six Sigma.

This issue is just one of several that can appear once your Lean Six Sigma is up and running, but that can be prevented or minimized by up-front planning. Let's look at:

1) How to adjust to requiring less time to do the work (and perhaps fewer people)

2) What to do about rotating Black Belts into management positions

Issue 1: What happens when you can do the same work in less time?

"You have to be careful because a lot of companies use value-added analysis as a rationale for laying people off," says Mike Joyce of Lockheed Martin. "There are two sensibilities here. The first one is that is just pure business, and I think most people understand capitalism. If there is no business out there, I've got to shrink. It has nothing to do with the work we do or how we do it, or the people or how good or bad they are. It's just the reality that this market is nonexistent anymore at the size that we need it. So if it's a market-driven thing, then yes, you've got to lay people off to survive.

"But that's a completely separate issue from 'I need people to help me get better,'" says Joyce. "The more distance you can put between those two realities, the better off you are. At Lockheed, we said, look, LM21 is definitely going to change the distribution of work and where people get deployed. It's going to happen, especially in areas like materials management, where we know our stockrooms are targets for eliminating idle inventory… we're going to have people that can be redeployed. **The key is that we know this a year in advance of its happening.** So it's management's job to decide how we are going to redeploy those people, and what we have to do to get them ready for redeployment."

A similar issue was faced at Stanford Hospital and Clinics, though in the early years, says Karen Rago, she was more concerned about getting enough staff to provide good care for Stanford's patients. She'd spend her evenings and weekends making emergency calls to staff trying to get them to work even *more* overtime. But then the improvement efforts starting paying off... and many areas were wildly successful in reducing the hours of care. Unfortunately, that happened at a time when patient loads were dropping, so she suddenly found herself overstaffed—and Rago was now making calls telling people to stay home. Fortunately, at that time she had enough staff who didn't mind losing the hours so she could let attrition take care of reducing the workforce without needing to lay off anyone. In fact, throughout her more than two decades at Stanford, there were very few layoffs thanks to proactive planning and attrition.

In other organizations, people freed up are used on teams to produce further improvements. Often, when demand outstrips available resources, the new improved processes are able to deliver more revenue with the same cost, but with much greater efficiency combined with greater job satisfaction. Where headcount reductions are unavoidable, careful upfront planning and instituting early retirement programs can be used to address these reductions.

Issue 2: Can you really rotate Black Belts into management positions?

One tradition associated with Lean Six Sigma is that the people chosen to be Black Belts are being groomed to segue into leadership positions after two or three years. The question you have to ask yourself is whether you can afford to make that promise to people.

The answer is yes. Caterpillar, for instance, went through a down cycle that started in the late 1980s and continued for six or seven years, where they simply didn't hire many new people. To them, using Lean Six Sigma experience as a way to quickly raise the professional skills of highly qualified people is a godsend that will allow them to more easily fill leadership vacancies that will open in the coming years. The Lockheed Martin SMEs (subject matter experts) are in a similar position: their intensive experience with Lean Six Sigma is viewed as an asset, and they are, indeed, being rotated into managerial positions. Experience has shown that the major problem is that Black Belts are promoted into management positions before their two-year assignment is completed.

Avoiding the Pitfalls in Lean Six Sigma Deployment

A *Fortune* 100 company involved in Six Sigma deployment commented to one of its suppliers who was in a similar situation, "We had the same vision as you, but we ended up in an entirely different place. We slid from a transformational change deployment back down to a targeted deployment because we let people have part-time Black Belts, we let people call this an initiative, we let other initiatives coexist with it and saw it as just one of many initiatives instead of the thing we're going to do to drive the strategy into reality." Oddly enough, this company has put some pretty significant results on their bottom line—but they said, "If we'd just had full-time resources, and created an environment where Lean Six Sigma was seen as THE best way to achieve corporate goals, we would have four times as much money."

This company was doing very well by some standards, but a few years into deployment recognized how much more they could have achieved had they taken steps to avoid some of the most common pitfalls:

1. Allowing projects to drift away from strategic management priorities or allow project scope to creep outwards, jeopardizing the results and schedule

2. Undertaking too many projects at the same time, which clogs the pipeline and reduces productivity the same way that too much work-in-process leads to delays and waste in any process (Little's Law)

3. Inadequate tracking of results

4. Little or no sharing of best practices

5. Forgetting about the people not directly involved in deployment

Pitfall #1: Drifting away from priorities

The problem of drift is most acute in organizations that do not have links between Lean Six Sigma resources and P&L management, that don't invest their Champions with the power to select projects based on shareholder value, and/or that allow projects to proceed without P&L management oversight. This pitfall can be avoided by using complexity value stream mapping to identify project opportunities, and by following a good DMAIC system that includes tollgate reviews by Sponsors and other managers between phases (see Figure 9.1). You need to decide:

- How often and in what way Sponsors, Champions, and others will review projects

- What metrics or indicators will be watched

- What other processes will be used to monitor progress and keep projects on track

Figure 9.1: The DMAIC Process With Tollgates

Define	Measure	Analyze	Improve	Control
1. Establish Team Charter	4. Confirm Team Goal	7. Determine Process Capability and Speed	9. Generate Ideas	15. Develop Control Plan
2. Identify Sponsor and Team Resources	5. Define Current State	8. Determine Sources of Variation and Time Bottlenecks	10. Conduct Experiments	16. Monitor Implementation
3. Administer Prework	6. Collect and Display Data		11. Create Straw Models	17. Mistake-Proof the Process
			12. Conduct Benefits & Concerns Analysis	
			13. Develop Action Plans	
			14. Implement	

In addition, it must be clear which people or roles have what accountability and responsibility (see Chp 8, p. 224). Monitoring and accountability provides the means to judge whether a project is on track to contribute to positive business results, or straying from its charter.

Pitfall #2: Too many projects in the pipeline

Avoiding the second pitfall requires your organization to be judicious in how resources are deployed. It's better to focus on getting a few high-potential projects done right than to just flood your workplace with dozens of less-important projects. When you have the right resources working on the right things, learning and results are maximized by short project cycle times.

Given that everyone's goal is to run projects that will give measurably significant results within a year, the tendency is to push as many projects into the improvement process as can be defined. But an example from Chapter 4 taught us one of the counterintuitive laws of Lean Six Sigma: you can *speed up* results by *reducing WIP* (a consequence of Little's Law). Pushing excess work into a process clogs the process and dramatically increases lead times. In the Chapter 4 case, a sales team needed to get quotes from marketing to complete a sales bid. Marketing was able to *guarantee* a fast turnaround time only by creating a Pull system. They capped the number of quotes they would allow into the process (their WIP) at 48, then developed criteria for triaging which quote request would be released into the process as soon as the WIP dropped to 47.

The same principles apply for the management of Lean Six Sigma projects. Let us assume that you have 20 Black Belts, and that the average time it takes them to complete a project is 4 months (for a completion *rate* of 1/4 projects/month/Black Belt). But now you've decided that you want to get projects completed in an average of 3 months. What is the maximum number of projects that should be "in process" at any one time? Applying Little's Law we have :

Basic Little's Law equation	$\text{Lead Time to Results (LT)} = \dfrac{\text{# of projects in process (PIP)}}{\text{overall project completion rate (CR)}}$

"Solve" for PIP	Maximum **PIP** to maintain Lead time $= \mathbf{LT * CR}$

Plug in the numbers	**PIP = LT *CR** = 3 months * 5 = 15 projects

Completion rate = completion rate/Black Belt * # of Black Belts
= .25 projects/month * 20 Black Belts
= 5

Since you have 20 Black Belts and only 15 projects, that means some projects will have two Black Belts assigned (or that there will be 5 "floaters" who go wherever they are needed). Intuitively, this equation makes sense: by doubling up 1/4 of your resources (= 5 Black Belts), you save 1/4 of the original lead time (= 1 month). The math won't work out this perfectly each time, but you should always do a reality check like this to see if the figures you get make sense.

Until your organization has a few years of project experience under its collective belt, this calculation will result in a ballpark figure only. You'll need to closely monitor results to see if you've overestimated (or underestimated) completion rates, lead time to results, etc., and make adjustments accordingly. But basically if you know how many Black Belts you have and can make reasonable estimates at their average completion rate, you will be able to put a cap on the number of projects and prevent excess projects (WIP) from clogging your Lean Six Sigma pipeline.

In this case, for example, if you want to get a completion rate of 2 months, then 10 projects is the maximum. Before another project is launched, one will have to be completed or scuttled. This discipline really forces people to prioritize projects around business objectives, ROIC etc. You will have to do some detailed planning to avoid competition for shared resources, but this first cut is a major step forward for the majority of companies.

The result makes intuitive sense on another level as well. A "lone wolf" Black Belt cannot possibly have all the skills and experience possessed by a complementary team, and experience shows that there is greater risk of a project producing disappointing results when a team and its project only have a single Black Belt as opposed to those with multiple Black Belts. If your organization can't afford to assign multiple Black Belts to a project, then be sure you don't overload any individual Black Belt with too many projects. Focus on developing Green Belts to the point where they can operate independently with Black Belt guidance. That's the best way to get the fastest velocity of ROIC generation.

Pitfall #3: Inadequate tracking of results

Chapter 8 (p. 235) talked about the need to establish metrics up front. Unfortunately, too many companies discount the necessity of having reliable means to judge project results and impact, or underestimate the difficulty in creating such a system. Lean Six Sigma results must be quantified to appropriately evaluate their impact and make good decisions about whether your resources are being used wisely. Guidelines given elsewhere in this book can help you identify metrics and establish a tracking system.

Pitfall #4: Little or no sharing of best practices

Rapid learning is at the heart of rapid results from Lean Six Sigma. Organizations gain the most by escalating the learning of each team across the organization through best practice sharing.

Therefore, as soon as you have projects launched (or even before!), you should be thinking about how you're going to leverage the lessons that team learns:

- Will the results be applicable to other areas of the company? Where? (Be sure to think of both lessons about the particular process *and* about making improvements in general.)

- How to document learnings in a way that is useful to others.

- How can you give others in the company open access to every team's results? Typical approaches include holding Best Practice symposiums, using web-based documentation in a searchable database (accessible by any employee), having teams present results at regular staff meetings, and so on.

Pitfall #5: Forgetting about the people not directly involved in deployment

Chapter 7 made a strong case for engaging the entire organization in Lean Six Sigma deployment, starting with key influencers and moving out from there. Ignoring people not directly involved can create resentment; involving them does the opposite. "We communicate our plans and metrics to all our employees via our quarterly all-hands meeting," says Manny Zulueta, the VP of Lockheed Martin's procurement center. "By keeping everyone updated on a regular basis, no one is surprised about what we're doing from an organizational standpoint."

Vigilance: Warning signals and decelerators

Morale among the Black Belts at a financial services company could best be described as mixed. Most of them loved the work: being able to work with different teams, applying their analytical skills to problem solving, seeing quality improve. But the stress was starting to get to them. They were having a harder time getting managers to pay attention to them or to assign people to projects. There was little commitment to putting team members through any kind of training, so the Black Belts had to spend more time dealing with conflict and confusion and less time helping team members improve processes. The Black Belts were also increasingly the butt of in-house jokes and resentment, and as a result had become a tight-knit group that didn't welcome "outsiders."

For organizations that are already in the midst of Six Sigma, there are warning signals of trouble. Sometimes, those signals are gut feelings or an uneasiness that employees are just paying lip service to Six Sigma. But in many cases, there are more concrete signals that Six Sigma has become disconnected from the core business.

1) Downward trends in deployment and results indicators (or no tracking of results)

- Projects take longer to complete; due dates are regularly missed

- Financial returns drop steadily (Black Belts begin working on smaller projects that would be better suited to Green Belt leadership)

- The time for completing Black Belt certification creeps upward

- Stated goals for projects become increasingly modest

- Projects get sandbagged ("under promised")

2) Flagging support for Six Sigma projects

- The company leaders no longer personally demonstrate a commitment to Lean Six Sigma (this happened at Honeywell, and Larry Bossidy had to return to reinvigorate the process)

- Black Belts and Champions have a difficult time recruiting people to staff projects

- Attendance at meetings drops off

- More and more people question their involvement in Six Sigma ("it's taking time away from my regular job"; "this isn't helping me get more efficient, it's just adding to my workload")

- Participation, commitment, and philosophy varies widely between locations and/or divisions

- Where once high-caliber employees were assigned to Six Sigma deployment and Black Belts were carefully screened, now "problem" individuals or those who don't have enough real work are assigned to the Six Sigma team

- Project selection is not or never has been driven by ROIC or other key strategic factors

- Black Belts start departing (see sidebar)

Watch for departing Black Belts

Lou Giuliano, CEO of ITT, has found that seeing Black Belts resign their positions is an indicator of trouble because they are typically successful people who have risked their careers to work full-time on Lean Six Sigma. They have a lot of initiative and relish the challenges of fixing business problems. They only leave Black Belt deployment if they are frustrated with a lack of support or if Lean Six Sigma becomes inconsequential. "It's my job to fix those problems," says Giuliano.

3) Evidence of Six Sigma isolation

- The Six Sigma staff show signs of becoming a clique of cowboys or commandos who take all the credit for improvement and are impatient with anyone who doesn't share their enthusiasm

- Project selection becomes a local activity leading to suboptimization of Six Sigma resources: some areas are overstaffed, some projects languish because of a lack of available Black Belts

- Cynicism mounts toward the Six Sigma initiative and cross-team collaboration problems start to develop

- Metrics for Six Sigma projects are set independently of corporate strategy, and are measured only in terms of cost reductions or amount of dollars generated per Black Belt (no customer, quality, or cycle time indicators)

4) People increasingly slide back into old ways of doing work

- The initial focus on customer needs dissipates; internally oriented metrics slowly creep in as the main measures used to select and monitor project success:
  - Projects are selected based on imposed executive mandates and/or managers' pet projects, not on objective criteria
  - Projects are chosen based on cost cutting criteria only (customer priorities are lost in the shuffle)
  - Projects aren't checked against corporate priorities

- Best Practices sharing is inconsistent or non-existent

- Senior executives' behavior contradicts the basic tenants of Six Sigma (they don't base decisions on data, react inappropriately to special/common causes, don't use good decision-making processes, focus on outputs [Ys] instead of the underlying drivers [Xs], etc.)

5) A gradual erosion of Six Sigma roles and responsibilities

- Champions are pulled into non-Six Sigma related work

- Black Belts spend more time on project selection and chartering than driving results by leading projects

- Master Black Belts are assigned to projects that really should be handled by Black Belts

- Sponsors focus solely on day-to-day operations, relegating Six Sigma to the zealots who are increasingly separated from the main culture of the organization

You may have already seen some of these warning signals in your own company, and may have even instituted some countermeasures in hopes of restoring the original enthusiasm and commitment to Six Sigma.

A Champion must be alert for these signs and engage the appropriate management to keep the momentum. Remember it is about RESULTS, it is not about meeting training goals, counting the number of teams kicked off, or presentations about what is going to be done. Management must insist there be a P&L financial validation to "book" the savings as real by constantly asking the right questions, specifically is the project on schedule!

One point of several earlier chapters was that you'll be more likely to reach the financial (and improvement) results if you are successful in changing the norms within the organization. For Lean Six Sigma to endure, it must become part of the culture. For that to happen, it must be part and parcel of the norms within the organization, "the way we do things around here."

Conclusion: Achieving transformational change

The last four chapters have discussed a number of ideas that can help make Lean Six Sigma a powerful engine for ongoing performance improvement. Some of the most important of those ideas are summarized in Figure 9.2 [next page].

To end this section of the book, let's hear once more from several of our contributors, starting with Nick Gaich, Vice President of Materials Management and Customer Service, Stanford Hospital and Clinics:

"There has to be some courage in the organization to allow these things first to be acknowledged and second, to support them. Because you're going to have so many cultural and political hurdles along the way, if you don't have a sound structure behind it, and you cannot clearly demonstrate what these changes mean, that's where I think most organizations fail long term, because it has become just the program-of-the-year. That's not what this is all

Figure 9.2—10 Deployment Principles that Always Work

1. Executive and key influencer engagement (training of CEO and direct reports)

2. A strong and respected Corporate Deployment Champion should report to CEO

3. P&L managers own Black Belt resources & are accountable for project results

4. Deploy critical mass of key resources full-time (1% headcount Black Belts/Champions)

5. Resources should be selected from "future leaders of the company"

6. Establish a process for value-based project identification and selection within the business(es)

   - Select value streams based on customer needs and value creation (ROIC%)

   - Prioritize and staff critical projects in the value stream based on delay time

   - Use Kaizen "blitz" for 5- to 30-day proejcts, Black Belt teams for 30+-day projects

7. Actively reduce Projects in Process to reduce project cycle times (Little's Law)

8. Track results rigorously: Lean Six Sigma results should "pay as you go" and be confirmed by CFO/Controllers

9. Black Belts must receive team leadership training.

10. Provide a "performance improvement" platform that allows for future innovations.

about. Instead of the term empowering, a movement towards 'self reliance' for both our customers and our staff has become our goal of ultimate achievement."

Geoff Turk, Corporate Six Sigma Champion, Caterpillar:

"There are a lot of ways to approach deployment. You can do a targeted deployment where you select certain areas and only do it there. You can do a functional deployment where you say, 'Let's take all the engineering guys because they understand the statistics stuff, and maybe the accountant guys because they can play with numbers too, and we'll just do it in these functional areas.' Or you can do the *transformational change* deployment where you affect the way work is done across the entire organization. And the people at Caterpillar who are bragging big-time about Six Sigma, who are putting up the big numbers on the scoreboard, are doing the transformational change."

But, Turk adds, Caterpillar didn't get there overnight. "We started with this huge grass-roots effort and a few big projects. It's kind of like starting fires around the middle and burning to the center, you know; you get the whole organization going. But if you don't start with enough breadth and magnitude down at the frontline level, it doesn't become the way you work. It doesn't become the common language."

And a final lesson from Lou Giuliano, CEO, ITT Industries:

"Bottom line: with Lean Six Sigma, everybody's job description changes. Everybody's number-one task becomes improving the processes for which they have responsibility.... The only thing that would make this not work was if our leadership skills weren't good enough to really demonstrate to people the value that we could get from this. Because I get tremendous energy, tremendous enthusiasm, fantastic feedback from everyone involved."

Part III

Improving Services

"Don't confuse action with results. Teams can show you all the slickest things, go through every tool in the book, but if they can't show you bottom line results, what have they accomplished? You need to stay focused on your business goals."

—Myles Burke, Master Black Belt,
Lockheed Martin

CHAPTER 10

Service Process Challenges

S uppose you asked a dozen people who all do the same kind of work in your organization to walk you through what they do, step by step. What are the odds, do you think, of getting the same answer from each person? You'll probably end up with a dozen different descriptions.

Here's the question: How can you improve a process that is really a dozen different processes? How can you *improve* something that doesn't really exist? In all likelihood, some combination of the dozen different procedures will comprise a better process, one that produces consistently better results, with less rework and waste.

The lack of a documented, standard process that everyone is trained on is just one of many reasons why improving service processes can be particularly challenging. Filling that gap is a critical point in service improvements, because it reduces variation and waste, and opens the door to significant Lean Six Sigma gains. This chapter explores the lack of process awareness and other barriers you may face in trying to improve service processes, and discusses ways to overcome or avoid typical problems.

Process Challenges in Service

The nature of service work makes it sometimes harder to identify what needs to be changed and how to fix it. Chapter 2 already discussed the fact that service processes are far less visible than manufacturing processes. You can't stand in an office and watch materials flow like you can on the factory floor. So one challenge will be to take full advantage of tools that take invisible work and make it visible. Post process maps and charts in the workplace. Other challenges include:

1) **Tracking of flow**: Manufacturing operations use a "router" to schedule and track the flow of materials through a process, so even if the process has not been mapped in the Lean Six Sigma sense, there is still an awareness of process flow. Service processes have no custom around using routers so there is no way to know where any given piece of work is at any point in time. **Consequence**: Encourage your staff to be creative in thinking up ways to know what stage of the process any individual work item is in.

2) **A tradition of individuality**: People working in service areas are typically given some guidelines or an overview of how their work should be performed, but they are generally left to their own devices to structure their daily tasks. This individual control over work has led to resistance to defining processes in service areas—people fear losing whatever creativity and freedom they have in being able to do their job anyway they see fit. (In fact, standardizing processes usually gives them *more* freedom to be creative in their jobs, but we'll explore that in more detail later.) **Consequence**: The only way to get people to accept process changes (relatively) easily is to involve them in deciding what has to change and how.

3) **The lack of meaningful data/the lack of data-based decision making**: Do you know how much work you have in queue at this very moment? Do you know how long, on average, it takes you to handle those work items, be they phone calls, requests, reports, bills, orders, etc.? Do you have a way to find out? Could *anyone* in your office answer questions about the quantity, quality, and speed of their work? Chances are the answer is no. **Consequence: Expect improvement teams to spend a lot of time on data collection issues.** Transactional environments have one universal metric of quality—the time it takes to complete a job or task—but almost anything else requires a lot of

The need for service data

A utility company operating in a deregulated environment suffered a great deal of "churn," losing existing customers about as fast as it gained new ones. This created a severe burden on marketing cost and effectiveness. The assumption had grown up that the churn was principally caused by high turnover among *new* customers who had just taken possession of their home from a builder and did not know who their utility provider was nor the many benefits offered. These new customers were, the reasoning went, unsuspecting targets of rival power suppliers. So the company sent a Welcome Pack explaining their services to thousands of new customers every week, at a cost of about $8 apiece. A Lean Six Sigma team subsequently collected data on churn and found that it wasn't these new customers who were leaving; they accounted for about 4% of the total. Most of the churn was the fault of long-term customers deciding to switch providers. The effort on churn was re-directed. Like most improvement projects that are not data driven, a complete victory of the Welcome Pack effort would have delivered negligible results to the bottom line.

judgment. And even if your organization has data, most likely it will be raw numbers sitting in an obscure file or database. Roger Hirt of Fort Wayne, for example, noted that they've got a lot of data, but often can't get it out of the software.

4) **People can't be controlled like machines:** Service processes are far more dependent on the interaction of people (both internal handoffs and working with customers) than are manufacturing processes. In a relative sense it is much easier to do something like "reduce the setup time on a piece of equipment" than it is to "reduce salesperson preparation time per sales call." People are your major asset but they are also your major cause of variation, and they can be resistant to changes imposed on them. **Consequence: Pay particular attention to people issues at each stage of improvement**. This is achieved by including people working in an area on the team. They should receive enough training so they understand why the data they are collecting is important. They understand the work process better than the Black Belt, so involve them in decisions about data collection; invite input on

improvement ideas; communicate plans for improvements before actions are taken; share results as widely as possible.

These challenges may sound daunting. But actually they make improving service processes more rewarding because people get to exercise their creativity, and gains come relatively quickly (at least in early projects). In fact, the pioneers chronicled in this book saw that behind each of these challenges lay enormous opportunity to outpace the competition. Just imagine what it would mean if your sales people were interacting with the customer twice as often? If you could reduce customer complaints by 80%? If you could serve your customers twice as quickly? Think how people in your organization would feel if they could hire a new sales agent in just 30 minutes as opposed to 21 days, as happened in one company. In every service business we have seen, the opportunities and pay-offs from application of Lean Six Sigma are enormous.

The best news is that these problems have already been solved in ways that you can apply. This chapter and Chapter 11 address how to approach making improvements in service processes; Chapters 12 and 13 describe actual case studies from organizations who have applied the lessons and principles described here.

And don't forget about customers or complexity...

Two other key issues with service processes discussed earlier in this book are that (1) customers can't be treated like inventory, and (2) complexity exacts an enormous cost on service processes. The pile of papers on your desk and the log of emails on your computer don't mind sitting there until you have a chance to get to them. But customers waiting for service are a very different kind of inventory. You can't pile them up and have them wait until *you're* ready to deal with them. That means you'll have to be creative in coming up with ways to continue meeting current customer needs while simultaneously improving a process. As for complexity, you'll need to focus on standardizing components, subprocesses, etc., as much as possible (as discussed at length in Chp 5). This will help reduce process and service complexity, and put you in a stronger position to *consistently* delight customers with on-time and low-cost service.

The Biggest Challenge in Service: Learning to recognize waste

> Imagine you are a self-stick note attached to an "overnight pack" entering Bank One's Wholesale Lockbox process (for processing remittance payments). By the time you had been through every step, up and down the elevators, back and forth between departments, you would have traveled one-and-a-half miles!

> Don't believe it? Neither did the lockbox staff at first. But as they traced the physical flow of the value stream, everyone was floored. "Well, I guess maybe it could travel that far!"

> What was even more astonishing was just how much that distance could be shortened. Bank One's team came up with a workspace design that required just 386 walking steps to complete the entire process (an 80% reduction in transportation).

The single biggest service challenges in Analyze—and, in fact, all of DMAIC—might very well be developing the ability to recognize service waste. Unfortunately, most services functions are in the same position as Bank One: they accept things like traipsing up and down hallways as simply part of the way work is done. Part of the Lean discipline is the "7 Forms of Waste"; here's how they translate for services:

Waste #1: Overprocessing (trying to add more value to a service/product than what your customers want or will pay for). The basic theme of overprocessing is doing more work than is absolutely necessary to satisfy or delight your customers. There are two elements to overprocessing: (1) If you don't know what your customers want, you could end up adding more "value" than what they are willing to pay for (e.g., wrapping each clothing item in layers of tissue paper might be seen as value-add in a high class boutique but would be seen as unnecessary delay at many retail stores). (2) Allowing non-value-add work to creep into a process. For example, examine a process in your organization that involves approval steps, or maybe a lot of handoffs. Think critically about each approval or handoff. Would your customer think that each of those steps is adding value? Would they be just as happy if the item only needed *one* signature, *one* handoff, so it could get to them quicker? If so, then you're overprocessing!

Waste #2: Transportation (unnecessary movement of materials, products or information). This is one of the problems that plagued Bank One's original lockbox process. Excess transportation is important because every move from one activity to another takes time (which is something Lean thinkers want to minimize), and creates a queue at the receiving activity. In many service processes, paperwork loops back on each activity several times… and waits in queue each time. Transportation in service processes almost always manifests itself as people constantly walking (or running) down hallways to collect or deliver materials, or the actual or virtual chasing of information ("Who has that figure? Marcy? Okay, I'll ask Marcy… Marcy says it's Hector…"). At one end of the spectrum, eliminating excess transportation can involve combining steps to eliminate loops (cut the hand-offs in half, and you will generally cut the queue time in half); at the other end is the option to rearrange the workspace to match the flow of the process.

Waste #3: Motion (needless movement of people). "Transportation" refers to the movement of the work; "motion" involves movement of the workers. Both are much harder to see in service environments than in manufacturing. Motion may show up as people constantly switching between different computer domains or drives; having to perform too many keystrokes to accomplish a computerized task, etc. Solutions can involve everything from rearranging people's desks to purchasing ergonomic furniture and equipment to using software that performs tasks offline (so information is waiting for your staff rather than vice versa).

Waste #4: Inventory (any work-in-process that's in excess of what is required to produce for the customer). Any work-in-process in excess of the amount actually needed causes non-value-add downstream costs of waiting, long lead times (per Little's Law), and the failure to meet customer expectations. Besides all the other evils of large amounts of WIP discussed earlier in this book, it increases the probability that the sequence in which work is done will not match the sequence in which it is needed downstream. This will cause additional queue time and more motion or expediting to meet a need-by date. In service, you need to look for physical piles of forms (in inboxes, for example), a list of pending requests in a computerized email program, callers on hold, people standing in line, and the like. This excess inventory of WIP is often the result of overproduction (see Waste #7).

Waste #5: Waiting time (any delay between when one process step/activity ends and the next step/activity begins). Because so much of the work in service process is invisible to the naked eye, process mapping techniques (and especially complexity value stream mapping) are essential for finding delays in a process. Such maps highlight where work sits around waiting for someone to do something with it. Figure 10.1 (below) highlights queue time and process time data that was previously invisible.

Figure 10.1: A Sample Process Map

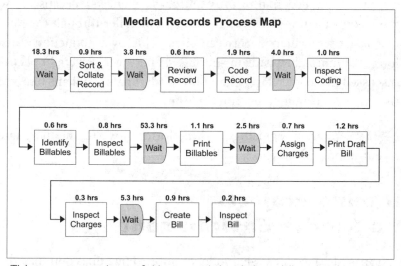

This team created a useful Lean tool simply by adding the time spent in each process step and highlighting wait time in a basic flowchart.

Waste #6: Defect (any aspect of the service that does not conform to customer needs). In services, a defect can be anything from missing information to missed deadlines that causes the customer to be unhappy with the results. Some defects are caused by activities upstream, such as when operators are given the incorrect version of process documentation (instructions, order forms, applications, etc.), others by a change in suppliers or supplied information/material. A defect is usually detected by a downstream person who either has to rework it or pass it back to the activity that made the error. The cost of fixing a service defect may be as small as a keystroke, but the opportunity cost downstream may be enormous, such as losing a customer to a competitor. (When first creating a complexity value stream map, make sure it includes the steps used to fix or repair defect-related mistakes.)

Waste #7: Overproduction (production of service outputs or products beyond what is needed for immediate use). How can overproduction be a waste? If you recall the Lockheed Martin MAC-MAR procurement example discussed at length in Chapter 2, you'll know the answer to that question. In their original process, buyers "overproduced" (processed non-priority purchase requests) because it was more convenient for them to do so than to suffer through the delays of constantly switching between sites. This overproduction caused long lead times, downstream shortages, and waste. Several tools to be discussed in Chapter 11 explain how to eliminate problems like setup time that contribute to overproduction.

The better you are recognizing all these forms of waste, the more effective your improvement efforts will be.

Running Projects in a Service Environment

For the past decade, one basic model of improvement has dominated the Six Sigma landscape. The experts would all tell you to...

- Train about 1% of employees to be full-time Black Belts

- Have the Black Belts lead teams of 5–8 people who have received at least a day of training in the "why and how" of Six Sigma, and which may include some Green Belts

- Have the teams meet regularly for however long it takes to complete the project (say, once a week for a few hours for a period of 3 to 6 months)

- Complete every step of DMAIC or some other improvement model

Data collected on many Six Sigma deployments shows that this model usually achieves the fastest results. Having full-time Black Belts, for instance, generates twice the results (or more) than when part-time Black Belts are used.

While some of these factors affect manufacturing projects as well, coordinating, scheduling, and conducting projects, and getting people trained seems to pose greater logistical challenges in services than in manufacturing. That's why many organizations find themselves adapting the basic model to fit their particular needs. Here are some options that may work for you:

1. Be creative in finding meeting times

2. Look for quick-hit opportunities

3. Include improvement "events" (Kaizen approach) to accelerate DMAIC

4. Reach out beyond team boundaries whenever possible

5. Set realistic expectations

6. Pay attention to team composition

Here's more detail on each of these options:

Tip #1: Be creative in finding meeting times

At Lockheed Martin's MAC-MAR procurement center, the answer to finding a common meeting time has often meant providing free lunches to employees. As professional office staff, employees were unable to give up their regular work hours, because they were already working long hours to get the job done, and they had to be available to respond to internal customers. Part-time Black Belts would stop regular work at 3PM to begin project work, sometimes working quite late into the evening. During the improvement process, people did work some uncompensated overtime to eliminate the non-value-add waste, but as a result are now working fewer hours than they had previously.

At Stanford, where staff work in three 12-hour shifts, they took a different approach. A common practice in healthcare is to have weekly staff meetings that included representatives from each group. Stanford used these meetings to conduct a brainstorming session, analyze improvement options, provide feedback on how changes were working, and so on. Data-gathering and the testing of solution ideas were conducted off-line by managers who didn't have the front-line responsibilities and/or by front-line staff who were able to free up small increments of time. If quick input or decisions were needed, management was charged with communicating with all their staff before decisions were finalized.

Tip #2: Look for quick-hit opportunities

When you first start to work on a process that has not previously been described or mapped, you're going to expose lots of ways in which that process can be improved. Employees will be brimming with ideas on what goes wrong and how to fix it. While in general its preferable to address opportunities through the DMAIC model—where you use data to validate opportunities, select between alternatives, and so on—early on you'll find a lot of ideas that fall into a "just do it" category. If the change is obvious and the risks are small, it makes sense to implement it without wasting a lot of time on additional data collection or process analysis. A just-do-it mentality is infectious; taking immediate action to fix problems will show everyone you are serious about change, and help overcome initial skepticism. Having a bias for action is a characteristic that will differentiate you from other companies.

Two hints if you choose a just-do-it approach:

1) Do a quick check to make sure the change won't hurt other processes or your customers ("We're thinking of doing _____, would that affect anything you guys are doing?")

2) Identify an indicator or metric that will tell you whether the change is having the desired effect ("we should see cycle times

The full-time/part-time Black Belt issue

It is generally acknowledged that full-time Black Belts achieve more than their part-time counterparts. But not every company has been able to devote people full-time to improvement work at the beginning. The issues surrounding the full-time vs. part-time Black Belts (and other resources) was discussed in some depth in Chapter 8 (p. 227).

drop within the next two or three weeks") and have someone monitor that indicator

Tip #3: Include improvement events (Kaizen) to accelerate DMAIC

Perhaps it was impatience with how long traditional projects take; often it was an awareness of how hard it is for people to concentrate on improvement when they keep thinking about getting their work done; to some extent it was a matter of their innate respect of the people who do the work. For all these reasons, years ago the Japanese inventors of Lean manufacturing came up with a different improvement model they called **Kaizen**.

As you may recall from the discussion of Bank One's improvement efforts, Kaizens are intensive "improvement events" where people work only on improvement for some period of time. In a traditional Kaizen project, the people from a particular work area come together with a few experts for 4 or 5 days straight and complete most or all of a DMAIC cycle on a limited high-priority issue ("we need to get materials to the shipping dock faster"). Kaizen events are a powerful improvement tool because people are isolated from their day-to-day responsibilities and allowed to concentrate all their creativity and time on problem solving and improvement. Companies who use Kaizens have found they (a) generate a lot of energy among those who work in the area being improved, and (b) produce *immediate gains* in productivity and quality.

If you can use this model of improvement, you will be amazed at the speed of results and the enthusiasm generated. However, there are a lot of situations where it is difficult to pull a handful of people off their jobs for a full week at a time. But there are ways to adapt the basic model that will allow you to still get the benefits of intensive improvement work.

For example, Lockheed Martin's procurement operations have gotten around this constraint by using a mix of off-line work by just a few people and intensive full-team work for much shorter periods of time, typically a half to a full day. This flexible, focused time is excellent for cross-functional or larger teams where trying to coordinate periodic meetings could be a project unto itself. They have developed a pre-Kaizen checklist that assures when the team does come together they are ready to work. "The beauty here is balancing the completion of the project with the team members' need to meet their daily job assignments," says Myles Burke, one of their Black Belts.

In one MAC-MAR project, for example, the team was brought together for a brief meeting where the problem was explained. Then the team leader, a Black Belt, and one team member worked offline over a period of several weeks to gather data and refine the problem definition. The team was then brought together for a day to rapidly Analyze the problem and come up with complete action plans (not just ideas!) for Improve. Since the changes likely affect the everyday work of the team members, they and others were involved in making the changes real-time on the job, and establishing a Control plan and responsibility.

Bank One sticks a little closer to the traditional model, but with a few twists. Their "Focus 2.0 improvement events" last from midday Monday to midday Friday, so participants are still pulled off their job most of one full week. They make this work, however, by having their internal consultants partner with the manager/sponsor to pick problems that are extremely high priority not only for that work area but also for the business as whole. (That makes it much easier to justify taking people off their regular jobs.) Also, the goal of a Focus 2.0 event is a little more modest than a traditional Kaizen: instead of having solutions up and running full-bore, teams are expected only to get through the simulation and piloting of solution ideas. The internal consultant will then assist the team with full-scale implementation. (You can find more details on the Bank One Kaizen model in Part I, starting on p. 91.)

What makes these Kaizen adaptations work well is that they still...

- Rely on the knowledge of the people who actually do the work.

- Use data-based decision making.

- Start with a narrowly defined problem or opportunity statement— often they may be examining how they can implement a Lean principle to their process, such as "how can we make information flow better?"

- Take steps to verify that the target is likely to bring important, measurable results (e.g., use a value stream map to confirm it is a leading Time Trap, causing the longest delays). Random or "drive by" Kaizens, chosen with little forethought, at best may lead to local improvements but not contribute to significant value stream gains.

Tip #4: Reach out beyond team boundaries

Participation in projects at Stanford Hospital and Clinics fluctuates with each phase of improvement. As noted above, brainstorming and idea generation are often done at regular staff meetings where a large percentage of staff are present. The manager of each unit then brings those ideas to the "service line team" responsible for making improvements. The cross-functional teams have representatives of each major group involved with patient care: a physician Champion, clinical specialists, pharmacists, social workers, case managers, respiratory therapists, and so on. Each of these representatives will also take ideas back to their group and present updates, ask for input on alternatives being considered, and so forth.

And don't stop at your internal boundaries. Evidence from cases you'll see in Chapters 12 and 13 show the benefits of partnering with suppliers and customers.

Tip #5: Set realistic expectations

Mike Fischbach of Bank One comes from a Six Sigma background, so it's no surprise he speaks the language when advising people about setting realistic expectations for team achievements. The mistake many organizations make, he says, is thinking that they achieve consistent best-in-class performance with a single project (see graph C in Figure 10.2).

In reality, most service process are both "out of control"—in the strictest sense, meaning littered with special cause variation, but in a more general sense, meaning not being managed with any understanding of process velocity and flow—and performing well-below any target. (See graph A in Figure 10.2, next page.) It's important to realize that these are two distinct deficiencies, and should be addressed separately. The initial

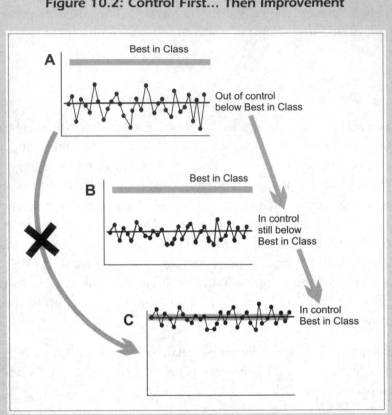

Figure 10.2: Control First... Then Improvement

A — Best in Class / Out of control below Best in Class

B — Best in Class / In control still below Best in Class

C — In control Best in Class

If your processes are currently not in control and are nowhere near being Best in Class (graph A), don't expect that you can simultaneously achieve both goals (graph C). In practice, it's easiest to bring the process in control first (developing process management skills) as shown in graph B, *then* work on improving its capability.

goal should be bringing the process in control (graph B in Figure 10.2) by application of basic process management tools and principles to remove variation, *then* strive to raise the performance level (graph C).

Tip #6: Pay attention to team composition

A big theme in this book has been adding rigor to decisions that previously have been based on judgment, experience, or gut instinct alone.

That theme holds true when creating project teams. In some situations, you may be limited in your options for who should or could serve on a project team. But when the stakes are high and you have to select a few representative team members from among a larger pool, there are techniques you can use to be more astute about team composition.

The most effective of these approaches comes from Dr. Meredith Belbin of Cambridge University. Belbin and his team spent nine years intensively studying management teams that were undergoing executive development and working in situations that simulated real world challenges. Every participant underwent detailed psychometric and mental ability testing prior to participating in the simulations. Belbin's group amassed a huge amount of data on the relationship between team success, personality factors, mental capabilities, and creativity (their work is described in the book *Team Roles at Work*).

When Belbin concluded his research, he had achieved his goal of being able to accurately predict which teams would succeed and which would fail. *The fundamental discovery was that individuals have one or more Preferred Roles, and that to be highly effective, a team needs a balance of these roles.* Belbin, in fact, identified nine roles, shown in Table 10.1.

You'll note that Belbin discovered that the personal attributes that enable a person to make a particular type of contribution generally come with "weaknesses" that must be accommodated. The footnote to the table points out another important lesson: seldom is anyone strong in all nine roles. Finally, there are no "good" or "bad" roles—each role is useful, and every person's preferred role is a good role, *if* they are aware of it and play it on the team.

Obviously, teams will do best with a combination of roles, and imbalances need to be recognized and dealt with. In fact, Belbin's research identified specific team dynamics that were predictive of team effectiveness (or lack thereof):

Factors contributing to *ineffective* teams

1) No *Monitor Evaluators*: without this role present, teams are unlikely to carefully weigh options when making decisions

2) Too many *Monitor Evaluators*: paralysis-from-analysis outweighs creative ability

3) No *Completer/Finishers* and *Implementers*: the team will create good strategies but not follow through

Factors contributing to *effective* teams

4) Having a *Plant* leads to more ideas and better strategies, but will also require *Monitor/Evaluators* and *Coordinators* (to shape and refine ideas)

5) *Resource Investigators* provide an external orientation

6) *Shapers* will keep alive a sense of urgency to achieve results, essential to high performance teams

7) Having too many *Shapers* leads to excessive conflict; make certain there is a *Team Worker* to facilitate relationships

8) Having a *Specialist* when specialized knowledge is required

9) Recognizing and compensating for the "allowable weaknesses" for each role

Belbin's findings show that:

- It is necessary to understand each person's Preferred Team Roles (there are usually more than one), which are the roles in which that person has an aptitude and learned skills.

- Companies should carefully consider the structure and composition of its teams.

- Each team must consciously use the different strengths of those on the team and manage their weaknesses.

- A team that does not have a balance of roles or a plan to address deficiencies can be *predicted to fail.*

- You can use this model to help *prevent* failure. For example, the team member with the strongest Shaper capability will be recommended as the tie-breaker in a team of Monitor/Evaluators.

Table 10.1: Nine Team Roles

Role	Team-Role Contribution	Allowable Weaknesses
Plant	Creative, imaginative, unorthodox. Solves difficult problems.	Ignores details. Too preoccupied to communicate effectively.
Resource Investigator	Extrovert, enthusiastic, communicative. Explores opportunities. Develops contacts.	Overoptimistic. Loses interest once initial enthusiasm has passed.
Coordinator	Mature, confident, a good chairperson. Clarifies goals, promotes decision making, delegates well.	Can be seen as manipulative. Delegates personal work.
Shaper	Challenging, dynamic, thrives on pressure. Has the drive and courage to overcome obstacles.	Can provoke others. Hurts people's feelings.
Monitor Evaluator	Sober, strategic, and discerning. Sees all options. Judges accurately.	Lacks drive and ability to inspire others. Overly critical.
Team Worker	Cooperative, mild, perceptive, and diplomatic. Listens, builds, averts friction, calms the waters.	Indecisive in crunch situations. Can be easily influenced.
Implementer	Disciplined, reliable, conservative, and efficient. Turns ideas into practical actions.	Somewhat inflexible. Slow to respond to new possibilities.
Completer / Finisher	Painstaking, conscientious, anxious. Searches out errors and omissions. Delivers on time.	Inclined to worry unduly. Reluctant to delegate. Can be a nit-picker.
Specialist	Single-minded, self-starting, dedicated. Provides knowledge and skills in rare supply.	Contributes only on a narrow front. Dwells on technicalities. Overlooks the "big picture."

Strength of contribution in any role is commonly associated with particular weaknesses. These are called allowable weaknesses. Few people are strong in all nine team roles.

A Final Tip: Be conscious of your audience

One common pattern seen in service organizations is that you're more likely to find people who will be totally new to (and possibly intimidated by) Lean Six Sigma language and methods. There are a number of ways to handle this issue:

- Translate Lean Six Sigma language into terms that will mean something to your employees (such as how "Kaizens" are called "improvement events" at Bank One). Build off any heritage language/terminology by blending Lean Six Sigma tools and methods into existing systems. The name isn't important; the results are.

- Relate the tools and methods to specific work in your organization.

- Make sure that all examples used in training are from service applications. Manufacturing examples act like an automatic shut-down button in service training.

- Lead by example. Lockheed Martin's Myles Burke was the first person to have his office area cleaned up ("sorted") and organized ("straighten & shined") according to a Lean method called "5S's." (See Case Study #9, p. 350 for details).

- Make sure your Black Belts and trainers are adept at explaining Lean Six Sigma terminology and concepts to people unfamiliar with data collection terms and methods.

- Emphasize the basic suite of Lean Six Sigma tools (like Pareto charts, value stream maps, and time plots) over tools that require more data sophistication (such as regression analysis or ANOVA)—but offer expert help from a Master Black Belt where needed.

Conclusion

The organizations profiled in this book can teach us an important lesson: None of them treated traditional Six Sigma guidelines as an "all or nothing" proposition. They have all adapted the methodologies to fit the specific history, environment, and business needs of their organizations. If you can't afford to devote resources to improvement full-time, use whatever resources you can muster to buy you enough in capacity and other gains to justify greater investment in the future.

CHAPTER 11

Using DMAIC to Improve Service Processes

No matter how you approach deploying improvement teams in your organization, they will all need to know what it is you expect of them. That's where having a standard improvement model such as DMAIC (Define-Measure-Analyze-Improve-Control) is extremely helpful because it provides teams with a roadmap.

There are a lot of resources out there that describe the DMAIC process. The purpose here is to focus on special considerations for using the *Lean Six Sigma* DMAIC process in a service environment, including both methods and tools that are particularly helpful as well as hints on how to handle the people side of each phase. You'll also find case studies demonstrating the use of many of the tools and concepts in Chapters 12 and 13.

A table of Lean Six Sigma tools is shown in Figure 11.1 (next page). One of the key advantages of Lean Six Sigma is its ability to prevent the creation of competing Lean or Six Sigma camps. By training your employees, and especially Black Belts, on both sets of tools simultaneously, they will understand why both process speed and process quality are necessary to maximize ROIC.

Project Chartering: The transition into Define

Typically, a Lean Six Sigma Champion will work with P&L managers/sponsors to create a first draft of a project charter before the team is officially commissioned because project ideas need to be better defined before they will be ready to undergo a final prioritization. Their task will be to turn the "postcard" of information generated during the project selection process into a more robust project description. The Champion needs to communicate sufficient detail about the project to other audiences like a project selection committee, the managers of the Lean Six Sigma program, and the company's senior management so they can make informed decisions about which projects to launch first. Some companies find it helpful to use a project definition form (PDF), similar to that shown in Figure 11.2 for this purpose. These forms become living documents that evolve as the project teams are formed and begin work on their project. While they capture more information than was represented on the postcard or in a spreadsheet, it is not necessary to go into excruciating detail yet because the project teams will augment and refine the information as they proceed.

Another reason for *simple* project definitions initially is the burden that will be placed on the selection committee in becoming familiar with each project they must prioritize. An ideal PDF therefore is just a single page, with an absolute maximum of two pages, and sufficient data to compute benefits, resource requirements, and ROIC estimates.

Figure 11.1: Lean Six Sigma DMAIC Tools

Define	Measure	Analyze	Improve	Control
• Project Selection Tools • PIP Management Process • **Value Stream Map** • Financial Analysis • Project Charter • Multi-Generational Plan • Stakeholder Analysis • Communication Plan • SIPOC Map • High-Level Process Map • **Non-Value-Added Analysis** • VOC and Kano Analysis • QFD • RACI and Quad Charts	• Operational Definitions • Data Collection Plan • Pareto Chart • Histogram • Box Plot • Statistical Sampling • Measurement System Analysis • Control Charts • **Process Cycle Efficiency** • **Process Sizing** • Process Capability, C_p & C_{pk}	• Pareto Charts • C&E Matrix • Fishbone Diagrams • Brainstorming • Detailed 'As-Is' Process Maps • Basic Statistical Tools • **Constraint Identification** • **Time Trap Analysis** • **Non Value-Added Analysis** • Hypothesis Testing • Confidence Intervals • FMEA • Simple & Multiple Regression • ANOVA • **Queuing Theory** • **Analytical Batch Sizing**	• Brainstorming • Benchmarking • **TPM** • **5S** • **Line Balancing** • **Process Flow Improvement** • **Replenishment Pull** • **Sales & Operations Planning** • **Setup Reduction** • **Generic Pull** • **Kaizen** • **Poka-Yoke** • FMEA • Hypothesis Testing • Solution Selection Matrix • 'To-Be' Process Maps • Piloting and Simulation	• Control Charts • Standard Operating Procedures (SOP's) • Training Plan • Communication Plan • Implementation Plan • **Visual Process Control** • **Mistake-Proofing** • Process Control Plans • Project Commissioning • Project Replication • Plan-Do-Check-Act Cycle

An integrated Lean Six Sigma training course for Black Belts typically covers all the tools listed here (Lean tools in bold). Some of the most important and most common tools are discussed in this chapter.

Figure 11.2: Sample Project Definition Form

Project Charter

Proposal Process Improvement

Description: Improve quality proposal development by defining a precise process, managing to the process, improving efficiency, and reducing cycle time such that we can accomplish 15% more proposal work without increasing budgets.

Background: Engineering analysis needs to be done up front. Using analysis, develop a clear understanding of work scope. Educate senior management on proposal content. Prepare team to write/estimate based on a clearly defined technical scope of work.

In Scope: Product line proposals

Out of Scope: Highly efficient quality proposals

KPOV: Proposal cost

Goals:

1. 15% reduction of proposal cost based on metrics derived from previous large scale proposals

2. Increase proposal capacity by 10% (no increase in budget)

3. Reduce rework in the writing process

Assumptions:

1. Improving efficiency and reducing cycle time will result in the ability to do 15% more proposal work within the same budget

2. Full time dedicated proposal manager

3. Move rework resources into up-front planning and education to realize back end savings

Other Benefits:

1. Improve quality of written material

2. A standard proposal process will improve training, repeatability, and employee efficiency

3. A database / archive of material that can be reused for future proposals

Role	Name	Utilization	Start	End
Project Champion	Blanck, Mike	50%	8/20/2002	1/11/2003
Black Belt	Parra, Derek	100%	8/20/2002	1/11/2003
Financial Approver	Martin, Rick	10%	9/24/2002	1/11/2003
Team Member	Clark, Kathy	25%	8/20/2002	1/11/2003
Team Member	Rubert, Rone	25%	8/20/2002	1/11/2003
Project Sponsor	Raney, Al	10%	8/20/2002	1/11/2003

An ideal project definition form captures enough information to allow a project selection committee to prioritize among many ideas without swamping them in detail.

Basic Elements of Define

In the Define step, a team and its sponsors reach agreement on what the project is and what it should accomplish. Presuming that a draft of the project charter is already in place, the main work in Define is for the team to complete an analysis of what the project should accomplish and to confirm their understanding with their sponsor(s). They should...

- Agree on the problem: what customers are affected, what their "voices" are saying, how the current process or outcomes fails to meet their needs, and so on

- Understand the project's link to corporate strategy and its expected contribution to ROIC

- Agree on the project boundaries

- Know what indicators or metrics will be used to evaluate success

The last two issues often prove particularly important in service environments. When processes have been mapped and studied, defining project boundaries is usually a simple matter of identifying the start and end points on the map. Since most service processes have *not* been mapped prior to improvement, there is often some dialog between a team and its sponsors in the early stages as the team creates a SIPOC or value stream map and then has the means to identify exactly what they should include as part of their project and what they shouldn't. Scoping the project is critical to success.

Setting project boundaries

Choose projects that are too big, and you'll end up with floundering teams who have trouble finishing in a reasonable time frame. Choose ones that are too small or insignificant, and you'll never convince anyone that Six Sigma is worth the investment. Choose projects that don't significantly contribute to financial payback (increased revenue or decreased costs), and everyone from line managers to the senior executives will quickly lose interest.

Another factor in project scope is the skill level of the Black Belt and participants. During their training period, Black Belts will likely work on only one project of limited scope. With experience, they can start to take on larger projects or multiple projects.

As for metrics of success, the issue isn't that people can't understand what metrics are, but rather just aren't used to thinking about how to quantitatively measure administrative or service processes. Here are some suggested metrics:

- **Customer satisfaction**, usually measured through surveys to ensure that all customer segments are represented

- **Speed / lead time** (see sidebar, next page)

- **Sigma level** (DPMO) improvement, which requires that a team carefully define "defects" and "opportunities" (see p. 25 for details)

- **Financial outcomes**, focus on revenue retention and growth, or on cost reduction and/or avoidance

If very little data has been collected on the process being studied, it's unlikely you will have numbers to plug into the lead time (speed) equation (aka Little's Law) or to estimate other key variables. If that's the case, make some reasonable sample estimates of these values up front, then be sure to revisit them once you have accurate data in hand.

Options for measuring speed or lead (cycle) time

One way to measure cycle time is to track individual items through a process. For example, put a tag or form on the printout of a purchase request and see that it gets time-stamped at each process step. Or use a stopwatch and physically follow an item through a process. This procedure is usually time consuming and subject to a lot of variation.

Alternatively, you can more quickly get a sense for lead time by recalling the now-ubiquitous Little's Law:

If you know or can make a reasonable estimate of average

$$\text{Lead Time} = \frac{\text{Amount of Work-In-Process}}{\text{Average Completion Rate}}$$

completion rate and can count the number of items in process, then just plug those values into the equation to determine lead time. This process is instantaneous, is easy to do even on a daily basis, and quickly highlights previously hidden problems with work-in-process.

Key Define Tools for Service Applications

The tools used in Define help in confirming or refining project scope and boundaries. Two common tools are:

- SIPOC Diagrams
- Multigenerational Plans

SIPOC diagrams

A core principle of Lean Six Sigma is that defects can relate to anything that makes a customer unhappy—long lead time, variation in lead time, poor quality, or high cost, for instance. To address any of these problems, the first step is to take a process view of how your company goes about satisfying a particular customer requirement. Because many organizations still operate as functional silos—and the fact that no one person owns the entire process, just steps in the process—it's likely that few if any people will have looked at the process from start to finish.

The tool for creating a high-level map of process is called SIPOC, which stands for:

Suppliers: The entities (person, process, company) that provides whatever is worked on in the process (information, forms, material). The supplier may be an outside vendor or another division or a coworker (as an internal supplier).

Input: The information or material provided.

Process: the steps used to transfer (both those that add value and those that do not add value).

Output: the product, service or information being sent to the customer (preferably emphasizing Critical-to-Quality features).

Customers: the next step in the process, or the final (external) customers.

A SIPOC diagram (see Figure 11.3) usually takes shape during the Define stage of DMAIC, but its impact is felt throughout the rest of the improvement project as well. The team will be *Measuring* the lead times and quality levels wherever the process fails to meet Critical-to-Quality (CTQ) requirements of the customer. In the *Analysis* phase, the team will be relating each CTQ and each Time Trap (the output, or Y, in Six Sigma parlance) to a few process parameters (the Xs) whose change will improve that CTQ or Time Trap. In *Improve*, the team makes changes to the inputs and process steps that affect the critical output; these improvements are then the target of *Control* measures to make sure the gains are retained.

Figure 11.3: SIPOC process diagram

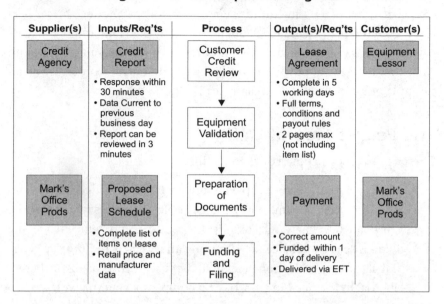

Supplier(s)	Inputs/Req'ts	Process	Output(s)/Req'ts	Customer(s)
Credit Agency	Credit Report	Customer Credit Review	Lease Agreement	Equipment Lessor
	• Response within 30 minutes • Data Current to previous business day • Report can be reviewed in 3 minutes	Equipment Validation	• Complete in 5 working days • Full terms, conditions and payout rules • 2 pages max (not including item list)	
Mark's Office Prods	Proposed Lease Schedule	Preparation of Documents	Payment	Mark's Office Prods
	• Complete list of items on lease • Retail price and manufacturer data	Funding and Filing	• Correct amount • Funded within 1 day of delivery • Delivered via EFT	

This figure shows a SIPOC diagram for an organization that leases equipment. It not only shows all the S-I-P-O-C elements, but also CTQ indicators (such as "complete in 5 working days").

Multigeneration plans

There are many reasons why you may want to look at defining different generations of improvement for the service or process being studied. For example, Chapter 10 presented a model for setting realistic expectations (p. 267) that had one message: you have to first bring your current process under control before you can aim for best-in-class performance levels. So an early project may be "bring the process under control," followed by a second project to "raise the performance level."

Similarly, if there are a lot of customer requirements you're trying to meet, you may divide them into groups to be attacked sequentially (e.g., first do a project to fill gaps in the minimum requirements your service/product has to meet, then do a second phase to improve additional features. A third factor is simply practicality: how much improvement you can reasonably hope to achieve within the timeframe of any single project.

A multigeneration plan helps capture this notion by setting out the current goals plus targets for future generations of the product or service. Having such a plan facilitates dialogue between the team and the leadership on which objectives are most important for the current project, and lets them be clear about the boundaries of the current project. For an example of a multigeneration plan, see p. 366 in Chapter 14.

The People Side of Define

There are two key people issues in Define:

- Making sure the right people are on the team. This decision should be influenced not only by which people are representative of the work area(s) likely affected by the project and which have the knowledge, experience, and training that match the project goals, but also by an evaluation of team dynamics (such as using the Belbin approach described in Chp 10 or a comparable alternative).

- Making sure that everyone involved in the project is starting from the same page, with the same expectations. That includes team members, process owners, Champions, Black Belts, other staff who work on the process but aren't on the team, and so on. The more that all these people understand what is going to happen and the importance of the project to the organization, the likelier it is that the project will go smoothly.

Communication is a significant challenge in any initiative involving change. The team should develop a communication plan to proactively provide information and solicit feedback on the progress and direction of the project. It is very important for the Black Belt to meet often with the Project Sponsor/Process Owner, the individual(s) from the leadership team who is championing the project and who will have responsibility for the results and process once changes have been implemented. The Sponsor's feedback and alignment with project direction is critical to its success and implementation.

Basic Elements of Measure

One of the major advances of Six Sigma is its *demand* for data driven management. Most other improvement methodologies, including Lean, tended to dive from identifying a project into Improve without sufficient data to really understand the underlying causes of the problem. The result was a lot of quick-hit projects with short-lived or disappointing results. Combining *data* with knowledge and experience is what separates true improvement from mere process tinkering.

If you've ever tried to gather data in your own work area, you've probably encountered one or more of the following roadblocks common in service environments:

1) The needed data have never been collected before

2) The data have been collected, but for all practical purposes are unavailable (e.g., they are not tracked by computer or they exist in an obscure part of a software program that only a handful of people know how to access)

3) So much data it's difficult to separate the wheat from the chaff

4) The data does not measure what it purports to measure

If a service process has not been studied before, you have to expect that any team trying to improve that process will spend a great deal of its time dealing with data problems. Here are some tips for those tools and techniques that are particularly helpful in service environments:

1. Establish baselines

Chapter 4 introduced a number of metrics associated with creating a complexity value stream map. Below is a recap of metrics you'll want to monitor:

Work-in-Process (WIP)/Things-in-Process: The amount of work that has entered the process but has not been completed.

Average completion rate: The average number of work items that are completed in a given time period (usually a day).

Cycle or lead time: How long it takes for any work item to make it through the process from beginning to end.

Demand variation: The amount of fluctuation in the demand for the output of your process. The amount of work that arrives at a given activity is measured in terms of units/day and as an average completion rate per unit. Variation can be used in queuing theory to estimate the resulting delays that this variation causes. (See p. 49.)

First-pass yield: The percentage of "things-in-process" that make it all the way through the process the first time without needing to be fixed or rehandled in some way. First-pass yield is a good overall indicator of how well the process is functioning. It also reflects both Lean and Six Sigma goals: in order to have a high first-pass yield, your process must operate smoothly (i.e., with good process flow) and with few errors.

Approvals or handoffs: Two characteristics almost always seen in *slow* processes are (1) a lot of approvals before work can be completed or (2) a lot of handoffs back-and-forth between people or groups. In contrast, Lean processes operating at high levels of quality are characterized by much fewer approvals and handoffs. While having low numbers of approvals or handoffs doesn't guarantee having a Lean process, this is relatively easy data to collect and will almost certainly drop as your process improves.

Setup, downtime, learning curves: Any delays or productivity losses that occur when people switch tasks. (See the Setup discussion later in this chapter, p. 292.)

Defects/Sigma capability: If you've studied Six Sigma principles before, you know that the Sigma level is the rate of *defects* that occur per *defect opportunities*. The key is to come up with definitions that: (1) everyone in the team will interpret the same way, and (2) are consistent with other definitions used in the organization. For example, when filling out a form, do you count every keystroke as an opportunity for someone to make a mistake? Or is the whole form one "opportunity"? Do typos count the same as omissions? One hint: focus on the things that are important to your customer. There are a lot of ways that a form, a report, or a service can be technically "defective" in some way without it mattering to your internal or external customers. For example, perhaps different employees do the work in a slightly different sequence. If "sequence" affects quality as perceived by the customer, then doing the steps in the wrong order is a defect that should be tracked. If sequence does not affect the customer, then you probably have bigger fish to fry elsewhere.

Complexity: The number of different tasks that an activity is called upon to process each day/week/month (which is a function of how many different options there are in your products/services). An estimate of this figure is needed to calculate the effect of the complexity-related WIP on process delays.

If your process has a lot of steps and/or a lot of throughput (volume of work), consider measuring on a sample basis at first (e.g., randomly sample key steps).

2. Observe the process

In the famous words of Yogi Berra, "You can observe a lot by watching." There simply is no substitute for impartial observation as a way to confirm what really happens in a process and identify waste and inefficiencies that are built into how work is currently done.

In an office environment, you can't easily observe "materials" and "products"; instead, you'd need to track things like e-mails, reports, phone calls, or inputs to screens—work products that may exist only in a virtual sense. Since we can't really observe these things directly, process observation in service environments means watching *people* and what they do. Think for a minute about how you'd feel having someone sitting at your shoulder, watching your every move, and you'll understand why this is a tricky proposition. Having a stranger barge in holding a clipboard and writing down notes will do more harm than good. Process observation works best when trained *neutral* observers are used, and you involve office staff in setting the goals for the observation ("what do we want to learn from this?") and in deciding when the observation will happen, which staff will volunteer to be observed, and so on.

Figure 11.4 shows a form that Lockheed Martin uses for process observation. They've found it to be invaluable in the early stages of improvement for verifying (or refuting) everyone's ideas about what they think is happening, and for helping them zero in on areas that need attention.

Figure 11.4: Process Observation Form from Lockheed Martin

	Process Observation Form					
Process Observed: _____					Date: _____	
Observer: _____					Takt Time: _____	

	Description	Distance From Last Step	Task Time	Queue (Wait) Time	Yield	Notes
	Totals					

3. Collect data by participating in the process

What better way to evaluate a particular service than by acting as a customer of that service? Roger Hirt of Fort Wayne recalls one project where a team wanted to improve the quality of response to citizen calls. Instead of doing an after-the-fact survey of callers, they used the increasingly common practice of using "secret shoppers," people who interact with the process just as real customers would. First, they provided the secret shoppers with standard scripts relating to different types of inquiry and complaint calls. They had these people call the city department at different times (so they would talk to different staff), then looked at how the staff had handled the calls. They discovered a lot of inconsistency in how staff recorded and categorized information, with the result that citizens weren't always provided with correct answers or responses. This information allowed the department to develop training for everyone who received calls. A second secret shopper trial showed dramatically improved results.

Collecting data this way is a sensitive issue. On the one hand, you want to know that the service you're getting is similar to what real customers would experience, but on the other hand you can raise people's hackles if the data collection comes as a complete surprise. There's no right or wrong answer here; your Black Belts and improvement teams will have to make a judgment call about how much to tell people ahead of time.

Key Measure tools

A typical Measure toolkit includes everything from data collection sheets to brainstorming methods and prioritizing tools (such as Pareto charts). There are a lot of Measure tools listed in Figure 11.1 that aren't covered here because you can find out about them in other books. The tools serve one or more of the following Measure purposes:

1) Process description

2) Focus/prioritization

3) Data collection and accuracy

4) Quantifying and describing variation

Here is a quick overview of some of the most common tools for each of these categories.

Measure Tools #1: Process description tools

- **Complexity value stream maps**: Process flow maps that label work as value-add or non-value-add and capture data on time and complexity (see Chp 4 for a detailed description)

- **Process cycle efficiency**: A calculation that relates the amount of value-added time to total cycle time in a process (see Chp 2, p. 28)

- **Time value analysis**: A chart that visually separates value-added from non-value-added time in a process (see example, p. 37)

Measure Tools #2: Focus/prioritization tools

- **Pareto charts**: A chart in which bars are used to represent the *relative* contribution of each cause or component of a problem. The bars are arranged in descending order. Typically, only a few of the contributors will account for most of the problem, as shown in Figure 11.5. A team will want to focus their efforts on understanding those few contributors. A flat Pareto chart (that is, where the bars are basically all the same height) is indicative that complexity may be involved or that you're looking at common cause variation in the process.

- **Failure Modes and Effects Analysis** (FMEA): a table relating *potential* types of failure of a product, service, or process to three criteria on a scale of 1 to 10:
  1) The likelihood that something will go wrong (1 = not likely; 10 = almost certain)
  2) The detectability of failure (1 = likely to detect; 10 = very unlikely to detect)
  3) The severity of a failure (1 = little impact; 10 = extreme impact, such as personal injury or high financial loss)

FMEA tables are gaining increasing popularity as a way for service teams to organized their ideas. (One example is depicted in Figure 11.6; you'll find another completed example from Fort Wayne on p. 329.)

Measure Tools #3: Data collection & accuracy

- **Gage R&R** (Gage Repeatability and Reproducibility) is a method for studying and adjusting measurement systems to improve their reliability. "Repeatability" means that someone taking the same measurement on the same item, with the same measuring device or procedure, will get the same answer. "Reproducibility" means that different people taking a measurement on an individual item will get the same answer. Gage R&R was historically used to make sure that manufacturing instrumentation was working properly and that operators were all using those instruments in the same way. In service situations, instrument accuracy isn't as much an issue as whether the people gathering data are all doing it the same way. E.g., are the people measuring cycle time all "starting the stopwatch" at the same point in the process? Are team members counting defects in the same way? Many Six Sigma references contain a description of the full Gage R&R methodology.

Figure 11.5: Pareto Chart of Freight Billing Errors

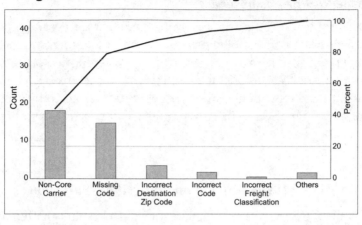

Pareto charts help a team focus on the biggest contributors to a problem. This chart shows how often different types of billing errors occurred. The team would want to focus its efforts on the first two types of errors, since solving those would reduce the number of defects by 80%.

Figure 11.6: FMEA Form

Process/Product
Failure Mode and Effects Analysis Form (FMEA)

Process or Product Name			Prepared by:					Page ___ of ___		
Responsible			FMEA Date (Orig): _____ (Rev):_____							

Process Step/ Input	Potential Failure Mode	Potential Failure Effects	Potential Causes	Severity	Current Controls	Occurrence	Detection	RPN	Action Recom-mended	Respon-sible	Actions Taken	Severity	Occurrence	Detection	RPN
What is the process step & Input under investi-gation?	In what ways does the Key Input go wrong?	What is the impact on the Key Output Variables (Customer Require-ments)?	What causes the Key Input to go wrong?		What are the existing controls & procedures (inspection & test) that prevent either the cause or Failure Mode?				What are the actions for reducing the occurrence of the cause or improving detection?		What are the completed actions taken with the re-calculated RPN?				

Identify Failure Modes and Their Effects · Identify Causes and Failure Modes and Controls · Prioritize · Determine and Assess Actions

Failure Modes and Effects Analysis is a planning tool that helps teams anticipate and prevent problems. For each step in a process, the team asks what can go wrong, and decides what they can do.

What Gage R&R means in services

Whether or not you follow the full Gage R&R method for evaluating a measurement system, you should pay attention to the underlying message: that no measurement system should be considered accurate until it is proven to be so! If you're on a team or reviewing a team's work, explore what steps they took to make sure that data collected by one person or at one time would be consistent with that taken at another time or by other people.

Measure Tools #4: Quantifying and describing variation

- **Control Charts:** A control chart shows data points charted in time order, with calculations performed to determine whether the variation seen in the data is a normal part of the process (known as "chance" or "common cause" variation) or if something different or noticeable is happening ("special cause" or "assignable" variation). The reason to use them in the Measure phase is so you can determine which type of variation is present, and respond accordingly (see Figure 11.7). They are also used in the Control phase for monitoring ongoing process performance. Though the theory behind control charts can initially seem intimidating to people unfamiliar with data, most teams can pick up the basic skills fairly quickly with support or training from a Black Belt.

The People Side of Measure

Unfortunately, the only experiences that many people in service environments have had with "data" are negative: figures used to prod greater performance or punish low-performers, facts used to justify layoff or cutbacks, statistics misused to justify spurious arguments. Therefore, you should expect some level of distrust or wariness when teams first begin data collection efforts. As with most people issues, the solution lies in communication and involvement: asking staff to help decide what data should be collected and why, how it will be used, getting their help whenever appropriate in developing data collection forms or gathering the data itself, and so on.

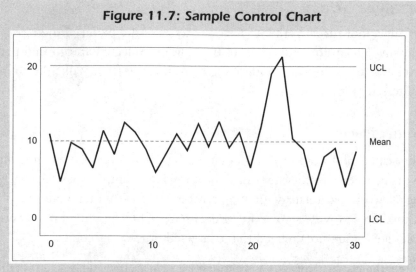

Figure 11.7: Sample Control Chart

The basic structure of a control chart is always the same. The charts show (a) data points plotted in time order, (b) a centerline that indicates the average, (c) control limits (lines drawn approximately 3 standard deviations from the average) that indicate the expected amount of variation in the process. If the variation in a process is the result of random variation due to factors that are always present, data points will be randomly distributed. Points that form patterns within the control limits, or points that go beyond the control limits, are indicators that something "special" is going on that requires immediate investigation.

Basic Elements of Analyze

The purpose of the Analyze phase is to make sense of all the information and data collected in Measure, and to use that data to confirm the source of delays, waste, and poor quality. A challenge that all teams face in Analyze is *sticking to the data*, and not just using their own experience and opinions to make conclusions about the root causes of problems. The most common tools used in Analyze are those used to map out and explore cause-and-effect relationships (5 Whys analysis, cause-and-effect diagrams, scatter plots, design of experiments, etc.).

Analyze Tools

The data tools used in the Analyze phase serve the pimary functions of allowing a team to make sense of the data it's collected and to find patterns that point towards underlying or root causes that will need to be addressed in Improve.

Scatter Plots

The **scatter plot** is a simple tool that can help determine if a relationship exists between two measures or indicators. For example does the "backlog of work" correlate with the "error rate of computer data entry"? Scatter plots provide a powerful visual image of how potential input variables are (or are not) related to the targeted process outcomes.

Often, the visual impression is enough to confirm (or rule out) a specific course of action—such as whether a potential cause should be specifically addressed by countermeasures. If necessary, more advanced statistical tools such as regression analysis can be used to quantify the degree

Figure 11.8: Scatter Plot

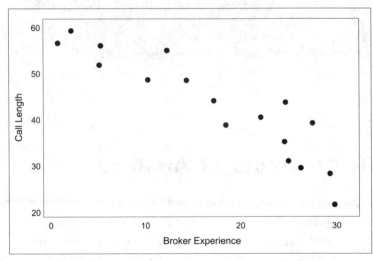

A team will look for the pattern on a scatter plot to determine whether two factors are related. This plot shows a "negative correlaion"—as "broker experience" gets larger, "call time" gets shorter. In other words, inexperienced brokers take longer to complete a call than more experienced brokers.

of relationship between the two factors (see Figure 11.8, previous page, and *Lean Six Sigma, pp. 199–200*).

Time Trap Analysis: Complexity value stream analysis

One of the major themes of Lean Six Sigma is that slow processes are expensive processes. In most processes, the work (forms, calls, requests) spends only 5% of its time in value-add and the rest waiting around, being reworked, and so on. By increasing value-add to 20%, you can reduce non-value-add work (and costs) by 20–50%. How to achieve such a substantial increase in value-added time in a process? Another theme of this book is that 80% of the delay is caused by a few Time Traps. By identifying these Time Traps, we can identify the improvement projects that will drive the cycle efficiency over 20% and hence make a major impact—typically improving operating profit by 5% of revenue and reducing WIP by 50%.

A trained Black Belt can facilitate a team through a value stream mapping event to calculate minimum batch size, identify the hidden Time Traps, and so on. As discussed in Chapter 4, specialized complexity value stream mapping software is available as a supplement to manual calculations. It can link traditional capacity planning capability that your company likely uses already and the new information needs associated with Lean Six Sigma projects.

The People Side of Analyze

The biggest people challenge in Analyze is overcoming the unfamiliarity that most team members will have with data analysis tools. Having expert guidance from a trained Black Belt or other coach is invaluable, especially if he or she takes the approach of helping the team do the analysis themselves.

Basic Elements of Improve

The sole purpose of Improve is to make changes in a process that will eliminate the defects, waste, costs, etc., that are linked to the customer need identified in a team's Define stage. Common tools and strategies you'll find referenced in any discussion of the Improve phase of DMAIC are those such as solution matrices that link brainstormed solution alternatives to customer needs and the project purpose, and methods for implementing desired solutions.

Lockheed Martin has developed its own version of a solution matrix they call a PICK chart that their service teams have found very useful to prioritize the ideas for implementation (see Figure 11.9).

Many of the Lean tools play their most important role in Improve. Pull systems have been discussed extensively in Chapter 2 and again in Chapter 10; here's a quick look at three others:

Lean Improve Tool #1: Setup reduction

A P&L manager who wants to prepare a monthly report starts gathering together the information he needs. He realizes that this month's sales figures aren't broken out by region, so he calls over to accounting and tells them to email the regional split as quickly as they can. He also discovers that he has updates on only three of the four Lean Six Sigma projects in his unit. The Black Belt for the missing project is out on the floor that day, so he spends a few minutes tracking her down and getting a verbal update. Then all he has to do is get the month's wages/benefits figures from HR, and he's ready to work on that report.

# # #

Dave, one of the more experienced technicians in IT knows more about PCs than nearly anyone else in the company. Trouble is, the graphic design group is on Macintoshes. So even though Dave spends 95% or more of his time supporting the PC users, he still has to answer a handful of calls each month from the Mac users. He describes the experience as having to "reconfigure" his brain so he can switch from thinking in Windows to thinking in OS X.

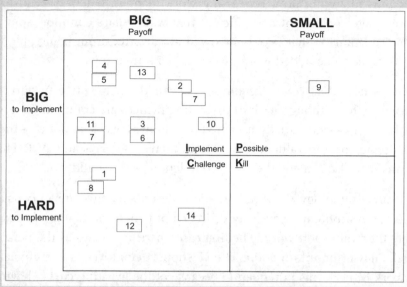

Figure 11.9: PICK Chart (sample from Lockheed Martin)

A PICK chart helps a team organize and prioritize its solution ideas by separating them into four categories: Possible, Implement, Challenge, or Kill. Here, most of the solution ideas were easy to implement and would have a big payoff—they fell into the Implement quadrant. Four ideas would have a big payoff but were harder to implement, so the team needed to Challenge these ideas (was the payoff really that big? were there easier ways to accomplish the same effect?). Only one idea had a small payoff, and therefore was considered Possible; no ideas fell into the automatic Kill category. The next step is to schedule, secure sponsor approval, and fund the activities selected by team consensus, implement them, and track the implementations.

#   #   #

Marcie over in Personnel is the gatekeeper of incoming job applications, some of which arrive by mail, some by fax, and some via the company's website. She's found it is more convenient if she waits until she has a stack of at least 20 applications that she can log into the database all at once, rather than trying to do them as they come in.

Odds are that at least one of these examples reflects what happens in your job—needing to track down information to finish a task, switching from one set of tasks to another, having some element of your job that you only rarely perform, processing work items in batches because it seems more convenient and efficient that way. What's common among these situations is that people involved are diverted from being able to perform the value-added work associated with their jobs.

Perhaps now that you're becoming a Lean thinker, you can start to recognize that although each of these job practices are common in service functions—and usually accepted as "the way work is done"—they each represent non-value-add work that increases delays and WIP. That means they also impede the *quick* completion of value-add work.

In Lean terminology, the three situations described above are all considered **setup problems** that delay or interrupt people as they try to complete their value-add work: The first case, there are delays as the person **tracks down** the information. The IT support employee is less efficient at work he performs infrequently because of the **learning curve**, having to switch his brain from one way of thinking to another. Job applications are delayed because the gatekeeper prefers to work in **batches**.

A good example of the impact of setup time was described in Chapter 2, where the buyers at Lockheed Martin's MAC-MAR procurement center ended up "locking onto" their internal customer sites (rather than purchasing all priority orders first) because of the length of time needed to switch from site to site, and the learning curve costs from having to remember 14 different sets of product codes. In that case, the solution was a custom software tool that allowed the buyers to see all customer requirements in priority order, rather than batched one customer at a time. Discussion of this example also showed how setup occurs anytime a change in task causes a drop in productivity, because it will force us to stay on that task for a longer period of time, delaying service to other tasks.

The tool for attacking setup time is the **Four-Step Rapid Setup method**. The principle of this method is to **eliminate anything that interrupts or hinders productivity**. Here's how it works in service applications:

STEP 1: *Identify and tabulate any process-related work that fits into one or more of the following categories:*

A) that delays the start of value-added work

B) causes interruptions to value-add activities

C) where it takes people time to get up to "full speed"

D) that is very similar or identical to another task in the process

This is where your ability to recognize waste really comes into play. Typically, it's the hardest part for people in service functions because there is so much waste and non-value-add work that is taken for granted. What you have to learn to do is objectively observe people as they perform the tasks of a process and note anything that *prevents them from performing the value-add work.*

- Try to develop an awareness of when you or the person you are observing is delaying, slowing down, or stopping value-add work and ask yourself why.

- As shown in the examples above, for instance, the "why" could be the lack of information, the need to refresh your memory if you are switching tasks or doing something you don't often do, the need to have a certain number of items in queue (batched) before you begin the work, and so on.

For the purposes here, focus only on delays or interruptions that are related to the process. For example, a buyer completing a purchase order may get a phone call from another employee who is requesting information. That buyer will likely interrupt the processing of purchase orders, but that delay is not caused by something inherent in the PO process.

The question about looking for work that is identical to other steps in the process is intended to help you recognize duplicative work that has grown up as product or service offerings/features have expanded over time. If you discover tasks that are similar to other tasks, ask yourself if they can be combined, thereby eliminating the need to switch tasks, do additional setup, and so on. If so, implement the change as quickly as you can.

STEP 2: *See if any of the interruptive/delaying tasks can be offloaded*

What you're looking for here is ways to handle preparatory work outside of the main process flow so the information or material ends up waiting for you, not vice versa. The goal is to have people zip through all the value-add work in a process without any delays or interruptions.

Focus in on any activity or task where you have to stop the process. Then ask yourself why those problems appear, and figure out how to eliminate that source of delays or interruptions.

For example, in the Lockheed Martin procurement story we've referenced multiple times, the solution was to develop a software application that could automatically log into the legacy systems at each of 14 sites *every night*, and then have all that information compiled and waiting for the buyers when they arrived at work in the morning. In other words, the "tracking down of information" was offloaded to a new software application so it was no longer a source of delays.

STEP 3: *Streamline or automate any interruptive/delaying tasks that cannot be offloaded*

In any process, there will be some delaying or interruptive factors that are deeply woven into a process. Be creative in trying to find ways to either eliminate or drastically reduce the amount of delays that these tasks inject.

In the procurement case study, one of the issues was that each of the 14 legacy databases used different part numbers for identical components. While "matching the part number to the component" was a step of the process that couldn't be eliminated entirely, the company did invest in developing a database that automatically matched the site part numbers to the needed component. So that was work the buyers no longer had to do each time.

Similarly, many pizza chains today just ask for your phone number the second time you order. They have eliminated the need to ask for your address, name, and directions a second time.

There are several streamlining approaches that can be used when the cause of the delay or interruption is related to "learning curve" issues associated with infrequently performed tasks. One is to funnel all the requests of a certain type to one highly skilled or specially trained person to increase the frequency (e.g., if 10 calls for Mac support came into the IT department described above, have Dave handle all 10 calls rather than having each of ten people only handle one Mac call a month). Or there are often ways to provide visual or automatic reminders that eliminate the need for people to remember the specifics of obscure processes (such as having pull-down or pop-up menus on a computer screen).

- Only batch if you can't solve the setup problem.

- Try to reduce complexity so you don't have so many setups in the first place. Remember, the greater the complexity of the tasks performed, the lower the frequency of performing any single task, which leads to a continuous loss in productivity due to learning curve issues.

STEP 4: Bring the process under statistical control

The final step in this method is another example of using intelligence instead of money to solve problems. The setup is not complete until the output of the process is "in spec" and under statistical control (meaning the amount of variation in lead time is within predictable limits of $\pm 3\sigma$). An automatic reporting system should note any deviations outside this limit. As you observe the new process in operation, look for any ways to reduce variability in how the steps are completed or in the time it takes to complete them.

Typically, the ideas require only a modest amount of capital. The amount of setup reduction accomplished by this step is very dependent on the complexity of the task, and can vary from 30% to 100%.

The examples we have given show both the importance of reducing setup time and the applicability of this tool to the service environment. It is clearly critical to reducing process lead times (along with Pull systems and other Lean tools). Moreover, the tool is cheaper and more effective to apply in service than in manufacturing.

A Lean tool by any other name...

If you use the *Four Step* terminology used here in a manufacturing plant, they won't know what you're talking about. The more common terms sound like rather poor English translations of Japanese terms. To find out more about this method, look for the following terms:

1. Separate internal from external setup ("Internal" setup means activities that can only be performed with the process "down." External setup activities can be performed in parallel)

2. Convert internal to external

3. Streamline any remaining internal setup

4. Eliminate adjustments

How much setup time should you allow?

In the Lockheed Martin procurement example, where buyers locked onto one site due to legacy software issues (as described in Chp 2), the original setup time was 20 minutes. This setup dropped to 0 minutes once the process was attacked with Lean thinking and tools. But even under the old system, the Buyers could have worked more efficiently had they known about the "ten times setup" rule, which says you should stay on one task only ten times as long as it takes to do the setup, because productivity falls off after that.[1]

In this case, that would have been just over 3 hours (10 x 20 min = 200 min)—you can see that the curve in Figure 11.10 rises rapidly until just around 3 hours (180 min). So even without other improvements, applying this rule—meaning buyers would switch after 3 hours even if they weren't done with that customer site—would have allowed buyers to cycle through all customers in less than 6 days. Since it often took them 14 days or more, this would have been a great improvement in a key customer requirement.

Figure 11.10: The "Ten Times Setup" Rule[1]

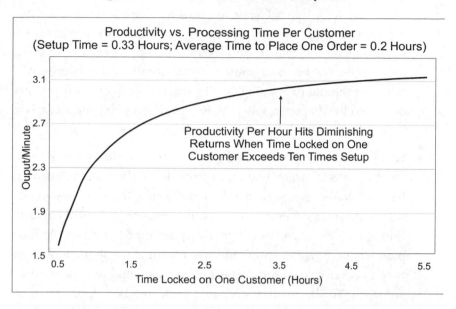

Productivity vs. Processing Time Per Customer
(Setup Time = 0.33 Hours; Average Time to Place One Order = 0.2 Hours)

Productivity Per Hour Hits Diminishing
Returns When Time Locked on One
Customer Exceeds Ten Times Setup

Ouput/Minute

Time Locked on One Customer (Hours)

The graph shows that the benefit of staying "locked on" to one customer before moving onto the next starts to rapidly fall off after roughly "ten times" the 20-minute setup delay (200 min or just over 3 hours).

Lean Improve Tool #2: Queuing methods for reducing congestion and delays[2]

Often congestion occurs because of variation in demand, much like the effect that variation in arrival time and check-in times had on the hotel check-in process described earlier in the book (p. 114). In that case study, though the average check-in time was 5 minutes, guests often had to stand in line 10 minutes or more due to congestion at the check-in counter. Variation in the time it takes to perform various tasks can also lead to congestion and delay, and follows the equation on p. 124.

Once identified, there are three principle techniques for reducing congestion that arises from variation in the demand for services:

- **Pooling**: Cross-training staff to step in during times of peak loads. One hotel chain, for example, trains office and other staff to help out with registration with both unexpected peaks and predictable peaks.

- **Triaging**: Sorting jobs into categories that reflect different levels of effort required. Typical schemes include: fast service times vs. medium times vs. slow service times; easy and small problems vs. real problems vs. catastrophic problems. Then develop different routings, strategies, or resources to deal with each category. We saw an example of triaging in the marketing quotatio`n process described in Chapter 2, where they ended up establishing a cap on WIP and "releasing" work into the process.

- **Back-up capacity**: Pooling and triaging are very effective in knocking the peaks off delays that result from demand variation. But what happens if the excess demand for a given offering is sustained? You've already used up all the possible alternate sources of capacity through pooling, and intelligently quarantined the troublesome products by triaging. You could use overtime for short periods of time to cover a peak, but this is an expensive and non-sustainable approach. To deal with a sustained peak, the best approach is to cross-train any operators/staff in the work areas that have high demand fluctuations. By juggling scheduled downtimes (such as lunch, coffee breaks, etc.) you can usually provide sufficient coverage to effectively add 20% more capacity. Finally, if the demand is

---

Triaging

The principle of triaging has been applied in a variety of situations with remarkable success. Take, for example, one auto body repair shop. As in traditional repair shops, each mechanic had three to five cars to work on (= lots of WIP), each with varying degrees of damage. The lead time to complete repairs was 2–3 weeks, much to the chagrin of customers and insurance companies. By triaging the incoming jobs based on the degree of damage, the light wrecks were repaired in an "index line" in which cars moved on to a new repair activity every four hours. Using this method, the lightly damaged cars could be repaired in just 2–3 days. Medium and heavy wrecks were sent to the more experienced/skilled mechanics in traditional bay repair. Costs were better understood, gross profit margins rose, and customer and insurance companies were delighted, and mechanics made more money through higher volumes. What was lost? The non-value-add cost!

truly sustained (as documented by trends on a control chart), you will have to add people or equipment.

- **Reduction of variation in processing time:** In the auto repair example (above), the variation of repair time within each of the triaged processes was dramatically reduced. For the procurement buyers at Lockheed Martin, there effectively was no variation in the time to place an order in many cases—40% of the orders were "point and click" once the commodities were put on contract.

Lean Improve Tool #3: 5S+1

Think about how you spend your time during the average workweek. How much of that time do you think you waste looking for the right folder, the right file, the right piece of paper? How often to you scramble through your office trying to find a self-stick note, a pencil, a marker, an envelope? Does your office look like Figure 11.11 below?

For some reason, clutter is something that most of have learned to live with in our professional lives. To some, it is even a badge of creativity.

Figure 11.11: A "before" workspace from Lockheed Martin

But the fact is that clutter and disorganization are significant contributors to wasted time in office environments. Putting effort into organizing your (and your work group's) workspace can sometimes have almost miraculous results in making your organization more efficient. The goals are to (1) eliminate wasted time as people perform their everyday tasks, (2) present a professional image to customers, and (3) enable staff (or temporary workers) to seamlessly step into a coworkers shoes during travel, sick days, meeting times, and so on. This is enabled by having a place for everything and everything in its place—clearly laying out a work area.

When combined with the Lean tool known as **visual management**, you can have a self-running, self-regulating organization. A visual workplace stresses communication via bulletin boards, graphics, status boards, web portals, dashboards, etc. that make performance of the process immediately visible to any one walking into the work area. The purpose is to assure that everyone knows the current priorities, status, and upcoming events, with no filtering.

Components of the 5S+1 System

Historically, the basic elements of getting a workspace organized were defined by the five S's:

Sort: Organize, separating the needed from the unneeded (SEIRI)

Straighten: Arrange and identify for ease of use (SEITON)

Shine: Clean and look for ways to keep it clean (SEISO)

Standardize: Maintain and monitor the first 3 S's (SEIKETSU)

Sustain: Discipline, stick to the rules and maintain motivation (SHITSUKE)

Lockheed Martin and other organizations often add on one more S (hence the notation 5S+1):

Safety: Removing hazards and dangers

The 5S method can be applied profitably to virtually any activity. In one case, a company was considering buying more computer servers and routers for an on-line banking application. Before the capital requisition was approved, a Black Belt decided to "5S" the servers. It turned out one of the servers had 70% of its capacity serving the data requirements of less than 5% of the users! Further investigation showed that the majority of this data was infrequently used and not required in real time. Major server capacity was gained simply by archiving that data. You'll find an example of how the 5S's are applied in Chapter 13.

Caution note:

"5S is normally the *first* thing performed in a manufacturing situation because of the need to see 'flow' of physical inventory. In an office environment it should be a third or fourth improvement action because office people are more likely to see it as threatening their personal work space than are machine shop employees. It must be 100% led and backed by the managers, and implemented by respected people from the work area. You are going for culture change."

—Myles Burke, Master Black Belt, Lockheed Martin

The People Side of Improve

Nothing really changes in a process until the Improve phase of DMAIC… which explains why you'll need to pay extra attention to people issues: communication, involvement, and commitment. Usually, team members are representative of a larger group of people who work on that process. A team can make implementation go much more smoothly by communicating with their coworkers regularly—especially if it is two-way communication that invites involvement and commitment. For example, the team can share their thoughts on potential solutions, get feedback from other coworkers, and ask for volunteers to help try out the changes on a small scale. The use of Kaizen events (see p. 52) to facilitate Define and Measure work can pull together the team and make communication proactive, preparing members for the Improve work.

Another people issue in Improve is getting **sponsor support** to the impending changes. The sponsor (and process owner, if he/she is not on the team) must be involved at this stage because they control the funding and systems that will be needed to accomplish the change.

Basic Elements of Control

The purpose of Control is to make sure that any gains made will be preserved, until and unless new knowledge and data show that there is an even better way to operate the process. The team must address how to hand-off what they learned to the process owner, and ensure that everyone working on the process is trained in using any new, documented procedures. Six areas of Control are critical in service environments:

1. Making sure the improved process is documented (and that documentation is used regularly)

2. Turning results into dollars (validated by the finance department)

3. Maintenance of gains is verified down the road

4. An automatic monitoring system is installed which will identify "out of control" performance

5. Piloting the implementation

6. Developing a control plan

1) *Make sure the improved process is documented (and that the documentation is used regularly)*

Service processes rely on the habits that staff develop as they perform their work. Changing those habits is a lot harder than changing the switches on a machine. You must document the new steps with a written procedure, train people on the new procedures, and make it easy for them to use the new process (and hard to use now-outdated procedures), so that people don't slip back into their old habits. The process owner must be responsible for seeing that this documentation and training occur, and for developing ways to ensure the methods continue to be used.

2) *Always turn results into dollars*

Lean Six Sigma is not a "feel good" undertaking like some of its predecessors turned out to be. It is not a "mile wide and an inch deep." Lean Six Sigma is focused on high value projects. Companies do it to make themselves more competitive and more profitable. Project results must be verified financially, before the project is launched, tracked thereafter (and reported to the CEO). Work with financial analysts in your organization to develop methods for verifying improvements and quantifying their financial impact (cost reduction or avoidance, increased revenues, etc.).

... and one Six Sigma Improve tool that's often overlooked in service applications (Design of Experiments)

Lean tools aren't the only ones that are often overlooked in the Improve phase of DMACI. Another under-used tool is Design of Experiments (DOE). DOE is a method for *simultaneously* investigating anywhere from a handful to dozens of potential causes of variation in a process. DOE used to be solely the domain of the statistician, but simple software tools have made it accessible to many. Here's one example of how it can be applied.

A large carpet company had hundreds of retail operations, with huge variation in sales per store. Over 1500 ideas were generated about the reasons for that variation. They boiled the list down to 12 major factors that could potentially affect why some stores sold more or less than others. By using a designed experiment to study these 12 factors and their interactions, they determined which were most critical for increasing revenue. The experiment showed that the biggest factors that consistently drove store revenue up were (1) the quality of the greeting of customers, and (2) displaying carpet under a variety of light sources (solar, fluorescent, incandescent) because customers really appreciated this differentiated offer. Being able to focus on just these two factors (instead of spreading its efforts among 1500 "good ideas") and standardizing the practices among all stores (investing in the light sources, training of sales people) generated a 20% average increase in store sales.

That said, however, it's also important to realize that not all gains can be easily quantified. Some gains are simply more easily tracked by current accounting systems than others, such as a reduction in the use of supplies, or increased sales volume due to increased capacity. Other types of gains are immeasurable, such as the increased confidence that comes when employees have been involved in improving their own process.

3) Verify the results at a later point in time

Organizations experienced with improvement know that it can take awhile for people to become comfortable with new procedures, so they usually perform a check two or three months after the project is officially done to verify the changes are still in place.

4) Set up an automatic alert system

The widespread use of computer systems has made it possible to add automatic warning systems that immediately alert staff about process performance, or, more specifically, provide warnings if something has gone wrong. Some companies use a web-based "digital dashboard" that displays real-time numbers on key process metrics; others have programs that automatically generate an email report on yesterday's (or last hour's) performance. As a minimum, implement a manual monitoring process for a few months after making a process change to assure the process is stable and producing the desired results.

5) Piloting implementation

A pilot is a small-scale test of the solution, and as many projects as possible should take advantage of the opportunity for a pilot. A pilot could be conducted over a specified region, at a particular facility, with a beta version of a technology solution, with just a few personnel, or it could be anything that simulates how the service will work when it is implemented. Run the pilot long enough for adequate data collection. The pilot data should be sufficient to prove to the leadership and those affected by the solution that the new service meets their requirements. Positive benefits of piloting include increased buy-in, early realization of benefits, and the possibility of minor modifications to the solution to improve it. The other significant benefit is risk mitigation. The team needs to learn as early as possible where potential issues are, and to manage the implementation to avoid unintended negative consequences.

6) Developing a control plan

The team will also develop a process control plan to ensure that the new process continues to satisfy requirements over time. A process control plan usually builds on the future state process map, indicating who is responsible for what in the new process. Also, metrics that will be critical to the ongoing process are identified, along with how the data will be captured and displayed. Control charts for costs, revenues, productivity levels, or customer satisfaction data are common. Visual process control tools are helpful for communicating performance. Ownership of the new service will be finalized, along with a process management team to monitor ongoing performance post-implementation.

The People Side of Control

Just as with Improve, the ability to Control a service process depends entirely on the people who work on that process day in and day out. The difference is that here a team has to make sure that it's the process owner who takes responsibility for seeing that process documentation and procedures are maintained (and used).

"The Control phase is normally a crossover point," says Roger Hirt of Fort Wayne. "When I was with GE, it was where the process owner took over. We had a control measure that required the process owner to sign off, indicating they understood and knew what the control plan was. The Black Belt stayed in only until the changes were in place, then the process owner took 100% ownership." The model being used at the City of Fort Wayne is a little different, he adds. "We are training the process owners directly, and having them work on projects in their work section to improve their job performance... and make their life easier." That means transition issues aren't as challenging because the process owners have been involved throughout the project.

Another important people aspect of Control is communicating with those who were not directly involved in the project... a lesson that Stanford Hospital and Clinics learned the hard way:

> The cumulative result of different projects focused on cardiac bypass graft surgery at Stanford Hospital and Clinics was that patients were able to be discharged much sooner and often experienced fewer complications. But the hospital team soon discovered they had ignored a vital link in patient care: The cardiologists who did the referrals would tell patients, "You need a coronary bypass graFort You're going to be in the hospital about nine days." So the patient would go through the surgery and four days later be told they were being sent home. While people aren't typically

*upset at being released early from the hospital, these patients—
expecting a nine day hospital stay—were convinced it was all a
cost cutting measure and that they hadn't really gotten their full
measure of care. They were also concerned because their family
members weren't prepared to take them home at day four. And
that's how Stanford discovered that part of their control plan had
to be communicating with anyone who dealt with patients.*

Control tools

One control tool, control charts, was already discussed under Measure
(see pp. 288-289). Two closely related concepts that are very helpful in
Control are **mistake prevention** and **mistake proofing**. Mistake prevention means working to find ways to make it difficult or impossible for
operators to make a mistake in the first place. Mistake proofing means
that even if a mistake occurs, it *cannot* be passed onto the next step of the
process.

In manufacturing processes, mistake prevention takes the form of designing components so that they can only fit together in one (correct) way;
mistake proofing occurs by making sure that a piece of equipment, for
example, simply won't accept a component or material that is incorrect.

In paperwork processes, mistake prevention increasingly occurs via software solutions. In one Fort Wayne process, for example, a field on a
computerized form will only accept numerical characters (operators
used to mistakenly enter alphabetical characters as well). The same form
also has pop-up windows to provide instructions if needed.

Improving Your Improvements

Manny Zulueta, the VP at Lockheed Martin's MAC-MAR procurement
center, has set his staff an ambitious goal of having all their teams complete the full improvement cycle in 30 days. They aren't there yet; typical teams take 3 to 6 months. So they decided to apply improvement
logic to getting better at improvements, and collected data on 25 teams
in operation during the first 6 months of 2002. They looked at whether

the team had followed the full DMAIC logic (and if so, how long the teams spent in each phase), had adopted an intensive Kaizen approach, had gotten together for a value stream mapping exercise, and so on.

What they discovered was that by far the teams spent the most time at their equivalent of the Improve stage—deciding on, implementing, and validating improvements. There were four main contributors to the long cycle time in this phase:

- Poor planning of improvements
- Poor project management
- Little or no sponsor involvement
- Project scope was broader than initially thought

As a result of this analysis, they have developed better training on planning and project management skills, and have made changes to their DMAIC process to ensure better involvement of Sponsors throughout the project. They are also working on ways to divide the "solve world hunger" problems into more manageable pieces.

Learning More About the Lean Six Sigma Tools

There are far more Lean Six Sigma tools than can be covered in this book, as shown in Figure 11.1. Note that the list encompasses Lean, Six Sigma, and complexity analysis tools. A balanced toolset like this is needed so you can tackle any problem that comes your way.

However, keep in mind the advice from Myles Burke of Lockheed Martin: "Of the literally hundreds of improvement and data tools, there's maybe a quarter you use regularly because they fit so many different situations. Focus on teaching and learning those. The other ones—I call them the exotic or sexy tools—are useful only in very specific circumstances and should be close by for quick reference when you see the need. All tools need not be mastered to be a successful Black Belt. My most used tool is asking 'why' five times to a team and seeing them 'get it.' Work with your Black Belts to identify those tools most likely to be needed by your teams, and customize training around that subset."

Conclusion

The final lesson on running effective projects comes again from Myles Burke of Lockheed Martin: "What's the right way to run a team? Whatever is quickest to get you where you want to be. We've had teams that didn't complete every step of our model, but they got out what they wanted and the results have stuck. Remember you are teaching people to see waste and value and non-value-added tasks. Do not let Lean Six Sigma be perceived as bureaucratic. Be flexible to what makes sense."

Endnotes

1. The "10 times" rule only applies if there is no variation in demand, no defects, no downtime, etc.

2. Much of these practical results of Queuing Theory are due to Professors James Patel and Mike Harrison of Stanford University Graduate School of Business

CHAPTER 12

First Wave Service Projects

There's a dynamic tension set up whenever a company embarks on a Lean Six Sigma initiative. Naturally, it wants to target resources at significant problems, where improvements will have a noticeable effect on quality, speed, and cost. Yet it's likely the majority of people recruited to make these improvements will be new to Lean Six Sigma: newly minted Black Belts, novice team members, untrained frontline staff. So a company needs to balance its focus on important issues versus not putting people into situations that just set them up for failure.

Fortunately, the opportunities for manageable, meaningful projects abound in the early stages of Lean Six Sigma, especially in organizations with no active program on improvement. You can make significant gains in lead time, quality, and cost reduction relatively quickly by...

- Having frontline staff collaborate on developing complexity value stream maps. Collaboration is key because it's through discussion that people realize there are differences in how they each *think* the process works. It's this realization that opens the doors for identifying and documenting best practices.

- Developing data collection systems (especially for value stream mapping), which is generally absent from service processes.

In addition, you'll want to use experienced Lean Six Sigma resources (Master Black Belts, Black Belts) to provide coaching on tools and methods.

Below is a selection of five case studies from our contributing organizations that illustrate how some of the basic tools and principles of Lean Six Sigma work in real life. These projects were all conducted by novice teams under the guidance of a trained Black Belt (or someone with equivalent skills).

None of these particular projects were done with novice Black Belts as part of their training, though such projects will occur in your own organization.

One last note: It is unlikely that the majority of the readers of this book will work in a procurement center, or a city government, a bank, or hospital. But as you'll see, the basic principles of Lean Six Sigma hold true for all processes, no matter what the environment.

Quick Reference Guide for the Cases

Case #1: Understanding the process

Kevin Fast, a Lean Sigma Black Belt and Manager of Quality Initiatives for Lifetime Support at Lockheed Martin in Moorestown, NJ, made an interesting observation: "You know," he said, "after you do a few Six Sigma projects, you come to expect certain things. When a project team comes together to define their as-is process, inevitably someone will say, 'You do that? I didn't know you did that!' Or 'You do this? I do this, too.' It's just amazing how people who have worked on a process for a long, long time often don't realize everything that goes on. And it's because they don't have the tools."

Kevin was right: Though we may think we know all about the processes we use every day, chances are we're wrong. When we start using Lean Six Sigma tools to document those processes, we all have moments of epiphany where we realize that what we're doing differs from what others are doing. In many cases, there's no flowchart, let alone a value stream map, that we can compare against our perceptions. And even if a process map does exist, chances are it documents only the value-add activities in a process not the other 50% or more of the activities that are non-value-add. A lack of process knowledge and documentation *always* means there is hidden non-value-add cost and waste that is ripe for elimination.

Why do this particular project?

As you may recall from Chapter 2, the Systems Integration MAC-MAR procurement operation at Lockheed Martin has a huge impact on overall costs and efficiency: more than 50% of the costs of their final products are determined by products and services that are purchased from outside the company.

But as in most service functions, until recently the purchasing process had never been studied in great detail. Process mapping is the first step toward developing the

Participants

Project team: Myles Burke, Scott Lovett, Joshua James

Subject matter participants: Ed Mikulski, Chris Davis, Judy Liang, Bill Statton, Gladys Alford, Carol Stewart, Lee Miller, Scott Fairbanks, Jennifer Sharpe data for a value stream map and ultimately a complexity value stream map. The initial goal therefore was to **document the current reality** of the early stages of procurement, from when an internal customer submits a request to when a purchase order is generated and the order placed. The goal was to find out how the process actually worked, where the value was, and where opportunities existed for improvement.

The Analysis

The initial steps for this project consisted of a lot of process mapping and data collection. They began with a basic flow analysis, but then continued to collect the data needed to generate a value stream map like that shown in Figure 12.1. This VSM shows the three different methods buyers used to obtain quotes from suppliers, which is typical in service processes.

The data they gathered led to the creation of a time value map (TVM), shown in Figure 12.2. In this sample, only 14 minutes of a 4-day turnaround time was spent on value-added work—and this reflects higher-performing buyers working on simple requests. (The median turnaround time for *all* orders was 11 days.) Other insights included:

- The TVM made it clear that even if the buyers doubled their productivity (completing twice as many orders a day), it would only shorten the total cycle time by 7 minutes over 4 days! Getting significantly faster wouldn't happen by getting buyers to "work harder"—it would take eliminating non-value-add time in the support process that delayed prompt PO placement.

- Originally, there was only one measurement of lead time, and the clock started the moment someone entered a request into the system—but it could take days before it reached the buyer. That meant measures of buyers' lead time looked much worse than they really were because they were penalized for time over which they had no control. Now, there are two distinct metrics: total cycle time and buyer cycle time. This better understanding of the metrics provided the data to start additional cross-functional teams to look at the whole process. (Measurement system errors are common in transactional processes mainly due to the lack of standard definitions.)

Figure 12.1: Value Stream Map

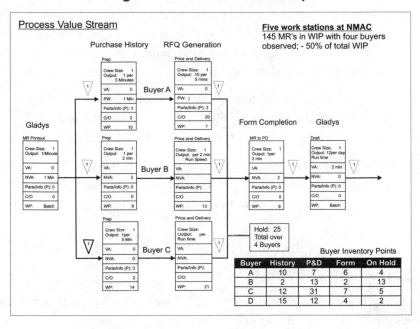

This "5000-foot view" of the procurement value stream shows three key stages: purchase history review, request-for-quote generation (where price and delivery are confirmed with the supplier), and finalizing the form for entry into the purchasing system. It has three separate paths because different buyers did the work differently.

Figure 12.2: Time Value Map for the Purchasing Process

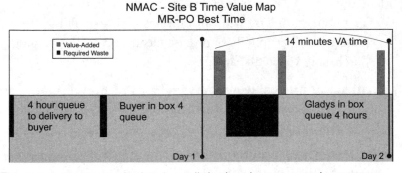

This time value map depicts how little time in a process is spent on value-added work compared to non-value-added delays. Here, only 14 minutes added value in the eyes of the customer.

- 41% of the requests were for materials or items that cost less than $50; another 38% was for items under $500. Estimates showed that the cost to place about half of all orders was more than the cost of the order itself—meaning a disproportionate amount of resources was being spent on low-dollar items.

- There was often insufficient information submitted by the requesters, which meant the buyers couldn't do their jobs and had to send the requests back for "rework" (pure non-value-add activity).

- Priority was often given to orders based on when the request was submitted, not when delivery was due because a key metric was not aligned with the true customer CTQs.

Solutions & Results

One question that arose for this team was "why isn't this a paperless system?" Having a method that eliminated paperwork would save a lot of time, especially on the small dollar-value requests (where it actually cost more to place the order than to purchase the goods). The team implemented numerous actions that revolved around training, new processes, best practice standardization, new computer functionality, daily status messaging, working with the customer, and so on. Here is a sample of just a few of their improvements:

1) A full-time position was created to focus on high volume/low dollar purchase orders, with an emphasis on expanding the use of master (blanket) purchase orders, electronic on-line catalogs, and purchasing via credit cards.

2) Adding a "material-request to purchase order" cycle time metric to the visual management boards allowed the group to track the daily pulse of work-in-process.

3) A second team developed a Buyer Training Aid pamphlet that had quick reference materials incorporating best practices.

What it took to make this work

- In any un-studied, un-documented process, you will *always* find easy improvements that lead to visible improvement—having people who work on a process talk about what they do inevitably leads to some quick hit improvements.

- A key element is *observing the process in action.* This project took three Black Belts and a core team of buyers three weeks (part-time) to capture the process details for the value stream map. (The Black Belts would sit with the buyers asking a lot of "dumb" questions, looking over their shoulders observing keystrokes, time on the phone, interruptions, etc. This only works if you have a good team with very people-friendly Black Belts.)

- The people who work on the process were integrally involved.

- This project, like many at Lockheed Martin, was conducted in a Kaizen mode—short, intensive sessions.

"With shorter lead times, people are not interrupted in the middle of a task to handle another customer. People in service take it for granted that we will have to constantly change tasks mid-stream, moving on to a second task before the first is completed. While some flexibility is good, too many interruptions lead to inefficiency. This was observed daily in the VSM by sitting next to the buyers being in their shoes. The Black Belts saw that the buyers' priorities would change two or three times within an hour."

—Myles Burke, Master Black Belt, Lockheed Martin

Case #2: Blaming the visible part of the process

It seems common in service functions for people from only one part of a process to receive most of the blame when something goes wrong. A delivery is late? Blame the delivery person. A hospital bill is wrong? Blame accounting. A maintenance person appears in the wrong location? Blame him or her. In all of these situations, there is *some* chance that the end-point person is at fault. But the vast majority of the time, factors from throughout the process are the root cause. Bank One ran into this exact situation early in one of their improvement efforts.

Why do this particular project?

In June of 2000, Bank One handled more than 210,000 transactions where an individual or corporate customer requested a paper photocopy of a cleared check. Though this check copy retrieval process wasn't as visible as other bank services, the quality of the process was critical in determining the attitudes of those customers who used it.

Data from that month showed that 10% of those transactions resulted in a service failure—the customer didn't get what they wanted, when they wanted it. And the rate rose as high as 25% on some days in July. So in any given month, the bank could create 10,000 or more unhappy customers. It was no wonder that staff were tired of dealing with angry customers calling to demand why their copy hadn't appeared as promised, or complaining that the copy was unreadable.

The Analysis

The cross-functional team brought together to improve the photocopy retrieval process quickly identified three main failure modes:

- The customer didn't get the check copy on time
- The customer couldn't read the copy
- The bank had no copy of the check

They then mapped each step of the process and determined what could go wrong in that step that would contribute to the failure mode (which is the essence of Failure Modes and Effects Analysis). It turned out that nearly every step of the process had serious problems. Here are just three of the many problems they uncovered:

- **Staff sometimes promised the wrong service level to customers.** The bank had a standing policy of providing 3-day turnaround... but that was good only if the check was kept onsite. Checks over two years old were moved to off-site storage—and it could take two or three extra days to produce copies of those checks. The retail branches didn't know about the two-year cut off, so they were unknowingly promising the wrong delivery dates.

- **The request may have incomplete or wrong information.** The staff trying to retrieve the checks often had difficulty identifying what it was they were supposed to copy because information was either missing from the request form or filled in incorrectly. (A Pareto chart revealed the most common types of problems, see Figure 12.3.)

Figure 12.3: Pareto chart of errors

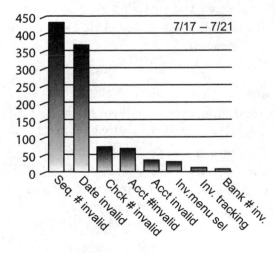

This Pareto chart showed that the two biggest types of errors made in the check retrieval process were having an invalid sequence number and an invalid date.

Fixing those two types of errors first will eliminate the majority of errors.

■ = # requests w/errors

- **Vendor service quality had a big effect.** Some check "copies" were actually images on microfiche film. The team tested a number of microfiche cartridges by exposing the film and returning them to the vendor, who would develop the images. They discovered that the vendor overexposed *one out of every ten cartridges.* So 10% of the time an image was unclear because of overexposed film—a problem that no one inside the bank could solve.

Solutions & Results

The team instituted numerous changes throughout the process to deal with the problems they had identified. Some common themes in the solutions were:

- **Mistake-proofing the process:** Improving the software used to submit requests prevented clerical staff from entering incorrect information (e.g., not accepting alpha characters where numerals were required). It also allowed an instant message to pop up whenever the check date was more than two years old so staff would know not to promise a 3-day turnaround.

- **Educating staff on the procedures.** New procedures exist that allow staff to adjust the microfiche equipment to make the photocopies better, and there is better documentation on making clear photocopies. There is also a new set of standard error codes used to communicate between the retrieval staff and other users. Having everyone trained on the new codes eliminated miscommunications where clerical staff didn't understand what information the retrieval staff needed.

- **Developing better tracking** so they could tell where, when, and under what conditions service failures were most likely to occur. The process includes regular business reviews where management and staff evaluate performance data an react quickly when problems arise.

- **Initiating preventive maintenance on key equipment.** When the changes were first made, vendors were required to perform frequent tests of their

Participants

Team: Melana Ackerman, Tim Bishop, Norma Borcherding, Allen Niven, Scott Richardson, Karen Zirkle

Internal consultant support: Tim Williams, Cathy Hayhurst, Rush Fozo

Management support: Chris Bobko, Lyle Myers, Elizabeth Petri equipment. The tests have gotten less frequent now that the process is stabilized.

Measurable Results

Soon after the team started implementing the new procedures, the error rates dropped substantially. Overall service failures were cut in half, from more than 15% to nearer 7%. Factors contributing to this drop were improvements in *preventing* the various types of service defects. Figure 12.4, for example, shows a drop in the number of requests the bank was unable to fulfill due to mistakes made in filling out the request forms.

Figure 12.4: Time Plot of Check Retrieval Errors

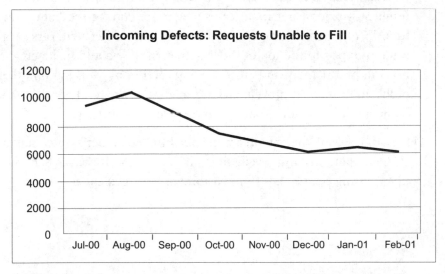

This time plot shows how many check retrieval requests the bank staff could not fill due to problems with how the initial request form was filled in. The data shows that the errors dropped steadily for months after the changes were made.

What it took to make this work

- **Having an end-to-end perspective of the process.** Bank One had tried to fix this problem in the past, but the efforts always focused just on the people who made the copies. This time, they included people from all parts of the process on the team: front office retail and commercial (the people who deal directly with customers); item processing (where the checks are originally converted into microfiche); and retrieval.

- **Devoting sufficient resources to the problem.** This project was not the first time the bank had attempted to improve this process. What was different this time was not only did they draw people together from all points in the process, end to end, but also devoting people to the team *full-time for four to six weeks.* (This kind of focus on an important project is possible only if you limit WIP—the number of "projects-in-process.")

- **Realistic expectations:** While six sigma levels of quality are always the goal, Bank One has found that's simply not practical in their environment—at least not in all cases yet. Here, cutting the failure rate from 15 to 7 percent was worthy of celebration. After that, other priorities popped to the top of the list (that is, they could make greater gains in productivity and customer satisfaction by working on other problems). Once improvements are made elsewhere, it may be that reducing this 7% failure rate will once again become a priority.

That said, it wasn't the data that convinced the customer service staff at Bank One that this improvement stuff was okay. It was when they stopped getting phone calls from customers yelling at them.

Don't forget the Intangibles

"Improving this process didn't require the use of advanced statistical tools. Success came from having a cross-functional team examine the end-to-end process and identifying the gaps that caused breakdowns through the use of simpler tools such as cause-and-effect diagrams and Pareto charts."

—Tim Williams, Ass't Vice President, Bank One

Case #3: Turning a customer hassle into a delighter

As a customer yourself, how often have you decided NOT to do business with a company because it was simply too much of a hassle? Customer surveys reveal that people often make their decisions about where to take their business based on their total experience with a company, not just on price alone. Here's an example from the city of Fort Wayne, Indiana, that demonstrates how much can be gained by removing hassles for your customers.

Why do this particular project?

Like many cities, Fort Wayne has suffered the loss of key employers throughout much of the 1980s and 1990s. Economic development efforts are therefore key to the city's long-term plans. Sustaining and creating the tax revenue base was clearly one of the largest "ROIC" opportunities facing the city.

Through some initial benchmarking, the city's Department of Economic Development discovered that the city was failing in a critical element of the building permit processes. While smaller cities nearby could turnaround site plan improvement applications in just 5 to 10 days, Fort Wayne was taking 50 to 60 days or even more. And it wasn't just turnaround time that was a problem: potential applicants were expressing a desire to build/expand in other locations to avoid Fort Wayne due to the protracted and intimidating permit approval cycle. They were hearing comments like, "I'm not going to put myself through that hassle. The permit process takes too long, there's too many restrictions, and I'm not going to go in there and be treated that way."

Obviously, this negative attitude towards dealing with the city was having a serious impact on jobs and business opportunities.

Participants

Heather Presley (Green Belt)

Team: Elissa McGauley, Rick Kunkel, Michelle Kyrou, Jim Norris, Pat Fahey,

Support: Andrew Downs (Champion), Stacey Stumpf (Black Belt)

The Analysis

A first step for this team was collecting the Voice of the Customer by conducting focus groups with representatives from other city departments affected by or involved in the permitting process, and with external customers (building contractors, engineers, and architects). Critical-to-quality factors turned out to be:

- Timely approval of permits and certificates of compliance

- Excellent service in face-to-face contact

- Timely and accurate reviews

- Quality of the communication between the city and the customer

To focus their efforts, the team created a process map (Fig 12.5) and then answered the question, "**What process steps most significantly affect whether customers get what they want?**"

Figure 12.5: Permitting process flowchart

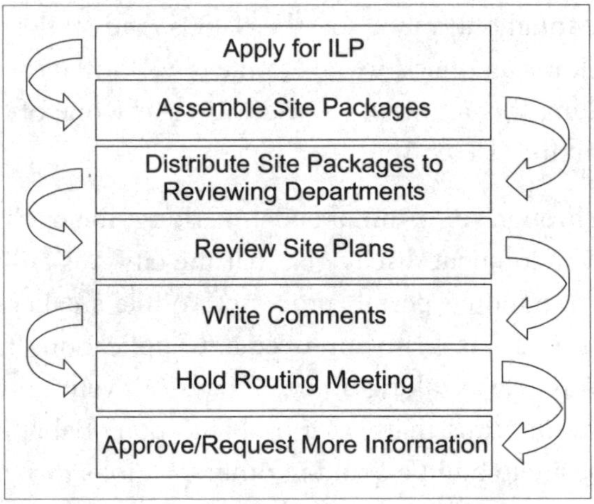

- Apply for ILP
- Assemble Site Packages
- Distribute Site Packages to Reviewing Departments
- Review Site Plans
- Write Comments
- Hold Routing Meeting
- Approve/Request More Information

They concluded that the following process elements were most critical:

- Reviews of the permit application documentation ("site packages")

- Routing meetings and attendees (where it is decided which city departments have to get involved in the review)

- Tools and guidelines used during reviews

- Communication back to the customer after the city's review

Their investigations revealed that the permit process was rife with non-value-added work and delays. For example, standard practice had been to send every application to every department, when in reality different types of permits needed reviews by only certain departments. As the process was originally structured, a lot of people ended up going through a lot of permits they didn't have to review. Eliminating that overproduction was a huge reduction of WIP which, according to Little's Law, will dramatically reduce Lead Time.

Solutions & Results

After studying each of the target process elements, the team came up with a number of process measurements, changes, and enhancements:

- Using a **punch list** to make sure that the permit requests are complete before they are accepted from the customer

- Developing **better tracking** capability through use of new software (see Figure 12.6, below)

- Developing **triaging criteria** (such as assigning "red flags" to permit types that had historically proven challenging or complex) and developing **alternative pathways** for simpler permit applications

- Changing procedures to **provide better collaboration and communication** between city departments

- **Collecting data regularly** to better measure and monitor turnaround times

Figure 12.6: Permit Tracker [Screen Capture]

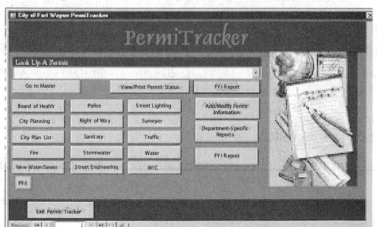

Results

The team tracked three different kinds of results: measurable improvements in lead time, cost avoidance, and anecdotal support.

1. Quantifiable results in lead time

The team saw dramatic improvements as soon as they began making changes (see Figure 12.7), and ultimately achieved even greater gains (see table below).

**Figure 12.7: Before & After Results
of the Permit Tracking Project**

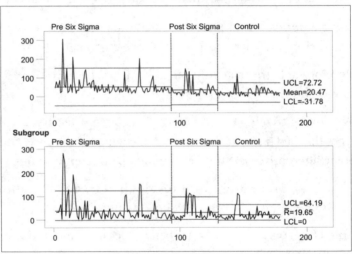

Before	After
None released ≤14 days	95% released in ≤10 days
Nearly 1/4 took 60 days or more	Only special causes exceed 41 days
72 requests in the cycle (WIP)	30 requests in the cycle (WIP)

2. Expenditures avoided:

The team Green Belt taught herself Access and did the programming—saving the city from spending $150,000 that had been budgeted for software purchases (funds that were freed up to provide additional services to citizens).

3. Anecdotal support

Feedback from customers has entirely changed in tenor from "I said I'd never build here" to "I never believed that the city could get this good." The builder's association was so excited about the gains that they invited the team Green Belt to give a presentation at an association meeting.

What it took to make this work

- **Giving teams the green light to immediately fix obvious problems.** As Roger Hirt says, "One of our philosophies with all of our Green Belts and Black Belts is that they shouldn't wait until the end of the project before making changes. Don't let it run on broken. We call it process hardening—get it done, put it in place, make it work, fix it."

- **Having a cross-functional team.** Typical permits need to pass through a number of city departments before they are approved, so no single department could have hoped to improve cycle time without cooperation from all the departments involved.

- **Using a process focus and data to build trust.** Team members drawn from different city departments were able to set aside historical finger-pointing blame games by focusing on the process and using data to isolate problems.

- **Direct contact with customers.** Holding discussions with various customer groups (contractors, engineers, realtors) proved invaluable in providing direction and focus to the project, and in re-establishing trust between customers and the city.

Case #4: Getting rid of backlog

Why do this particular project?

For years, the problem of "curb cut restorations" was a real headache in the city of Fort Wayne. A curb cut is when a builder or contractor cuts away part of a curb and the adjoining frontage property in order to add a new driveway, create a handicap-accessible sidewalk ramp, and so on. In theory, the entire process from making the cut to complete restoration (pouring the concrete, re-seeding grass) is supposed to be done in 30 days. Then, also in theory, it would be inspected by the City and cleared off the books.

What happened in practice was twofold: (1) sometimes the restorations never got done, and (2) it could take as long as three years for the inspection to be done.

By early 2001, there was a backlog of over 2800 curb cut permits that were unresolved (= WIP), clogging the permit process.

The Analysis

Ideally, once an individual or company receives a permit, the process should flow through just three steps: the permittee makes the cut, the permittee restores the cut, and the city clears the permit. But along the way, as the team discovered, there was a lot of opportunity for errors.

For example, the original information was copied several times by hand before being put into a database. As you probably know, one way to minimize errors in paperwork/information systems is to minimize the number of times the information is touched. Also, there was often poor communication between city departments. When one department would confirm

Participants

Departmental team members: Rick Orr (Black Belt), Elenore Petroff, Sunnie Heddon, Harvey Meyer, Mike Burkart

Expert resources: Bill Simmons, Peter Hill, Bob Bowen, Gary Merriman

Support: Ted Rhinehart (Champion), Michele Hill (BB), Roger Hirt (BB)

restorations ("clear the permit"), they threw the paperwork in a box without updating the central records. When a team member asked why the department had so many open permits, they responded "Oh, we got all those done."

Overall, the team confirmed four main problems with the process:

- Cuts not being restored quickly enough

- Permits not being finalized quickly enough

- Customer satisfaction is too low

- Wasted dollars due to process inefficiencies

Solutions & Results

The team performed a Failure Modes and Effects Analysis (FMEA) to identify the ways the process could fail that would contribute to the problems they had just confirmed. A portion of this analysis is shown in Figure 12.8.

Figure 12.8: FMEA table

Process Step/Input	Potential Failure Mode	Potential Failure Effect	S E V	Potential Causes	O C C	Current Controls	D E T	R P N
What is the process step/ Input under investigation?	In what ways does the Key Input go wrong?	What is the impact on the Key Output Variables (Customer Requirements) or internal requirements?	How severe is the effect to the customer?	What causes the Key Input to go wrong?	How often does cause or FM occur?	What are the existing controls and procedures that prevent either the cause or the Failure Mode?	How well can you detect cause or FM?	
Restore understanding of City expectation	Expectation of 30 day cycle time not understood	Lengthens cycle time	4	Permitee subcontracts restoration work	4	Performance bond, contractural agreement	8	
Restore understanding of City expectation	Expectation of 30 day cycle time not understood	Lengthens cycle time	4	Inexperience with City requirements	4	Handouts, familiarity with applicants	7	
Restore understanding of City expectation	Expectation of 30 day cycle time not understood	Lengthens cycle time	4	Assumption that applicant already knows expectations	3	Familiarity with permit applicants	7	

By looking at ways in which the process could fail, the team discovered factors that led builders to unintentionally exceed the 30 day limit (such as when inexperienced permit holders subcontracted out the restoration work without informing the subcontractor of deadlines).

In response to their FMEA analysis, the team initiated the following changes:

- Regularly communicating expectations to applicants

- Better documentation of key information (e.g., recording anticipated completion dates on permits)

- Identifying locations where restoration was not required

- Instituting daily updates on particular types of restoration work

- Triggering inspections based on expected completion date rather than waiting for notification of completion to arrive at the office

- Working with customers so they would not request permits until the work was scheduled (originally, if a contractor or the power company was going to develop 40 sites, they'd get permits for all 40 at once even though work on the majority of those sites wouldn't be started for weeks or months)

- Working closely with their largest customer (who always had numerous permits-in-process) to foster better awareness of its progress, delays, etc.

The team also immediately and easily reduced the current WIP by examining open permits and determining which were in fact still open and which were completed but the city had not been notified. This cleared a lot of the backlog.

Results

Goal #1: Reduce WIP: The original level of 2,843 backlogged permits dropped to 342 within just a few months.

Goal #2: Having all the permits cleared (the cuts restored and confirmed) within 45 days. The extra 15 days beyond the 30-day limit stated on the permit was to allow the grass to grow. The actual results can be seen in Figure 12.9 (where a "defect" is any permit not cleared in 45 days).

In addition, the database on completed and outstanding permits is now essentially defect-free (and more likely than before to remain that way).

Figure 12.9: % defective, before and after

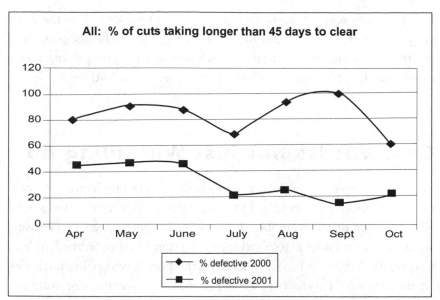

The data points here are percentages of defective curb restorations (those not cleared within 45 days). The upper line shows that originally often times less than 20% of curb restorations were cleared within the target time frame. Post-improvement (lower line), the situation is completely reversed: 80% of the curb cuts are restored within target, and only 20% do not make the deadline.

What it took to make this work

- **Looking at the process from the customers' viewpoint.** The team members realized they needed to understand the contractor's process and its relationship to their process.

- **Making changes in both their processes and their customers' process.** Achieving the faster lead time required modifications in both the contractors' and Fort Wayne's processes. The work with customers had to be conducted in a non-costly and non-threatening manner.

- **Recognizing that a "one size fits all" process was inefficient and prone to delays and errors.** They needed to develop alternative pathways depending on the substance of the permit.

A last bonus case...

Due to space considerations, we were unable to present all of the cases our contributors have shared with us. We have compiled the cases described in this chapter and others at our website (www.georgegroup.com). Here's a quick peek at just one of the additional cases you'll find there.

Case #5: It's not just WIP piling up

When you're in charge of Robbery cases in the City of Fort Wayne, the people you're concerned about aren't just "customers," they're crime victims. So when you see that the number of unresolved robbery cases is increasing faster than the number of resolved cases, you start to get concerned. At least Captain Art Norton, a 16-year veteran on the Fort Wayne police force, did. So he launched a project to see if the lead time for the disposition of Robbery cases could be brought down from 2 months to less than 30 days.

Captain Norton and a team of nine police officers and administrative staff mapped out the robbery case process, from assigning of the cases to five potential outcomes: an arrest is made, there is a warrant request, the complaint was unfounded, the case is closed because the likelihood of solving it is extremely low, or the arrested person is prosecuted for different crimes ("exceptional clearance"). The mapping exercise and subsequent data analysis revealed a number of procedural problems in the process, such as the lack of controls over staffing levels in the typing pool, no backup procedures in place if the Sergeant in charge of assigning a case is away, a lack of use of guidelines on determining solvability, and so on.

The team made a number of relatively simple changes:

- Establishing guidelines for minimum staffing levels in the typing pool. This eliminated delays in report preparation due to illness or vacation, etc., among typing pool staff.

- Training officers on new quality control guidelines. This eliminated delays due to the problems with the report forms.

- Assigning backup responsibility among section Sergeants so cases could always be assigned for investigation within 24 hours. This eliminated delays in assigning cases.

- Establishing a triaging procedure (see pp. 299–300) such that cases determined to have a low probability of being solved were diverted out of the mainstream case assignment. This eliminated WIP and cleared the pipeline so officers could spend their time on cases that were more likely to be solved.

Results: Average days to disposition was 58 days prior to this project, now it is 24 days. And even those that can't be solved are being handled better: The new process for the "no solvability" cases includes upfront communication with robbery victims. Whereas in the past they'd be kept hanging for months at a time as their case languished in the pipeline, now they're told that the likelihood of solving the case is slim and it will not be actively investigated. Having an earlier resolution to the case, even though the resolution does not include charging a criminal, has been a welcome change among the robbery victims.

Lessons We Can Learn

Here are some tips for running first wave projects:

- Have teams focus on projects within their work area, because that is where they will have the greatest amount of control, subject matter expertise, and support.

- It's important to select projects that will mean a lot to the people involved. Ideally, the selection would be based on the Voice of the Customer and/or management's key business needs.

- Be patient with process mapping and data collection; expect some confusion and mistakes the first time around.

- Try a few Lean things—get rid of WIP, visible waste, and hassles by improving flow, and everybody will be happy with and learn from early results.

If all you get is a value stream map and data out of the initial efforts, that's quite a bit… and it won't be "all"! In getting people to agree on flow as it is now and should be, you'll eliminate waste. And even without any sophisticated analysis, you'll be able to use the data to pinpoint areas where delays and complexity are greatest ("identify the Time Traps"). Often, just a few simple improvements will eliminate waste and delay… once the data on the value stream map has been compiled. So invest the time to get it right.

CHAPTER 13

Raising the Stakes in Service Process Improvement

Inevitably, both the types of projects you select and the methods you use will evolve as your skills in and understanding of Lean Six Sigma increase. The main reasons why some projects aren't addressed until after you and your organization have gained experience with Lean Six Sigma are:

- The problem has proven resistant to improvement (which likely means the underlying causes are complex or interwoven).

- Achieving *significant* gains requires application of more sophisticated Lean Six Sigma methods or tools, or tools that will work only after people have developed a basic trust of the underlying methodology.

- Solutions require the involvement of external suppliers or customers.

- The culture needs to evolve to a point where people are more accepting of the fact that they need to change the way they do their work.

- There is no single silver bullet solution, and there needs to be the resolve to make multiple (incremental) changes in parallel and avoid quick hit "solutions" that won't produce the desired results.

Notice that these issues encompass not only the need for technical expertise, but situations where teams also need well-developed people- and project-management skills. In such situations, the challenges and risks are elevated. Failing to solve a long-standing problem could disillusion staff and be a setback to your initiative, just as asking teams to apply methods they don't understand can create frustration. And you wouldn't want to involve external customers or suppliers on a poorly run project, even if the solutions didn't require any particular expertise.

This chapter looks at case studies from our contributors that are more suitable for second-wave projects—that is, after the organization has some experience under its belt—either because of the need for more sophisticated tools or because they involve cross-functional and/or customer collaboration.

A Quick Guide to the Cases...

Case #6: Gaining control over process complexity [a service Kaizen project]

Why do this particular project?

In February 2002, Bank One held a strategy meeting where key operational managers talked about and prioritized improvement specific opportunities. The issue of "overnight courier packs" used in their Wholesale Lockbox operations rose to the top of the list. This involves corporate-to-corporate payments that customers would overnight to Bank One and want processed ASAP the day the payments arrive.

As described at the beginning of Chapter 5, what started out as a modest service comprising a few deposits each day soon exploded into a high volume, highly complex operation with a lot of "exception processing" (where staff would need to follow non-standard procedures because of varying customer needs). Besides the obvious cost associated with excessive complexity, Bank One was also losing a revenue opportunity—the competition charged for similar services, but Bank One didn't feel comfortable doing so until they could guarantee a specific service level. As one of the largest Wholesale Lockbox providers nationwide, the lost opportunity was estimated at millions of dollars per year to be had if the process was improved.

The Event

An initial improvement event in this area had generated some improvements, but the changes recommended to achieve a quantum improvement in service were deemed to risky, so a second event was launched to reexamine the process. The project was launched using the NEO's group standard improvement event (Kaizen) format:

Day 1: Training and Define. Team members receive baseline training in Lean and Six Sigma concepts, such as the 7 types of wastes.

Day 2: Measure and Analyze. Team members physically walk through the process, following the path that an item of work would follow. They collect data on cycle time, queues, travel distance, and so on to complete the value stream map.

Day 3: Improvement testing. Generating ideas for process improvements continues with an impact/effort analysis to focus in on areas contributing the most to waste. The team then brainstorms solutions for the high-impact areas, and reorganizes the value-stream map to reflect appropriate changes via "should" (future state) mapping (how they'd like the process to operate).

Day 4: Improvement simulation. Participants gather data to evaluate the selected improvements, document proposed changes to the procedures, and simulate the process with these new procedures (as much as is feasible).

Day 5: Evaluate and report out. The team reviews results with the sponsors and celebrates the results.

A portion of the value stream map developed by this team is shown in Figure 13.1.

Figure 13.1: Lockbox Value Stream Map Data

Process Step	List in OWL by Deadline	Transport to Staging	DP-TL Prioritizes Work Based on Deadline	DP Operator Encodes by Numeric Amount	Transport to Reassocia-tion	Clerk Reassociates Work
Functional Area	**LISTING**		**DP**			**Reassociate**
VA vs NVA	NVA	NVA	NVA	VA	NVA	NVA
Operator Cycle Time (sec)	50	**540**	30	5	**1680**	60

This chart shows the data collected by the Lockbox team to quantify various forms of non-value-add (NVA) time in their process.

Solution ideas

The team generated several dozen process improvement ideas they thought would have the biggest impact on turnaround time for the least investment. In general, they covered areas such as:

- **Establishing clearer policies about what would qualify for an guaranteed 4-hour turnaround time.**

- **Being clear about their capability.** This topic had several aspects. First, the team evaluated what staffing levels would be needed under the redesigned process in order to deliver a 4-hour turnaround time. Second, they also identified a keystroke limit beyond which they would knew it would take too long to process the request, which allowed them to establish guidelines around when they could promise a 4-hour turnaround time.

> **Participants**
>
> Team members; Sohail Khan, Stacey Hartman, Yolanda Johnson, Mike Gallagher, Keith Guarneri, Tammie Jones, Karyl Miller, Dannie Paz, David Medina, Karen Mieszala
>
> Support: Doug Hartsema (executive sponsor), Mike Hendershott (project sponsor), Jim Kaminski

Results

Together, these ideas allowed for a 35% improvement in cycle time, and a *reliable* turnaround within the promised service level of 4-hour turnaround. That means the company can now feel confident in generating a revenue stream (see Table 13.1, below, and Figure 13.2, next page).

Table 13.1: Before/After Lockbox Results

Objectives	Pre	Post	% Improv	Type of gain
To charge a fee that reflects the added value that customers receive from this service	$0	$MM *(Identified)*	100%	**Revenue**
Reduce Operator Processing Time	1:03	:38	39%	
Reduce Transportation/Delays	1:33	1:02	32%	
Reduce Total Cycle Time	2:36	1:41	35%	

Figure 13.2: Total Cycle Time (Before/after)

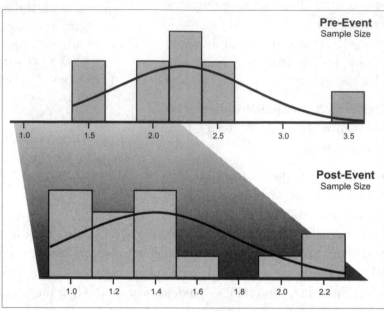

This frequency plot shows the results before and after process changes. The lower, dotted "before" curve reflects an average cycle time of over 2.5 hours. The "after" curve shows a 30% gain in cycle time.

What it took to make this work

- **Adjusting to the readiness of the organization:** As noted, Bank One's NEO group had actually held an initial improvement event in the overnight courier pack process where there were no limitations on what the team could try. The team came up with some radical ideas, including the application of some Lean principles to completely redesign the workspace. But at the report out from that first session there was some pushback. The sponsors told the team they could go back in and hold a second event (the project discussed here) designed to just make process improvements without radically changing the infrastructure of the operations.

- **Sponsor involvement:** The sponsors were involved prior to the project helping to identify priorities and define the project scope. During the improvement event, they met with the team at the end of every day to hear updates and provide input.

- **Wise use of IT:** In most service organizations, the IT resources are already running at or beyond capacity. In some cases, the NEO group has told teams not to even considering IT-related solutions, which they've found actually produces a greater level of creativity. For this project, the IT staff didn't participate in the entire event, but came in during the solution phase where they could help recommend solutions.

- **Best Practice dissemination:** The project described here was conducted at just one of the Bank One sites. But Bank One is a nation-wide company, and they needed to be able to guarantee the same service level at *all* sites before they could start advertising and charging for the service. The internal consulting group therefore had to evaluate the other sites where overnight courier packs were handled, and communicate and adapt what this team learned in order to build company-wide capability.

Case #7: Collaborating with internal customers

At one point, the procurement operations at the Lockheed Martin facility we've visited many times in this book discovered there was a very low first-pass yield on certain types of purchasing requests—meaning few requests made it all the way through the process without being stopped because of some defect (such as missing or incorrect information). The buyers could not solve this problem themselves because many of the problems originated with the internal customers (the people making the requests).

In many ways, this project could be considered "first wave" in that it used basic Lean Six Sigma tools and principles—developing work standards, mapping the process, and so on. But to use these tools effectively, the buyer team had to work effectively across organizational boundaries, carefully avoiding any appearance that they were simply trying to blame others for problems. Working across boundaries takes both credibility (so people outside your work area will be willing to support and/or participate on the project) and a degree of comfort with the tools. That's why significant cross-functional projects are often more suitable as later projects.

Why do this particular project?

Improving cycle time is a strategic goal for any service function. Here, a cross-functional team, which included a customer representative, was assigned to investigate situations or factors that contributed to significant delays. In this case, they realized that 2% of purchase requests (over 1600 annually, or a 3.38 sigma level) were "rejected back" to the requester because of defects (missing, incorrect information, etc.). These rejects extended the lead time from a mode of 11 days with an average of 37 days—more than tripling the cycle time. That meant on any given workday, there were at least three irate customers and helpless buyers on the phones expediting an order impacted by these rejects.

The Analysis

The first issues the team encountered should sound familiar by now: they discovered there was no consistency in how request rejects were handled, no data available on just how many rejects there were, no documentation on how the process should work, a lot of differences in defining what a "reject" was, and so on. The team manually collected data for two months just to establish baselines. In fact, the majority of its work (75%) was spent developing standard work definitions and data collection procedures.

Participants

Team members: Tony Ceneviva, Dave Anderson, Luis Escalante, Catherine Jeffries, Ken Mortimer, Rich Schneider, Zakiya Slayton, Ron Varnum, Myles Burke (BB)

Support: Dan Grant, Martha Derry, Gary Harrer, Rolf Eklund, Lou Diapollo, Ken Klobus

Once they had clear definitions of reject types, the team took a natural first step, analyzing the data on the reasons why a request would get rejected. The results are depicted on the Pareto chart shown in Figure 13.3.

Figure 13.3: Pareto Chart of Reject Reasons

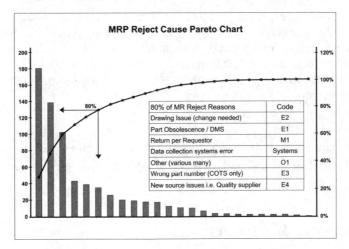

80% of MR Reject Reasons	Code
Drawing Issue (change needed)	E2
Part Obsolescence / DMS	E1
Return per Requestor	M1
Data collection systems error	Systems
Other (various many)	O1
Wrong part number (COTS only)	E3
New source issues i.e. Quality supplier	E4

Pareto charts give a team a focus and set the goals for the remaining DMAIC steps. Here, five causes drove 80% of the rejects.

The team also performed an impact/effort assessment for each of these reject reasons (how much effort would it take to solve that problem;

what kind of impact would it have if they could). The results are shown in Figure 13.4. As you can see, most of the issues that scored highest on the Pareto would also require a lot of effort to address.

Figure 13.4: Impact/Effort Analysis for Reject Causes

Classification of MRP Reject Causes				Define _____
		LEVEL OF EFFORT		
		L	M	H
H		Underlined requirement	**Technical Approval**	Drawing issue (change needed)
		No requirement		Part obsolescence / DMS
				New source issues
M		Return per Requester	Wrong P/N	Export/Import license
				Poor Quality
				Supplier Process Change
L		Min Buy	**Single Source**	Exceptions to T's & C's
		No manufacturer identified on MR		
		On Hold for GPA		
		Wrong Quantity		
		Load time issue		
		Incorrect unit of measure		
		Over Target		
		Wrong OEM/ Wrong Cage Code		
		Sub Process Function		
		Engineering is BLUE	Process is BLACK	
		Mat'l Ordering is GREEN	MAC-MAR is YELLOW	

This matrix was used to identify causes that had both a high impact on the observed problem (rejected purchase requests), and the amount of effort needed to fix them. Drawing and Part obsolescence scored "high" on both scales, so you'll see them in the upper right corner (they were the top two in frequency and also in effort to correct).

Other data analysis included looking at what factors contributed to the length of time a rejected request would sit "in queue" before being addressed.

Solutions & Results

The key ideas the team implemented were to...

- Document the process and standardize work

- Address technical approval, which is a restriction that engineering puts on certain purchases

- Process improvements on Single Source Justification (a federal requirement) to put the form online and add mistake proofing features to assure the initial submittal to the buyer is complete and acceptable

- Implement queue ownership to monitor aging. Give all staff access to upgraded computer system that provides email notification and a daily downloading of the MRP reject queue. This will help prevent excessive loss of lead time.

As a result of the many actions:

- Reject rate dropped immediately from just over 2% to 1.7%

- Verifying Single Sole Source problems went from 100% reviews to just 30% needing review

- All remaining MRP rejects are now corrected in 50% less time than before due to having the standardization and training in place

What it took to make this work

- This team overcame one of the biggest barriers to improvement in service functions: developing reliable data collection and analysis systems. It's not easy work. It took them four months to get the basic system in place, and even longer to refine it. Part of the problem was that in order to collect data, buyers had to perform extra work to enter codes when a request was rejected. It wasn't time consuming, but it is an add-on to the way they were used to doing their work. After the team realized its goal the manual data coding ended.

- Another key lesson they learned was the need to be open-minded to new ways of envisioning their work. What might have historically been viewed as a good use of buyer expertise (using their knowledge to correct mistakes and make sure customers got what they wanted) was soon viewed as total waste. Setting up a system to simplify the process and automate key steps prevented the need for all the rework. In fact, the buyers are now able to use more of their professional skills in value-added work such as developing relationships with suppliers and customers.

Case #8: Improving response time on signature services

Every business has signature services, the ones that are most visible and therefore have the biggest effect on how customers view you. In the city of Fort Wayne, one of the most visible departments is Street, responsible for everything from leaf collection to paving streets (they even have their own asphalt plant). Here's one of their case studies:

Why do this particular project?

Anyone who's driven on streets in the northern states knows that the continuous freeze-thaw cycles wreak havoc on pavement. And the problems are made worse if the city Street department is too busy to do preventive maintenance. Pothole repair is therefore a highly visible city service, and a failure to provide timely response has significant impact on citizen satisfaction and on the number and cost of claims filed against the city. Historically, it has also been the cause of huge overtime expenses that provide another drain on city services.

Employees of the Fort Wayne Street department knew that street repair and maintenance had suffered in recent years. The result was a large and growing number of complaints. Under new leadership, the department began a two-pronged initiative to get the problem under control:

- Increase the number of miles of streets that receive preventive maintenance treatments, such as sealing of cracks, asphalt paving, and so on (services that are largely invisible to citizens but failure to do them results in highly visible problems)

- Improve response time to repair existing potholes

There was one more reason for putting effort in developing the pothole repair system. "We have a heavy concentration of street department workers in the leaf season and the snow-removal season," explains Mayor Graham Richard.

Participants

Support team members: Brad Baumgartner, Jill Morgan, Brooks Beatty

Bob Kennedy (Black Belt), Ted Rhinehart (Champion)

"If we didn't have other work for them to do at other times, we'd have tremendous dips and valleys in employment."

The Analysis

The first question most teams want to answer is "just how bad is the problem." Figure 13.5 shows a dotplot of response times once a complaint was received. The average response time was well over 20 hours, with many trailing off much longer.

Figure 13.5: Quantifying the Problem

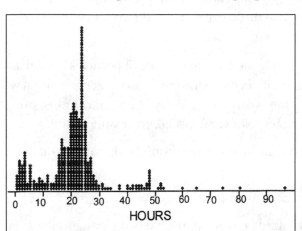

On this chart, each dot represents the amount of time it took to complete one repair. The plot shows a typical pattern seen whenever time is being measured: there is more than just one peak, and the points trail out on the long end. Patterns like this are seen when there are some types of jobs that go quickly (the small peak toward the left), a majority of work that has almost a normal distribution, and a few jobs that, for whatever reason, take a long time to complete.

The team also mapped out the process then brainstormed ideas about possible causes of problems. The team discovered that there was a lot of inefficiency in the repair process. For example, if a crew had a repair on the northeast and one on the southwest, they'd go to the northeast and then to southwest and do nothing in between. Furthermore, standing orders were to repair only the potholes for which they had repair orders—so a team could drive over a pothole in one block on their way to fix one in the next block, and not do anything about it. (Actually, most processes have some version of this problem.)

In discussing problems with the process, the team decided to focus on:

- How the work orders were filled out (timeliness and correctness)

- Communication of the work orders to the appropriate supervisor

- Factors affecting delays in completing the repairs (such as whether there was sufficient staff, weather conditions)

Solutions & Results

The process changes made by the team improved communication about where the problems were and made better use of the crews' time. The key changes were:

- "If you see it, fix it." The new norm is to fix all potholes even if an official complaint hasn't been lodged or hasn't reached the crew. (This type of solution works when delays because of transportation time are far longer than value-added processing time.)

- Supervisors started picking up orders from the dispatchers at least 3x/day.

- Repair orders are checked daily instead of weekly.

- Creation of a specialized crew for pothole repair during leaf season (so the repair work can continue in parallel with leaf collection).

- Using the 3rd shift to provide additional capability when needed.

- Centralizing control over repair assignments and completion.

Each truck is now equipped with communication equipment so crews can be updated immediately of any changes in their work orders.

Results

Defining a defect as any repair not completed within 24 hours, the original Sigma level was 1.2, which quickly went up to 3 Sigma. (In fact, that continues to rise: by December 2002, the average pothole repair time was less than 9 hours, with 100% of all reported pot holes repaired in less than 24 hours—meaning their defects have held at zero for a number of months). With lead time reduced so dramatically (see Figure 13.6), there essentially is no WIP to clog up the process. Perhaps the most important result is that positive citizen response has inspired the crews, and increased their job performance, job satisfaction, and self-image.

Figure 13.6: Improvements from the Pothole Repair Project

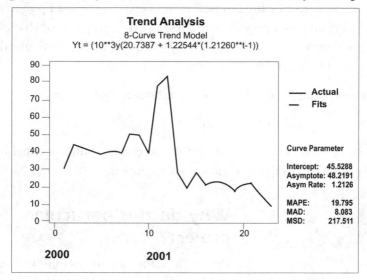

This time plot shows a dramatic (and sustained) drop in repair time soon after the project was launched in September 2001. Currently, 98% of the repair orders are addressed within 24 hours.

What it took to make this work

- **Waiting until the time was right.** Mayor Richard points out they staged the timing of this project purposefully so that the head of the Street department could build rapport and actually get everyone to the point that when the project started, they knew they could accomplish it. "We have so many people looking over our shoulders that part of our challenge in building trust and pride of spirit is project choice," says Richard. "Project definition and managing expectations are key."

- **Empowering employees to act.** The traditional command-and-control style of bureaucracy had contributed to waste and inefficiency. Instituting the "see it, fix it" policy allowed employees to exercise initiative and use their time more effectively and complete repairs more quickly.

Case #9: Cleaning up your workspace (a 5S+1 visual office project)

Disorganization and clutter in a workspace are big contributors to wasted time in service functions, and, if allowed to exist in public areas, will give customers a poor first impression. The way out of that clutter and dis-organization is a Lean technique known as the 5S's, introduced in Chapter 11 (see p. 301–302). The five steps are:

Sort—>Straighten—>Shine—>Standardize—>Sustain

...and some add a 6th S —>**Safety**

The buyers at the Lockheed Martin procurement center decided to put the 5S+1 method to the test. Here's what happened...

Participants

Team: Jennifer Sharpe, Judy Liang, George Sholtis, Natalie Stewart, Glenn Harden, Nicole Plair

Resources: Manny Zulueta (Champion), Ranga Srinivas (coach), Myles Burke (BB)

Why do this particular project?

During a value stream mapping event, it became obvious just how much variation there was among the buyers in how they performed the same job. The data showed the more productive buyers were also those who were the most organized in folder management, files, and general workspace usage. The team therefore launched an initiative called "Visual Workplace" with a very simple goal: To reach the point that when anyone was away from their desk, someone else could easily fill-in temporarily without spending all their time searching for the right files, information, or status. The scope of the effort was defined as follows:

- Paper/desktop organization (visual workplace) to clearly identify the status and backlog of work-in-process

- Labeling

- Paper consolidation, dissemination of the use of some Best Practices in organizing electronic files, schedules, contacts, queuing tools

The Project

The team studied other companies then held weekly meetings to develop a plan for achieving a clean, organized workspace. For each "S," they talked about what it meant in their situation, and talked about how they would achieve that goal. For example, the first S is **Sort**, getting rid of unneeded work (usually paper files or other documentation) from the area, and keeping only what's truly needed. To achieve this goal, the team follows the **Red Tag process:**

1) Each person examines their workspace and puts a red tag on anything they don't immediately need

2) The red-tagged items are all dealt with:

   – All "live" but currently unneeded folders are moved to a central file room; they are taken out when needed then moved back upon completion of a task

   – Outdated publications are removed

   – File cartons are removed from the work area

3) All remaining work (which is "needed") is organized in the workspace according to its purpose

In the next step, Straighten—based on the simple phrase "a place for everything and everything in its place"—any extraneous paperwork, furniture, etc., is eliminated. The team continued this way through all of the S's, developing guidelines for desk organization that would make it possible for anyone to easily find information in someone else's workspace, etc.

This same process works for both physical and computer workspaces; in the latter case, people delete old files, archive files that should be kept for business reasons but are no longer active, and so on.

Results

The team estimated it cost about $100 per person on average to complete this project, which included purchasing of standard supplies to make the work organization possible (In/Out boxes, hanging file baskets, file dividers, etc.). The time investment per person included a 1-hour introduction to 5S+1 process, plus 6 hours on average to complete all the sorting, straightening, shining, and so on (see Figure 13.7 for examples of improvements). The results are priceless in productivity and attitude.

Figure 13.7: Before and After Workspaces

Team member Judy Liang shows her office before the 5S+1 project (left). One action taken by the team was to post charts that help them track daily work (right).

What did it take to make this work?

- Having the project originate from the buyers rather than a management edict. This is an important factor since the issue boils down to having people rearrange their own personal desk space.

- Allowing some degree of flexibility based on job function and personalities. The team did not want to mandate that all desks look exactly the same. Rather everyone just had to have their work organized such that "strangers" could easily navigate in their workspace.

- Translating what could be perceived as a manufacturing tool to the office environment.

- Maintaining focus on 5S+1 objectives.

"I was at a customer's facility in Florida and received a panic call from my boss about a hot placement that needed to occur that morning. With my workplace organized it was simple to walk my coworker through the status to exactly describe where the files were for her to place the order."

—Natalie Stewart, MAC-MAR Buyer, Visual Workplace team leader.

Case #10: Knowing what's here (and where it is)

Most programs at Lockheed Martin rely on Government Furnished Property (GFP), equipment or materials that are owned by the U.S. government and furnished to Lockheed Martin. Knowing exactly when this equipment arrives and getting it to the proper location at the needed time has been challenging in the past. An earlier initiative failed to produce the desired results, so a team at the Naval Electronics Surveillance Systems–Moorestown, NJ, location (NESS-SS) was commissioned to take on the effort.

Why do this particular project?

There are two very powerful reasons why Lockheed Martin wanted to gain better control over the GFP it receives:

- First, the use of GFP is to be controlled in accordance with strict Federal regulations. Violations occur if property is not utilized in accordance with the terms of the government contract.

- Second, and perhaps more importantly, many times the GFP is being used to support programs that are crucial to national defense. If the GFP tracking and delivery system fails, critical program schedules may suffer.

The project goal was straightforward: getting the GFP equipment to show up in the right place at the right time. High level goals of the project were to:

- Develop better metrics

- Reduce cycle time

- Reduce labor

- Document the process

Participants

Team members: Edna Winans, Glenn Carlson, Steven Ezzyk, Jeffrey Lewis, Edward Maisel, Robert Ogbin, William Quail, Robert Wolfe, Paul Zurcher, Richard Winans, Joanne Smith, Kevin Fast (BB)

Support resource: Lara Cribb

Naval / Customer representatives: Charles Deitch, Kenneth Hornback

Before the Project – Picking the Team

In this project, team membership would be an important determinant of success. Rather than limit the team to like-minded individuals, the Black Belt pushed for a significant cross-functional team, ending up with 15 people representing diverse functions inside NE&SS-SS and 2 customer representatives. This positioned the team to define and understand the process many times better than if they had limited themselves to one or two functional groups.

Analysis

After some discussion the team defined the boundaries of its project from when the GFP was received at the warehouse until it was delivered to its final destination. The box was drawn here to ensure that the project was not too large and to ensure that the tasks remained within the team's sphere of influence.

Once the boundaries were clear, the team developed a flowchart then started measuring the performance of the process. Fortunately, a wealth of data was at their fingertips: by the nature of the process, documentation is well maintained and data mining was relatively straightforward. In addition, the team conducted a survey to understand how well participants and stakeholders understood the GFP processes. The data exposed numerous defects in the process:

- 69% of the deliveries had incoming documentation that was not consistent with engineering's definitions

- 48% of the deliveries had no local point of contact identified who could determine program use and resolve issues

- 29% of the deliveries had not been defined in their contracts

- 21% of deliveries were unauthorized direct shipments to end users (bypassing the warehouse receiving point)

- 19% of the deliveries had incomplete or missing packing lists for warehouse inventory

Because of these problems, GFP tracking and delivery occurred seamlessly only 10% of the time (a low first-pass yield). The other 90% of the time, some data was missing or incorrect: orders *without* problems had a cycle time of 2 days on average; orders *with* problems could take 2 days to 2 weeks. What the team discovered:

> "Not only didn't people know what they were doing wrong, they did not know what they were doing right."
>
> —Glenn Carlson, GFP Lead

- The survey revealed that engineers who initiate orders or request GFP for use on their programs did not understand the process nor the ramification of incomplete information.

- The requirements definition and the ordering processes (and related documentation) were inconsistent and often incomplete. It was difficult for staff to ascertain the nature of the GFP.

- In some cases, inconsistencies were the result of naming conventions.

- There was no single process owner to monitor process performance.

- There was no one procedure to integrate the processes across the organization. While most individual functions had work instructions, they were not defined and integrated as a system.

- Though the GFP receiving point was the warehouse (for in-processing functions to be performed), sometimes direct end-user deliveries occurred. This resulted in the need for additional personnel and trans-shipping, thereby delaying the availability of the GFP for the program.

Solutions & Results

It was obvious that NE&SS-SS employees needed to be trained, and convincing the stakeholders of the need was easy. What was most exciting, however, was the active participation the customer (= the Navy) assumed in order to train those in government. Other improvements included:

- The team developed and implemented a standard procedure that applied to the entire organization, not just local functional areas.

- Process owners were identified who are responsible for managing the process across the organization.

- The database used to generate required documentation was enhanced to provide more information to identify the equipment received.

- A feedback mechanism was implemented that automatically raises a flag if the proper internal documentation isn't timely. Management is involved, by design, to encourage proper behavior.

- Key stakeholders have volunteered to help educate everyone touched by the GFP process.

> "No one was doing anything wrong. The Navy ordered a Gateway computer, Gateway shipped a Gateway computer. And our defined requirement was for a 'simulator'—which was a Gateway computer."
>
> —Glenn Carlson, GFP Lead

Results:

- When you add up all of the labor across the organization required to resolve various problems and combinations of problems, this team estimated that more than 2,700 work hours may be saved a year. A tremendous return on a $30K investment!

- The team eliminated potentially huge liability and customer satisfaction issues.

- The new process encourages people to follow the procedures without penalizing a program for last minute fire drills.

- The process ensures that GFP is delivered on time—eliminating potential impact to important military program schedules.

What did it take to make this work?

- Having the right people on the team—including customers. Issues with the customer that would have otherwise been outside of the NE&SS-SS's control were addressed (a continuing partnership ensured continued accuracy). Team members realized they each had knowledge of only a portion of the process, and they needed everyone on the team to participate in order to get an accurate picture of the process as a whole.

- **Convincing people of the importance of process documentation.** Because employees have gotten along "just fine" in their jobs without documentation, they take some convincing of the necessity for establishing procedures. As Kevin Fast puts it, "Today, more than ever, procedures mean something, they have teeth. These documents can no longer be put on a shelf like they may have been in years past—they must be followed."

- **Ability to recognize an over-reliance on "heroes."** In every organization, there are heroes like Edna Winans. With her 20 years of experience she was so familiar with the way the GFP system worked that she could usually overcome limitations in the documentation or process (by accurately guessing where certain types of equipment should be delivered, etc.). But when Edna was gone, or a new employee came on board, no one could perform to Edna's level. The conversion of tribal knowledge to standardized procedures reduces the complexity of the process.

- **Using stakeholder influence.** This team leveraged stakeholders to obtain authority and buy-in necessary to be successful. On this project the customer proved to be the ultimate stakeholder and friend to the team.

"We considered starting at the beginning of time—when an engineer thought that he might just need some sort of GFP. However, as we considered all of the variables—all of the different development engineers, many scenarios, vendors of all types, GFP of all types— it was clear that such a scope would be too large and too complex. Keeping the project manageable is a key to success."

—Kevin Fast, GFP Project Black Belt, Lockheed Martin

A few bonus cases...

As in Chapter 12, we were unable to present all of the cases our contributors have shared with us. We have compiled the cases described in this chapter and others at our website (www.georgegroup.com). Here's a quick peek at two of the additional cases you'll find there.

Case #11: Changing professional practice

Once we're trained on a given way to perform any work, be it a simple task or heart surgery, it's human nature to continue doing the work that way (as long as we think it's working). One example of this phenomenon comes from Stanford Hospital and Clinics. For several years, staff had been aware that different cardiac physicians prescribed different pre-discharge procedures for their patients. But the issue of asking physicians to change their practice was deemed so politically charged that the topic sat on the back burner... until the cardiac surgery team decided to confront the issue head on. As it turned out, one set of pre-discharge practices was more expensive than another, with no perceivable advantage to patients. A standard practice was then adopted by all the physicians in the group.

The solution to this problem turned out to be relatively simple, but the key lesson is that the outcome may not have been so positive had the issue been tackled at the very beginning of Stanford's quality initiatives. Rather, over several years of being on and around improvement teams, the physicians (and everyone else at Stanford) started developing an "improvement mentality" that made them more open to critically examining their own practices.

Case #12: Developing supplier relationships through Lean Six Sigma

The basic philosophy that drives MAC-MAR's service is that their customers deserve to buy the *best* products made from the best suppliers in the world. "And if the best suppliers in the world are not our current suppliers… then we must make them the best!" They use a formal four-phase, fourteen-step engagement process with a goal of having the suppliers be self-sufficient in their Lean Six Sigma journey and to bring these suppliers into design efforts early on (and they'll have the opportunity to become a sole source supplier for their product). They make it a win-win engagement by telling suppliers, "We are after your waste, not your margins."

But the challenge here was that most of MAC-MAR's suppliers fall closer to the "mom & pop" end of the spectrum than to "worldwide conglomerate"—that is, they are small operations without a lot of flexibility in staffing or spending. The last census showed 75% are facilities of less than 250 people. Small suppliers have fewer managers to deploy strategic plans or drastically reorganize work to cut costs while improving outputs. There are few green fields, a lot of heritage, and many single sole sources. They are always asked to reduce cost without always having corresponding reductions in their own costs—and thus eventually they hit a price wall.

To decide which of their thousands of suppliers to work with, the procurement staff rated each supplier according to…

- How much business they do with each supplier
- Which suppliers were strategically critical either because they were sole source suppliers or because of the volume, technology, or criticality to providing Lockheed Martin's services and products
- How much leverage Lockheed Martin has with the supplier
- The current relationship between Lockheed Martin and the supplier

This evaluation was balanced against decisions concerning how much Lockheed Martin could afford to do ($s and personnel) to help suppliers improve. The result of this analysis was a list of 200 suppliers that Lockheed Martin's MAC-MAR and specific programs wanted to work with, and an understanding of WHY for each one—e.g., to reduce lead times, improve delivery, improve new product introductions, improve risk management, reduce cost, and so on. Over the past few years, they have used this information to help them structure and launch dozens of supplier development projects, which ranged from holding Kaizen improvement events (centered around value stream mapping) at the suppliers' locations, to holding supplier symposiums, to deploying Lockheed Martin experts full- or part-time to work with the suppliers.

Lessons We Can Learn

There is no substitute for conducting a rational project selection process, such as that described in Chapter 4. But the final list of candidate projects should also be filtered against the likelihood that your organization can complete the project successfully. There are no hard and fast rules about what kinds of projects an organization should work on first, or second, or not at all. But, in general, the kinds of cases in this chapter work better once an organization has some experience because they...

- Crossed organizational boundaries—both in terms of bringing together multiple internal departments and in including suppliers and customers

- Used tools/methods that might seem threatening to someone new to Lean Six Sigma (such as the 5S method, which requires people to change their own workspaces)

- Required a degree of cultural readiness and enthusiasm for improvement

These types of projects *can* be attacked by novice teams, *if* they have expert coaching by Black Belts or Master Black Belts who have both excellent people skills and technical skills.

CHAPTER 14

Designing World-Class Services
(Design for Lean Six Sigma)

By Kimberly Watson-Hemphill (George Group)[1]
and Rod Skewes (Caterpillar, Inc.)[2]

In the summer of 2001, an employee from Caterpillar's Malaga, Spain, facility was trying to book into a hotel in Peoria, Illinois, but his corporate credit card wasn't accepted. The employee called the Corporate Travel office in Peoria thinking they might be able to help, but no one there knew anything about his credit card. Corporate Travel called Corporate Treasury, but they didn't know anything about it either.

Eventually everything was straightened out, but this one incident set off a chain reaction once the corporate departments realized that it was the very small tip of a very large iceberg:

- There were a number of credit card programs that existed at each of Cat's global sites
- These programs weren't connected in any way
- There was no way of knowing how many credit cards they had, how much was spent on those cards, or the rebate dollars (financial incentives), if any, that the company was getting from the overall program

That meant Caterpillar would have to *invent* a process if it wanted to be able to manage its corporate credit card program.

The DMAIC model illustrated by cases studies from previous chapters works great if you're trying to improve processes, services, or products that already exist. But the basic DMAIC toolkit used by many organizations doesn't incorporate the type of rigor needed when you want to invent a new service, product, or process (or overhaul something that is already in place). Myles Burke of Lockheed Martin, who's been mentioned frequently in this book, found that some of the procurement processes were so complicated, and had so much variation from person to person that he gave up on value stream mapping and went into process redesign. There was just no way that procurement was ever going to satisfy its 14 external customers in terms of lead time with improvements to the existing "process" (using the term loosely).

In Caterpillar's case, you couldn't really say the value stream was "broken" because it had never existed at a macro level in the company. A rough cut at the cost benefit showed it might be worth $500,000 in hard savings per year for a relatively modest investment of available resources (that is, the "lead time to results" was favorable). The key would be pulling together all the disparate pieces into one coherent value stream designed to meet their business needs and those of the people using the credit card system.

Designing Services with DMEDI

The key issue when you want to design a new product, service, or process (or overhaul an existing process to the point where it's almost like starting from a blank slate) is that there are a lot more unknowns than when you are just tweaking what you already have. You don't really know what customers want. You don't really know which models or approaches are workable. You may not have existing capabilities to provide the needed functionalities.

The preferred improvement model used for these situations goes by a number of names: DMEDI (for Define-Measure-Explore-Develop-Implement), DMADV (for Define-Measure-Analyze-Design-Verify), or just Design for Six Sigma or Design for Lean Six Sigma (DFLSS). In this chapter, we use the terms DMEDI and DFLSS interchangeably. Though the labels differ, all are basically business strategies for executing any high-value projects that require a significant amount of new design. They all incorporate a greater emphasis on capturing and understanding the customer and business needs than does DMAIC, and establish clear links at every step from translating "needs" into "requirements" and ultimately to the processes used to create the new service or product. While DMEDI requires additional tools, it builds on the basic DMAIC methodology, and remains fact-based and data-driven:

Define: The project team comes together with its sponsor to develop well-defined charter that has clear ties to the business strategy and line-of-sight linkage to significant financial benefits

Measure: The team focuses on understanding the Voice of the Customer, information that will be used to design best-in-class products and services

Explore: The team innovates to develop multiple solution alternatives and selects the most promising concept and confirms a high-level design

Develop: The team uses Lean and Six Sigma tools and simulation to create a robust design

Implement: The design is piloted, a control plan is developed, and the new product or service is launched

In addition, all the process management basics established for DMAIC apply to DMEDI (see sidebar, next page).

Like many of the methods discussed in this book, Design for Lean Six Sigma (DFLSS) arose in manufacturing (in product development departments). But DFLSS tools work as well for designing services and processes as they do for products, and the overarching methodology evolved in what is essentially a service function (design). DFLSS has been successfully used on a wide range of service projects, such as developing new marketing channels for existing offerings, IT solution development and outsourcing, establishing a new process for managing intellectual property, developing new financial services offerings, and so on. This chapter walks through the DMEDI model, using the credit card case study introduced at the beginning of this chapter to illustrate the key activities and tools in each phase.

> **Using DMAIC for Product/Service Design**
>
> Caterpillar uses both DMAIC and DMEDI in the new product introduction process. DMEDI tools are preferred when, as described in the text, the number of unknowns is large or addressing a customer need requires significant new knowledge or capabilities.

All the DMAIC basics apply

Design for Lean Six Sigma projects—under the names of DMEDI or DMADV—are run using the same infrastructure and guidelines described for DMAIC teams:

- Projects are led by Black Belts with help from Master Black Belts, Champions, and Process Owners.
- Broad, cross-functional teams work on projects to mitigates risk and develop a solution that is acceptable to all areas of the business.
- Software tracking tools allow the executive team to monitor overall program status and financial results.
- Projects should be managed and monitored as usual, with Phase/Gate reviews between phases conducted by the Champion and sponsor(s)—this guards against having a team just dive into developing a process/service/product without proper decision making along the way.
- Design teams should be part of a project Pull system (where the number of projects is limited by the capacity to work on them).

Define

The key objective of the Define phase is the development of a well-defined charter. The elements of a DMEDI charter are similar to those discussed in Chapter 11 for DMAIC projects: a product/service description, business case, project goals, project scope, a high-level project plan, and team members. The charter should be sufficiently detailed so that the business objectives and the scope are clear to both the team and the management.

In addition, there are two major elements of risk to be considered in a DFLSS project. First, the risk that the project will not meet its objectives, which would primarily be a risk to the schedule and to benefits (technical, cost, schedule, and market risk). Second, there are the risks that the project poses to other elements of the business.

Phase/Gate Review for Define

To advance to the Measure Phase, the team should have a solid charter with a validated business case and a clear, attainable scope and ROIC.

A cross-functional team should be created, with representation from different areas that will be affected by the project and a balance of effective team roles (as discussed in Chapter 10). Initial planning work on communications, project management, and risk should be complete.

CASE STUDY:
Caterpillar Global Credit Card Project – Define Phase

When confronted with all the questions it could not answer about corporate credit cards, Caterpillar formed a global team consisting of representatives from corporate treasury, corporate travel, corporate accounts payable, shared services (United Kingdom), European tax, the Geneva subsidiary, and Asia Pacific treasury. Initial efforts showed that no process currently existed, so the team knew it would need to follow the DMEDI model to develop something that would meet Caterpillar's needs.

The charter stated that the project should quantify the number of cards currently used globally by Caterpillar, the total dollar amount of credit card purchases, and the cost to administer the cards. The team would then investigate and implement improvement alternatives.

The Business Case

Caterpillar is currently receiving significant rebates on cards for U.S. operations. The expectation was that that amount could be

---

Complexity Prevention vs. Complexity Cures

Recent advances in Design for Lean Six Sigma include a focus on reducing product and service complexity—both non-value-add (transparent) complexity, that which is invisible to the customer, and also customer-facing complexity, which exists in features and functions thought to be desired by the customer, but that don't add shareholder value. As you may recall from Chapter 5, the key is to use a platform design approach, where you standardize as many components, steps, modules, etc., as possible. This platform approach is a complexity "prevention" technique that served external customers; the process/service redesign case in this chapter is a complexity "cure" that affects internal customers. In both cases, the team had to incorporate a deep understanding of the Voice of the Customer in all phases of the project.

doubled if the team looked at the purchases outside those covered by the current U.S. program. Targeted benefits included:

- doubling rebates (financial incentives) received by Caterpillar
- improved VAT tax recovery (the European equivalent of sales tax)
- improved ease-of-use for employees who are traveling and doing business around the world
- visibility of purchases for greater purchasing leverage

The team managed the scope with a multigeneration plan (see Figure 14.1). The current project would establish a worldwide program for Caterpillar's two basic types of credit cards (Travel & Entertainment and Procurement) using a limited number of provider banks (the ultimate target was one bank, but that would turn out not to be achievable), and maintaining current electronic capability for those areas who had it. This would be supported with a standardized process to obtain cards, collect purchase information, and collect data. All information would be connected electronically worldwide from all credit card providers.

Figure 14.1: Multigeneration Plan for Global Credit Card Project

	Generation 1	Generation 2	Generation 3
Vision	Travel and Entertainment Cards and Purchasing Cards with worldwide accessibility with a limited group of provider banks. Current electronic capabilities will be maintained.	Travel and Entertainment Cards and Purchasing Cards with few partners and rest of world booking to ledger and paying electronically.	Buy anything - including direct material - with credit card. Payment and booking are done electronically.
Product/ Service Generation	Standardized process to obtain cards and to collect purchase information (traditional credit cards).	Same as Generation 1 except that everything is done electronically.	Integrated purchasing and payment functions.
Technologies/ Platforms	Transmit data files from credit card providers.	Software to link ledger systems.	Integrated software to purchase, pay, and book transactions.

Measure

The key objective of the Measure phase is to understand the Voice of the Customer (VOC)—or Voice of the "Process Partner" if you're working on an internal process (see sidebar, below)—and to translate the customer feedback into measurable design requirements. Chapter 3 discussed a wide range of techniques for capturing VOC data; the discussion here focuses on the tools and methods most helpful in design efforts. The degree of VOC emphasis may come as a surprise to those who have only been involved in DMAIC projects in the past. While customer needs play a central role in shaping priorities in a DMAIC project, here, a good understanding of customer needs is the single most important determinant of success.

Capturing the Voice of the Customer

The first step in capturing the Voice of the Customer is determining the appropriate customer segment. While in theory anyone in the world could buy your services, there is a particular subgroup, or segment, that is *most likely* to buy. If you're interested in achieving maximum performance, you want to focus your products and services on the customer group where it is most likely to resonate in the marketplace. Customers should be segmented or grouped according to similar needs. Focus on the customer segment(s) that aligns with corporate strategy, are attractive from a size and profitability standpoint, and align with the business's capability to satisfy them.

Once the customer segments are known, they need to be prioritized. As with other areas discussed in this book, the Pareto principle works here: 20% of your opportunities will bring you 80% of the value. (That is, the greatest value may come from a small portion of the customer base.)

Internal Customers or Process Partners?

A central tenet of Lean Six Sigma and most other quality methodologies is that "only customers can define quality." Historically, a distinction was made between "internal customers" (those to whom an employee hands off work) and "external customers" (the end purchaser or user).

Some companies, like Caterpillar, have found it helpful to reserve the term "customer" for those who purchase and use the end product or service— because they ultimately determine a company's fate in the marketplace. What used to be called "internal customers" are now called "process partners" to emphasize the idea that everyone inside the company should be working together to best serve the ultimate customer.

Start the VOC process by taking advantage of existing and available information (see sidebar, below). Once you understand the gap between what customer information you already have and what is needed, use proactive methods to gather additional information. The most important part of using any of these techniques is having the approach well planned in advance.

Typical existing sources of customer information

Every company has customer contact that can provide a baseline for service/product design. Some sources to look at are complaints, compliments, returns or credits, contract cancellations, market share changes, customer referrals, closure rates of sales calls, market research reports, completed customer evaluations, industry reports, available literature, competitor assessments, web page hits, or technical support calls.

If you survey customers and ask which features they would like to see in your services, they will undoubtedly say, "All of them!" However, customers attach different values to feature combinations, and we know that there are certain features that would be preferred by the customer over other options. That's why the process described below incorporates a rating by customers of the importance they place on different features or functionalities. You might also benefit by doing a Kano analysis, where service or product features are separated into three categories (expected quality vs. normal quality vs. exciting quality) based on customer expectations (see the original *Lean Six Sigma* book, pp. 140-142, for details).

Translating needs into requirements

The next step is to translate the Voice of the Customer into the Voice of the Designer. The method to do this is called Quality Function Deployment (QFD), a highly structured and very effective approach for converting customer needs into design requirements. The secret to QFD's success is that it establishes design requirements that are:

- Measurable (quantifiable)—so you can tell if you met them

- Solution-independent, meaning the requirements aren't linked to predefined solutions that the design team might have in mind (allowing for much greater creativity)

- Directly correlated to customer needs, so you know that you're addressing issues that are important to customers

- Easy to understand

To achieve these goals, QFD walks through a series of steps:

1) Identifying customer needs from the VOC data you gathered

2) Prioritizing those needs

3) Establishing design requirements that address all customer needs

4) Prioritizing the design requirements (to focus the design effort)

5) Establishing performance targets

These steps are linked together very deliberately, so that at the end you can trace a path directly from customer needs to specific elements of the service/product design. Along the way, you'll be asked to answer questions such as:

- What are your current strengths and weaknesses relative to the competition?

- How do these strengths and weaknesses compare to the customer priorities?

- Where are there gaps that need to be closed?

- Are their opportunities to learn from the competition?

- Are their opportunities for breakthroughs to exceed competitors' capabilities?

- Are there any customer needs that you do not know how to measure? If yes, how will you meet these needs?

- Are there design contradictions that cannot be resolved?

- Are the performance targets achievable?

The team will also assess the impact of failing to meet the targets and specifications, including an assessment of different risks (to the customer, to the business) and whether the organization's current competencies are well matched to meet the performance targets. Because there is so much learning about the project in the Measure phase, teams often discover quick wins: changes that look to be a sure thing, are easily reversible, and require little or no investment. The team should take advantage of quick wins as soon as possible, and begin accruing financial benefits. A Kaizen event (see p. 52) can be conducted to facilitate immediate implementation.

Phase/Gate Review for Measure

The Measure phase closes with a Phase/Gate Review. The team and the leadership should feel that the Voice of the Customer is thoroughly understood, and that clear design requirements have been established. The team will have assembled critical metrics and begin tracking them on a scorecard. The next phase will generate high-level concepts.

CASE STUDY:
Global Credit Card Project – Measure Phase

The focus of the Measure phase was to understand the Voice of the Process Partner via a series of global surveys. The surveys addressed the needs of Cat's "Road Warriors" (frequent travelers), of those using procurement cards, and of the business.

Survey #1: Voice of the Business

This survey was sent to all business units so the team could understand what business requirements a global credit card system would need to meet, and to gather data to shape the requests for quote they would later send to potential vendors. Sixty responses were received, covering all major business units. There were many different provider banks for 25,000 cards total, working in 23 different currencies, and almost 800,000 transactions a year. The fees varied widely, and there were virtually no rebates being collected outside of the United States. Administrative costs were also quantified for the first time.

What turned out to be important to the business units was:
- worldwide acceptability
- good expense reporting capability
- flexibility in purchasing card usage

Respondents also indicated they'd be interested in combining Travel & Entertainment and Procurement cards, which Caterpillar hoped would reduce process complexity.

Survey #2: Voice of the Process Partner (Travelers)

220 surveys went to frequent travelers in Europe, Asia, Australia, and the U.S. The heart of the survey was a list of 17 credit card attributes that the travelers rated on importance. Responses showed that all 17 features were critical, and no additional feature requirements surfaced from a user standpoint. (Conveniently, all of these features turned out to be present in most card offerings that were later considered.) The survey also gathered information about where customer satisfaction was the highest and lowest among provider banks.

Survey #3: Voice of the Process Partner (Procurement)

136 Procurement Card users worldwide were surveyed. This survey polled customers on the importance of 12 key criteria. Similarly to the previous survey, all were deemed important, and no criteria added. Information about high and low quality providers was also tracked.

Armed with the Voice of the Process Partner, the team developed a series of QFD houses. The first house took the needs from the surveys and translated them into measurable critical requirements (see Figure 14.2, next page). The requirements that were the most important were that (1) the card would be useful for travel, purchases, and phone, (2) the card would be accepted in many countries, (3) transferability between Caterpillar facilities, (4) software compatibility, and (5) the number of settlement currencies.

The next house of quality transferred the requirements to more detailed card functions, or design requirements. This house was instrumental in providing criteria for evaluation of different designs in the Explore phase.

The Gate Review confirmed that the project was on track to achieve anticipated benefits.

Figure 14.2: First House of Quality (excerpt)

This is an excerpt of the first House of Quality the Caterpillar team developed as part of the credit card project. This house relates customer (or "Process Partner") statements of needs (left column) to critical requirements (top columns). The individual scores for each requirement are multiplied by the importance (far right), then summed at the bottom to get a Priority rating.

9=strong / 3=moderate, / 1=weak — **Voice of the Travelers**	Rebate	Cash Advance Fee	# of Countries Covered	Transaction/Vendor Restrictions	Credit Limits	Administration Costs	Ad Hoc Reporting Capability	Software Compatability	# of Settlement Currencies	Limited Liability if Lost/Stolen	# of Countries with ATMs	Fraud Monitoring	On-line statements	Downloadable statements	Customer Importance
ATM in home country		3	9		1						9	9			3
ATMs worldwide		3	9		1						9	9			8
Widely Accepted	3		9	9	1	3				9	9	9			10
Customer Service			3		9	3	3	9	9			9	1	1	10
Insured purchases			9						1		9				6
Travel Insurance			9						1		9				10
Useful for travel, purchases, and phone charges	9		9	9	9	9	9	9	9	9	3	9	3	9	6
Transferable between facilities (currencies)			3			9	3	9	9				3	3	8
Internet purchases	3			9	9							9			6
Flexible credit limit					9	3	1			3		9	1	1	9
Priority	102	33	441	198	300	213	117	216	232	171	351	468	61	97	

Explore

After defining requirements, the team needs to answer the question: *What is the best way to meet our customer needs at a conceptual design level?*

This is where innovation occurs. Usually, teams will discover that there are conflicts between customer needs and the company's ability to meet those needs, conflicts between different design parameters, or conflicts between cost and performance. Often, trade-offs or compromises are made—though finding solutions to resolve these conflicts rather than compromise leads to more innovative products and services.

At the Measure Phase/Gate Review, the team has to convince its sponsor and other leaders that it has a solid understanding of the Critical-to-

Quality (CTQ) customer requirements. Now they have to combine that market and customer knowledge to generate specific concepts. The reaction at this point? "Now that we're about to work on solutions, how do we get started?"

Functional Analysis

Every service or product has certain things that it must do in order to perform acceptably from a customer's viewpoint. Functional analysis breaks the service down into its key tasks. This will help generate multiple solution ideas for each function, usually displayed in a tree diagram. Functional analysis also helps break down the problem into more manageable pieces to improve the odds of developing the best concepts. For example, rather than brainstorm concepts for a new fast-food service at a system level, the team would identify the functions (take order, fulfill order, collect payment) and then brainstorm solutions for each of the functions (e.g., take order—pencil and paper, cash register buttons, Internet).

In the Measure phase, the team developed the first House of Quality with QFD (see Figure 14.2, p. 372). Here, they continue working with the QFD matrix, completing House 2, which links the functions with the design requirements. The goal is to prioritize the functions that have the strongest link to the Voice of the Customer/Process Partner, because those will be the foundation of any new design. You can also use this work to flow down the high-level design targets into smaller design elements.

In completing House 2, the team will understand what functions the product/service must have, and how those functions rate in priority. Now they will investigate how those functions can be filled. The secret here is to be as creative as possible:

- **Brainstorm ideas**: With a little creativity and planning up front, brainstorming can be both a great source of new ideas and a lot of fun! There are many different twists on idea generation to help spark creativity within the team. (Check any good facilitation book for many different types of brainstorming.)

- Use **Benchmarking** to broaden awareness of what already exists out in the marketplace, and also what's possible. If you use benchmarking in this context, be sure to look at best practices that exist elsewhere in your organization, not just what other companies are doing. Review your existing products and services for ideas: Are their some technologies that you have used in other areas that might be of advantage for this new product/service? In the past, what have you done particularly well?

- If you are working on consumer products or services, **visit** places (such as local stores) where customers purchase or use the type of product or service you're designing or visit customer sites to observe similar products/services in use.

Create an open atmosphere

Most teams find Explore to be the most enjoyable part of DMEDI because they of the creativity. The team leader and coach should work to create a team environment that is open to new ideas, and to prevent teams from latching on to any one solution too early. Most importantly, the team leader should act as a facilitator, cultivating and emphasizing inquiry vs. advocacy skills learned in team leadership training.

After generating many interesting concepts, the team will need to narrow the field to the one or two most promising alternatives. (Notice the key assumption that the team has *multiple* concepts to consider!) You want to be sure that all feasible alternatives have been explored before deciding on a single concept. World-class innovations don't come from a one-horse race. If the investigation of concept ideas only brought about one or two options, it is strongly recommended you develop a plan to create additional options before moving forward.

Explore tools

A powerful tool to synthesize and select concepts is the **Pugh Matrix**. The team establishes the evaluation criteria from the Voice of the Customer and the Voice of the Business, and weights the criteria using an analytical tool such as the Analytic Hierarchy Process (an advanced form of pairwise comparisons where stakeholders can both compare the criteria and weight the differences). Once the criteria and weights are established, each concept is compared against the other concepts on the individual criteria, assigning pluses where the concept is superior and minuses where it is inferior.

Each concept will need to be developed sufficiently so that it can be compared to the other alternatives for each criteria. Information such as cost and time to implement will need to be gathered before the comparison process. This will lead to determining the winning concept. However, another significant benefit of the Pugh process is the opportunity for idea synthesis, generating even better concepts based on enhancing the pluses and minimizing the minuses of the different alternatives. (See the example of a Pugh matrix in the Caterpillar case study, p. 377.)

Phase/Gate Review for Explore

The Gate Review for the Explore phase presents the conceptual alternatives to the leadership and walks them through the process that the team used to select the winner. The high-level design is presented. Depending on the project, it may be necessary to have an additional leadership review earlier in the phase to get feedback on the initial concepts. For example, if the project involved selecting a software vendor, the team would want to make sure that the leadership agreed with the selection of potential providers. Get feedback sufficiently often so that the project does not backtrack. The end of the Explore phase is too late to realize that your team overlooked a concept that the management team sees as a viable alternative.

CASE STUDY:
Global Credit Card Project – Explore Phase

In the Explore phase, the team took the prioritized functions that needed to be provided by all concepts and developed a high-level design. For this program, the high-level design would be the proposal from the bank (or banks) selected as the prime candidate to provide the service worldwide. Steps included:

- Developing a list of requirements
- Developing a Request for Information (RFI), which covered 22 questions corresponding to the prioritized functions in the second House of Quality

- Sending the RFI to 10 banks, selected from current Corporate banks and current Credit Card providers
- Evaluating the responses from the 7 (out of 10) banks that responded, and selecting 4 of those banks for further investigation
- Sending a formal Request for Proposal (RFP) to the 4 selectees
- Selecting a final provider based on the responses

The proposal from the finalist was the preferred high-level design taken into the Develop phase.

The key tool utilized in this phase was the Pugh matrix (see Figure 14.3, next page), used to evaluate responses to the RFI and RFP. As it turned out, credit cards are mostly a commodity business from a user point of view, so all the providers scored about the same on those criteria. The differentiators arose in the Voice of the Business criteria. The key differentiators for the winning bank were that the rebates were the simplest and most robust, the bank offered the lowest fees, and also offered a single global contract. Caterpillar also had a long standing credit card relationship with the winning bank, so their performance history was known.

With utilization of the Pugh matrix and clear criteria for the preferred bank, it didn't take the team long to select a winning bank/proposal. Caterpillar would have a process by which they could offer cards around the world that had an established, known level of service quality with little variation. In addition, Caterpillar would now have availability of the purchase data put on those cards, along with significant financial gains.

At the Gate Review, the team reviewed previously identified risks and determined that the project was on-track to move forward. The leadership also acknowledged that the implementation timeframe would be driven by contract negotiations.

Develop

The Develop phase is where the detailed design occurs. In addition to designing the core service, attention should be paid to developing information technology elements of the project, establishing a plan for human

Figure 14.3: Pugh Matrix of Provider Candidates

Criteria	Weight	Bank A (Baseline)	Bank B +/-	Bank C +/–	Bank D +/–
Coverage - Ability to meet our needs around the world.	2	S	–	S	–
Contract Term - Will they agree to our preferred term	1	S	–	–	S
Fees	1	S	-	-	-
Rebate - Simplicity	2	S	-	--	-
Rebage-Amount we're likely to receive based on a standardized set of assumptions	2	S	--	-	-
Customer Service / Administrative Support	1	S	S	S	S
Insurance Coverage	1	S	S	S	S
Flexibility - Ability to work with our current level of inconsistent practices	1	S	S	S	S
Data - Consolidation and access / consistency	2	S	S	S	S
Data - Report writing / costs	2	S	S	-	S
VAT Identification	1	S	S	S	+
Additional Flexibility - Support from VISA or MC	1	S	S	S	S
Change-over	2	S	–	S	–
Counts					
Count of Positives			0	0	1
Count of Sames			13	7	8	8
Count of Negatives			0	7	6	4
Totals					
Sum of Weighted Positives				0	0	1
Sum of Weighted Negatives				12	10	9
Positives minus Negatives				-12	-10	-8

resources, developing sites/facilities, and purchasing materials that will be required for implementation.

As the solution is developed, the team should take advantage of Lean and Six Sigma tools to maximize speed and minimize waste in the new process. In particular, Value-Added Analysis is beneficial to many projects. The process map of the to-be service is reviewed and each step analyzed and assigned to one of three categories, as discussed in Chapter 4:

- **Customer Value-Add** – Tasks that the customer would be willing to pay for (i.e., adds value to the service, provides competitive advantage)

- **Business Non-Value-Add** – Tasks required by business necessity (i.e., financial reporting) but that do not provide value to customers

- **Non-Value-Add** – All other tasks (approvals, rework, waiting)

Develop tools

The Develop tools in DMEDI are similar to the Improve tools in DMAIC, including:

- Mistake-proofing (or poka-yoke, its Japanese name) is the science of preventing defects before they occur. Pull-down menus and pre-formatted data fields in technology solutions are just two examples.

- Design optimization and refinement can be done through Design of Experiments (DOE). DOE is a systematic methodology where input factors are varied to understand their impact on the output of interest, and a cause-and-effect relationship can be determined. In a service environment, outputs would be important outcomes of the project, such as cycle time, cost, revenue, efficiency, or customer satisfaction.

Phase/Gate Review for Develop

The Develop Gate Review presents the detailed design to the leadership team and solicits their feedback. Keep in mind that depending on the size and complexity of the project, an additional review might be needed mid-phase.

CASE STUDY:
Global Credit Card Project – Develop Phase

The objective of the Develop phase was to take the concept of the program (from the winning bank and team's ideas), turn it into specific contract language, and prepare for global implementation. The first contract draft didn't match the team's expectations, so the team reviewed their current skill set and decided that additional expertise was needed. They hired legal counsel with banking expertise to review aspects of the contract and also hired a consultant with significant credit card industry experience to help optimize the functionality. While these costs were not identified in the project charter, the team obtained permission for the extra expenditures from their management sponsors.

Concurrent with negotiations, the team reviewed the process that would be needed internally and evaluated it from a design element standpoint: service/process description, process methods, human resources, information systems, and materials. The team prepared for implementation by finalizing the process owner (Corporate Treasury), designating an ongoing process management team, and developing a detailed communication and rollout plan. The Develop phase concluded with a gate review after the contract was finalized. Based on a review of the project scorecard, the project continued to be on track to meet all of its objectives.

Implement

The objective of Implement is to successfully conduct a pilot, transfer ownership of the project to the new process owner, and implement the new service (very similar to the Control phase of DMAIC). One of the key benefits of Six Sigma methods is the rigor around implementation and process control. Everyone has worked on a project that started off well only to watch it fall apart when the solution was implemented. With solid up-front work in the Implement phase, these issues can be avoided.

CASE STUDY:
Global Credit Card Project – Implement Phase

This project is currently on track for a global implementation in 2003, with improved functionality for the travelers, a simplified process, better data gathering, and significant financial benefits. A pilot is planned for the UK, as a first step in the international launch. Controls are being developed that will maintain the improved functionality through the life of the program.

Conclusion

The case study here described a streamlined QFD approach that still gives a team a high return on its invested time. Some lessons learned:

1) Don't get so caught up in the process (filling out the QFD matrixes) that you fail to draw conclusions from the information.

2) Take the time to address conflicts in requirements.

3) Keep the amount of information at a manageable level. If one hundred customer needs are identified, and these were translated into an equal or even greater number of design requirements, there would be more than 10,000 potential relationships to plan and manage. Use importance ratings to find out what is most critical to customers.

Design for Lean Six Sigma is the logical next step for a company pursuing excellence in designing new products and services. Lean Six Sigma focuses on delivering both Lean speed and Six Sigma defect-free quality. Design for Lean Six Sigma takes the next step by focusing on new development to eliminate unwanted complexity, and deliver streamlined, customer-focused, defect-free services.

Endnotes

1. Kimberly Watson-Hemphill is a Master Black Belt with George Group Consulting and lead author of their Design for Lean Six Sigma curriculum. She has trained and coached hundreds of Black Belts and Master Black Belts throughout North America and Europe. She has a wide background in all areas of Lean Six Sigma, new product development, and project management and has worked with Fortune 500 companies in both service and manufacturing industries. She is a certified Project Management Professional, has a Bachelor's degree in Aerospace Engineering from the University of Michigan and a Master's degree in Engineering Mechanics from the University of Texas.

2. Rod Skewes is a Master Black Belt with Caterpillar Inc. covering administrative areas such as Accounting, Treasury, Tax, Auditing, and Legal Services. His career at Caterpillar has spanned more than 16 years and included economic analysis and forecasting, marketing research, and accounting before joining Caterpillar's 6 Sigma effort. He is a Certified Management Accountant, has a Bachelor's degree in Business Administration from Morehead State University in Morehead, KY, and a Master's degree in Agricultural Economics from North Carolina State University in Raleigh, NC.

INDEX